POLITICAL CONCEPTS
AND POLITICAL THEORIES

POLITICAL CONCEPTS
AND POLITICAL THEORIES

GERALD F. GAUS

Tulane University

Westview Press

A Member of the Perseus Books Group

Copyright © 2000 by Westview Press, A Member of the Perseus Books Group

Published in 2000 in the United States of America by Westview Press, 5500 Central Avenue, Boulder, Colorado 80301-2877, and in the United Kingdom by Westview Press, 12 Hid's Copse Road, Cumnor Hill, Oxford OX2 9JJ

Find us on the World Wide Web at www.westviewpress.com

Library of Congress Cataloging-in-Publication Data
Gaus, Gerald F.
  Political concepts and political theories / Gerald F. Gaus.
      p.   cm.
Includes index.
  ISBN 0-8133-3331-8
  1. Political science.   I. Title.

JA71.G28   2000
320'.01—dc21   00-027305

The paper used in this publication meets the requirements of the American National Standard for Permanence of Paper for Printed Library Materials Z39.48-1984.

10   9   8   7   6   5   4   3   2   1

To John W. Chapman

CONTENTS

Part Two
Political Concepts

Figures

PREFACE

The first great question of political theory was posed by Socrates: "What is justice?" It has been joined by others, such as, "What is liberty?" "What is equality?" and "What is political authority?" Anyone with political ideals sooner or later will face these sorts of questions. They also provide perhaps the best entry point for the study of political thought; if you understand these questions, and the answers that have been proposed, you understand the main debates and issues in the history of political theory. This book is intended for both sorts of readers: those who have already asked these conceptual questions and those who seek an introduction to political theory. I have tried to write a book that is interesting to those who have already thought about these matters, as well as accessible for those with little background in political theory.

Academics' writing (including, I confess, my own) too frequently falls into two classes. On the one hand, we write sophisticated and complex works that can only be grasped by graduate students (perhaps only advanced graduate students) and fellow academics and, on the other, we write textbooks for beginning students that are of little interest to anyone else (and perhaps not even to them). In the first sort of book, we present our arguments fortified by all our defenses and qualifications in order to withstand the scrutiny and criticism of our colleagues; in the second, we rehearse the familiar and acknowledged positions. Understandably, we are reluctant to bridge these safe shores. To present our views without their full fortifications, to interest our readers without overwhelming them with defenses, to introduce while challenging our readers and inviting them to disagree—all of these are fraught with obvious dangers. Yet, I think, some of the most interesting political theory occurs in this no-man's-land between the rigorous scholarly book and the elementary textbook. In this book, I seek to present my own view of the analysis of political concepts, one that I hope will be interesting to the expert and useful to the novice.

I have presented much of this material to my students—both first-year and more advanced—at the University of Queensland in Brisbane, Australia, and the University of Minnesota, Duluth. My thanks to all of them for letting me think things through in front of them, and for their reactions to my ideas. I would also like to express my appreciation to Westview Press; I thank them not only for their much-appreciated early interest and support, but for their patience in the face of delays brought about by my too-frequent movements back and forth across the Pacific. Richard Dagger and Michael Freeden provided extremely helpful comments for which I am most grateful. Last, and in this case most important, I would like to express my profound debt to John W. Chapman, my own teacher. From him I learned not just what political theory is about, but what academic life is all about.

Gerald F. Gaus

PART ONE

CONCEPTUAL ANALYSIS AND POLITICAL THEORIES

1

WHAT ARE
POLITICAL CONCEPTS?

1.1 Socrates's Question

Political Theory and Political Concepts

Western political philosophy begins with Socrates and Plato, and especially the *Republic*.[1] In this imaginary conversation among a group of Athenians, Socrates poses what may be the most fundamental of all questions in political philosophy: "What is justice?" Indeed, one of the great legal theorists of the twentieth century called this "the eternal question of mankind."[2] We all wish a government that is just—but what is justice?

To a large extent, the study of political theory is an exploration of different ways of understanding core political concepts such as justice, liberty, power, equality, and authority. From Plato onward, political theorists have asked—and have provided conflicting answers to—questions such as "What is justice?" "What is liberty?" "What is power?" and "What is equality?" In the first part of this book, I shall try to get a bit clearer about what sorts of questions these are. Are we asking for a definition, and if so what constitutes a good definition? Or do we seek something other than a definition when we inquire, "What is justice?" Unless we know what we are asking for, we shall not be able to distinguish good from bad answers. After this clarification of what sort of question we are asking, Part II of the book will explore some of the enduring answers that have been advanced in political theory.

Three Definitions of Justice

Let us return to the beginning: Socrates's inquiry, "What is justice?" The first proposal in the *Republic* is made by Cephalus, who has had a long and honorable life in business. To Cephalus, justice is a straightforward matter of telling the truth and paying one's debts—a view, no doubt, that has guided his own life. But Socrates immediately casts doubt on whether this is all there is to justice. Suppose, says Socrates, that a friend from whom you have loaned a weapon has gone mad and now demands the return of the weapon. Would it be right to return it? Cephalus agrees that it would not be right to do so; and if it is not right, it cannot be what is required by justice.

At this point, another Athenian, Polemarchus, speaks up; he believes that he can provide an account of justice that rescues the crux of Cephalus's definition while also showing why it would not be just to return the weapon. He suggests an abstract definition of justice—giving each man his due. But, asks Socrates, is not the mad friend due his weapon? It is, after all, *his* weapon. Polemarchus invokes a view that was common among the Greeks, that justice demands doing good to friends (since that is what is due to friends) and harming enemies (since that is what is due to enemies). Thus, since the madman is a friend, and it would harm him to return the weapon, it cannot be just to do so; it would not be appropriate to return the weapon because it would not be giving him what is his due. Socrates also rejects this view, though his argument against it is not as straightforward as his criticism of Cephalus's definition (that is, that justice is simply repaying one's debts):

> *Socrates:* Can it really be a just man's business to harm any human being?
> *Polemarchus:* Certainly; it is right to harm bad men who are his enemies.
> *Socrates:* But does not harming a horse or a dog mean making it a worse horse or dog, so that each will be a less perfect creature in its own way?
> *Polemarchus:* Yes.
> *Socrates:* Isn't that also true of human beings—that to harm them means making them worse men by the standard of human excellence?
> *Polemarchus:* Yes.
> *Socrates:* And is not justice a peculiarly human excellence?
> *Polemarchus:* Undoubtedly.
> *Socrates:* To harm a man, then, must mean making him less just.
> *Polemarchus:* I suppose so.

Thus, Socrates concludes that "if the just man is good, the business of harming people, whether friends or enemies, must belong to his opposite, the unjust."[3]

It is important to see that Socrates is not appealing to a widely accepted definition of justice; rather, he is rejecting a popular Greek view (that a just person does good to his friends and harms his enemies) by appealing to (what he sees as) a necessary connection between being just and doing good. If a just person is inherently one who does good and who never makes others less just, then this widely held Greek view of justice must be wrong.

At this point, Thrasymacus breaks in on the conversation. Thrasymacus is a teacher of rhetoric—effective public speaking—and questions whether all this philosophical argument really makes sense. Thrasymacus advances an apparently hardheaded and skeptical definition: "justice" is whatever promotes the interests of the stronger. As a man of the world, rather than a philosopher, Thrasymacus insists that he sees the hard truth that the stronger make the laws, these laws serve their interests, and "justice" is simply the name we use for what these laws require of us. Socrates immediately points to a problem. Suppose the stronger make a mistake and pass a law that is not in their interest. If justice involves obeying the law, then justice would require an action that is not in the interests of the stronger. Thrasymacus replies by switching his notion of a "ruler": if a ruler makes an error and proclaims a law that does not promote his interest, then at that point he is not really a ruler:

> Would you say a man deserves to be called a physician at the moment when he makes a mistake in treating his patient and just in respect of that mistake; or a mathematician, when he does a sum wrong and just in so far as he gets the wrong result? Of course we do commonly speak of a physician or a mathematician or a scholar having made a mistake; but really none of these, I should say, is ever mistaken, in so far as he is worthy of the name we give him. So strictly speaking—and you [,Socrates,] are all for being precise—no one who practices a craft makes mistakes. A man is mistaken when his knowledge fails him; and at that moment he is no craftsman.[4]

Thrasymacus now depicts a ruler as someone not simply with superior force, but with superior knowledge. This leaves him having to explain what type of knowledge is required for a (true) ruler. Thrasymacus has compared a ruler to a mathematician or a physician, but Socrates quickly points out that the knowledge that they must possess is not knowledge about how to advance their own interests, but knowledge of their craft; although they benefit from the exercise of their craft because they are paid, when exercising their skill they are seeking the good of others, as physicians seek the health of their patients not their own. If this is the case, however, the "ruler" is one who, in the appropriate way, seeks the good of the subjects over whom he exercises authority. Socrates thus turns Thrasymacus's conception of justice upside down: rulers rule for the sake of justice, rather than justice serving the interests of the rulers. This last move by Socrates leads to the subject of the rest of the *Republic*, which is concerned with the nature of the ideal state and the tasks of rulers and citizens in such a state.

What Socrates Is Looking For

We shall return to Socrates's own proposal in Section 9.3. Right now, I want to draw attention to the sorts of criticisms Socrates makes of others' answers to "What is justice?" This will help show us the sort of answer he is seeking. Cephalus, the honest merchant, illustrates what Socrates takes as our normal condition: he can identify instances or examples of justice but confuses this with an understanding of what justice (itself) is. As an honorable person, he has acted justly throughout his life, but when asked, "What is justice?" he provides a definition (justice as repaying debts) that is based on his own experience and is easily shown to be inadequate as a general definition. Socrates, though, is not interested in particular examples—he is searching for that common element that all instances or examples of justice share, and by virtue of sharing it are cases of justice.[5]

Polemarchus does better at providing a general account. His first proposal—giving each his due—is a vague formula, and Socrates is unclear what it means; even worse, it does not seem to explain why it is not just to return the weapon to the mad friend. To clarify it, Polemarchus relies on a commonly accepted view (among the Greeks), that justice consists in doing good to friends and harm to enemies. Socrates shows here that traditional or widely accepted views can be, indeed usually are, defective. One can imagine Polemarchus saying to Socrates that "doing good to friends and harm to enemies is what we Greeks mean by 'justice.'" Socrates points out, however, that relying on shared, common views is objectionable because they can be inconsistent or incoherent. It is clear, Socrates says, that a just man does not make others less perfect, and true harm to another makes the other a worse man. Since this firm conviction about justice is inconsistent with the widely held view, Socrates believes that we must reject the widely held view. Socrates, then, is seeking neither examples of justice nor popular definitions about what "we think"; he is seeking the *correct* definition that locates that common feature or property of actions, people, and conditions that renders them just.

Last, Socrates shows the inconsistencies of those who analyze concepts such as justice by debunking them—that is, those such as Thrasymacus who insist they are simply masks for power or domination. If Thrasymacus was content to say that talk of justice is simply nonsense or babble (as, we shall see, some have indeed claimed; see Section 1.2), he could avoid Socrates's criticisms. Instead he tries to show that "advancing the interests of the stronger" is what "justice" means—rather than ignoring the question, "What is justice?" he seeks to answer it in a hardheaded way that reduces it to the pursuit of interests. As Socrates shows, however, as soon as one accepts that terms like "justice" make sense, efforts to explain that sense in terms of mere interest or power lead to muddles and inconsistencies. Whatever we mean by "justice," we surely do not mean that which promotes the interest of the stronger. Thrasymacus finally learns this lesson and walks away from the conversation; unable to explain what justice is, he ignores it.

To sum up, then, we can identify three basic convictions of Socrates about concepts such as justice:

- Rather than examples of justice, he seeks that common element that all just things share; it is because it possesses that element that anything can rightfully be said to be just.
- The correct account is coherent and explains all genuine examples; we cannot arrive at it simply by rehearsing what "we say" justice is. Ordinary conceptions can be confused and contradictory.
- "Justice" is a meaningful and important term. As soon as we take it seriously, we see that it is not plausible to debunk it by showing that it reduces to something hardheaded or more obviously "real," such as interests.

1.2 Words, Definitions, and Things

Plato's Conceptual Realism

The three convictions listed at the end of the previous section led Plato and Socrates (it will be recalled that Plato wrote the Socratic dialogues) to a distinctive, if not especially plausible, view that I shall call "conceptual realism." Simply put, Plato believes that conceptual terms such as "justice" refer to a special realm in which the concepts themselves exist. As Plato put it, our conceptual terms refer to the world of "forms"—pure instances of the concepts.

To better see what Plato has in mind, let us focus on an example outside of politics. In another dialogue, the *Meno*, Socrates asks, "What is shape?" Now, the first impulse might be to point to examples of shapes—round, square, oblong, and so on. But as we saw in the case of Cephalus's definition of justice, this will not do; Socrates wants to discover that property shared by round things, square things, oblong things, and so on, such that all can be said to be "shapes." There must, Socrates is convinced, be some feature that *makes* round things, square things, and oblong things all shapes. A *definition* of shape would identify this "shape-making" feature. Socrates ultimately proposes this definition: "Shape is the only thing that always accompanies colour."[6] Plato is seeking a similar definition of justice.

For Plato, then, a definition identifies an essence—a shared feature of many otherwise diverse examples. Now, recall also that Plato is convinced that notions such as justice make sense; he is out to explain them, not debunk them. Thus, on Plato's view, if "justice" is a sensible term, *it must refer to something;* and his theory of definitions leads him to conclude that it *must refer to that essence,* that common thing shared by all examples of justice. It would seem to follow, however, that the essence must in some sense exist; if "justice" is sensible it must refer to something that actually exists. The essence that is shared by all cases of justice must, somehow, somewhere, exist. As Plato sees it, "justice"—that is, the pure essence shared by all instances of justice—exists only in what he calls the realm of "forms," a realm of pure concepts.[7] Plato seems to believe that at some point before we are born, we had direct access to the world of concepts and retain in our present world a more or less hazy recollection. Thus, people like Cephalus can generally recognize examples of justice, as he has some recollection of the concept and can group cases together as sharing the essence. But because our recollection of the world of concepts is incomplete and hazy, definitions of this essence are often wrong.

Why Plato's View Is Not as Alien as It May Appear

It might seem that Plato's conceptual realism is implausible and alien—no one thinks that way today. Although it is true that there are not too many strict Platonists around today, three of the convictions that led Plato to his conceptual realism are still widely shared. In particular, many of us believe (1) Words such as "justice" make sense and are important. In addition, we accept (2) that if a word makes sense we should be able to give a definition of it. A definition, let us say, aims at providing a set of conditions for use of a term that is both necessary and sufficient for (properly) using the word. To say that condition X is *necessary* for properly using word W is to say that *only if* condition X applies to a case can we properly describe it by W; to say that condition X is *sufficient* is to say that if a case has X, then W is an appropriate description. Thus, for example, "is mortal" is not a definition of human beings; for although being mortal is *necessary* to make a creature a human (one can be human only if one is mortal), it is *not sufficient*; it is not always the case that if one is mortal one is also human, as all other animals are mortal too. A definition of humanity aims at identifying that feature that is distinctive of humans—that all humans have, and only humans have. When asked, "What is justice?" most people seek to provide a definition of "justice" that provides the essential feature (or features) that governs the proper use of the word.

(3) Last, many us share the conviction that if a word makes sense and is important, and is not about fiction or fantasy, it must at least purport to refer to something real. When we are most comfortable using them—or at least so it seems—words refer to things. Thrasymacus would not seek to provide a debunking account of "house" or "horse": they obviously refer to real things in the world. He seeks to debunk "justice," as he doubts whether "justice" really refers to anything at all; his proposal that it refers to what is in the interest of the stronger, although in one way cynical, at least does seem to show that "justice" refers to something that is real.

Taken singly, none of these convictions seems outrageous. But taken together, they lead us to a new appreciation of Plato's proposal, for his conceptual realism explains all three of these convictions: it shows that the word "justice" is sensible because it refers to a real thing (the concept of justice), which identifies the essence, and so provides proper definition of "justice."

Words and Things

Many people are attracted to some version of claims (2) and (3) above; that is, many of us are convinced that to understand a term is to grasp its definition, and that sensible terms refer to things, or parts of the world. Those who approach the study of political concepts based on these two convictions often draw their inspiration from the early work of Ludwig Wittgenstein (1889–1951)[8] and a group of philosophers known as the logical positivists.[9] Wittgenstein's basic proposal in his *Tractatus Logico-Philosophicus* was that our language provides pictures of the world. Interestingly, Wittgenstein tells us that this basic picture theory of language was suggested to him by the Paris traffic courts, in which a collision between two cars would be examined by using toy cars and toy people to recreate the accident.[10] For Wittgenstein, the crucial thing was the way we connect moving the toy cars and toy people to the real accident. In some sense, the toys must *stand for* things in the real world. More than that, their relative positions and movements must also correspond to the positions and movements of the real things they stand for. That is, the placement of the toys forms a pictorial representation of the real world: each toy stands for a certain thing in the world, and the arrangements of the toys pictures the arrangement of real things. The recreated accident, then, provides a picture of the world.

In his *Tractatus*, Wittgenstein argued that language does the same job: our language mirrors the world by giving us pictures of it. Roughly—and I can only give an approximate account of his complex theory here—Wittgenstein maintains that the world is composed of *objects* that are related (or arranged) in such a way as to form *facts;* language is composed of *words* that name objects; when these words are arranged in *sentences* they mirror facts. Simple sentences mirror simple facts (that is, simple sentences arrange names is such a way as to mirror the arrangement of objects that form facts), whereas complex sentences are composed of a number of simple sentences mirroring a complex fact in the world.[11] It is important to stress that on the picture theory, language is not just a catalog of names that refer to things; the names must be arranged in such a way as to mirror the way objects are related in the world. As Wittgenstein says, "What constitutes a picture is that its elements are related to one another in a determinate way."[12] Of course, Wittgenstein realizes that sentences do not *look like* the world—they are not pictures in that sense. His point is that they *model* the world insofar as the relations between elements of a sentence represent the arrangement of facts in the world.

Now, to say that language presents pictures is not to say all these pictures actually correspond to facts. "A picture agrees with reality or fails to agree; it is correct or incorrect, true or false."[13] Thus, "in order to tell whether a picture is true or false we must compare it to reality"[14]—"it is impossible to tell from the picture alone whether it is true or false."[15] Language, we might say, is an attempt to describe the world; if the picture is an accurate one—if it corresponds to the arrangement of objects into facts—it is a true sentence; if it does not accurately picture the world it is a false sentence. Roughly, we can say that sentences make sense when they *seek* to mirror the world, and are true when they *actually do* mirror it (false sentences are thus meaningful). This led the logical positivists—who adopted a very similar theory of language—as well as Wittgenstein himself (at least for a time) to adopt a *verificationist* theory of meaning.[16] Sensible or meaningful sentences can be verified in the sense that we can imagine a test that would allow us to determine whether or not the sentence presented a true or false picture of the world. We need not actually conduct the test; in fact, we may not at the present time have the equipment to carry out such a test. The important claim is that if the sentence is meaningful, it presents a picture that, in principle, could be tested to see whether it is or is not accurate.

The Picture Theory and Political Concepts

We have arrived at a crucial juncture. Many of the sentences in which we are interested seem in principle unable to be tested in this way. Consider

(1) It is not just to return a weapon to a madman.
(2) Justice is that which is in the interest of the stronger.
(3) A basic income for all is necessary for social justice.
(4) Liberty is the supreme political value.
(5) We ought to have more equality in our society.
(6) All authority should be abolished.

Sentences (1) to (6) do not seem verifiable by any test, because they contain terms ("just," "justice," "social justice") that do not name any objects we could ever observe. To be sure, Plato thought there were such objects, but not only are most of us skeptical that "justice" refers to any such object, but even if it did, it is impossible to imagine a test in which this object plays a part. Sentence (4) has an additional problem: not only does it refer to the abstract value "liberty," but it also asserts that this value is "supreme." How could we verify the supremacy of liberty? Last, (5) and (6) do not picture the way the world *is*, but the way it *ought* to be. Whereas descriptive statements seek to fit themselves to the world—they seek to conform to the way the world is—ethical claims such as (5) and (6) seek to fit the world to them—they advise us to change the world so that the world fits "the picture" they draw.

Wittgenstein drew a similar conclusion. In the *Tractatus*, he held that because these sorts of ethical statements do not even seek to describe the world, they are without sense. In this he was very close to the logical positivists, who insisted that moral and value statements were "nonsense" because they could not, in principle, be verified. Wittgenstein's view was more subtle. Although he agreed that ethical statements do not describe the world and so are without sense, he does not deny that ethics is important and he does not think it should be abandoned. Rather, he believes, ethics is mystical: it cannot be talked about because it cannot be conveyed in language since it does not seek to mirror the world. "There are indeed," says Wittgenstein, "things that cannot be put into words. They make themselves manifest. They are mystical."[17]

Recall the three common convictions about the meaning of political concepts that I noted above:

(1) Words such as "justice" make sense and are important.
(2) If a word makes sense we should be able to give a definition of it.
(3) If a word makes sense and is important, and is not about fiction or fantasy, it must at least purport to refer to something real.

For all its problems, Plato's conceptual realism is attractive insofar as it makes sense of all three convictions. If, however, we take a more modern view and refuse to accept that there is a realm in which value-laden concepts exist, our devotion to (2) and (3) tends to undermine conviction (1). The logical positivists, accepting (2) and (3), thus denied that value concepts make sense and that they are important; in the *Tractatus* Wittgenstein accepts that they are important, but still denies that they make sense. In either case, it seems clear that if we combine a commitment to a close connection between sensible words and things to which they refer while rejecting Platonic conceptual realism, it will be hard to make sense of political concepts such as justice or affirmations of the value of liberty.

Perhaps if we eliminate any reference to goodness or value, we might still be left with some "value-neutral" political concepts. Or perhaps we should say, we might be left with the value-neutral remnants of our concepts such as justice, liberty, and equality. Some philosophers, inspired by Wittgenstein's *Tractatus*, have argued that we can separate out the "value" component of concepts such as liberty from the "descriptive" component, allowing conceptual analysis to focus on the latter.[18] I shall not pursue this possibility for two reasons. First, even if "value-neutral" understandings of concepts such as liberty and equality are possible, and even if they have their uses in some technical or social scientific theories, these value-neutral explications are silent regarding our main interest in studying political concepts: we want to know, for example, not only what liberty is, but why it is or is not important, and whether it is something we should strive for. Second, some concepts—the best example of which is justice—seem to have very little purely descriptive components. An analysis of justice that left out of the account why it was to be sought, or why it should guide our actions, would tell us very little about justice. Like Socrates, we wish to know what justice is so that we can know what sort of political and social life to strive for.

1.3 Wittgenstein's Later Analysis

Wittgenstein's Rejection of the Picture Theory

Wittgenstein begins his most important work, *Philosophical Investigations*, with a quote from *Confessions,* in which Saint Augustine (354–430) tells us how he learned to speak a language:

> When they (my elders) named some object, and accordingly moved towards something, I saw this and I grasped that the thing was called by the sound they uttered when they meant to point it out. Their intention was shewn by their bodily movements, as it were the natural language of all peoples: the expressions of the face, the play of the eyes, the movements of other parts of

the body, and the tone of voice which expresses our state of mind in seeking, having, rejecting, or avoiding something. Thus, as I heard words repeatedly used in their proper places in various sentences, I gradually learnt to understand what objects they signified; and after I had trained my mouth to form these signs, I used them to express my own desire.[19]

Wittgenstein comments that this gives a particular "picture" of the essence of language. "It is this: the individual words in language name objects—sentences are combinations of such names."[20] The meaning of words, then, is the object for which they stand in the world. This view, of course, is not simply Saint Augustine's—it is the view of Wittgenstein himself in his *Tractatus Logico-Philosophicus*. Wittgenstein thus begins the *Philosophical Investigations* by showing why his earlier picture theory of language is wrong.

To better understand the shortcomings of the naming theory of language, Wittgenstein explores a simple language in which it seems correct.

Let us imagine a language for which the description given by Augustine is right. The language is meant to serve for communication between builder A and an assistant B. A is building with building-stones: there are blocks, pillars, slabs and beams. B has to pass the stones, and that in the order in which A needs them. For this purpose they use a language consisting of the words "block," "pillar," slab," "beam." A calls out;—B brings the stone which he has learnt to bring at such-and-such a call.—Conceive this as a complete primitive language.[21]

This seems to be the sort of language one might be able to learn in the way Saint Augustine describes: it is a method that takes naming objects as the most basic use of language. But two considerations show that even in this extremely simple language, the assistant is not being trained simply to connect words with things.

What Is the Thing? Categorizing Under Concepts

Just what constitutes a "slab" has to be learned by the assistant. It is easy to suppose that when a builder points to a piece of stone and says, "Slab," the assistant will then connect the object to the word "slab." But this seemingly easy connection presupposes a great deal. Suppose that the assistant knows nothing of building or what the master builder is trying to do; the builder simply points and says, "Slab!" The assistant must know, first, what pointing is. If you try to point a bit of food out to a dog, the dog will sniff your finger; the assistant must have already learned that ☞ means that he should look in a certain direction. Having accomplished that, he must decide just what is being pointed to. A shape? A color? A rock? Do all slabs have to be the same color, the same thickness, the same shape? Be made of the same material? What is the *thing* to which the builder is pointing?

One of the points Wittgenstein stresses in his later work is that we only know what is the thing that the word names as we come to use the word in new situations and gradually come to differentiate, for example, slabs from a variety of other things. Another example may help. I knew a very bright two-year-old, and as with most children beginning to learn language, he began by naming favorite animals—in his case, it was "doggie." His parents, in the manner of Saint Augustine, had pointed to the various dogs in the neighborhood, to which he would correctly say, "Doggie." Had he learned what a dog was? Well, one day we were looking at a picture book, and pointing to a picture of a cow, he said, "Doggie." I corrected him, saying, "No, cow." For a moment he looked puzzled, and then suddenly he exclaimed, "Oh! Cow-doggie!" When his parents pointed to the things they called "dogs," were they pointing to the object "animal," "four-legged animal," "furry walking thing," or what we call a "dog"? Only by using the word in different ways in new situations could the two-year-old come to identify the thing we call a dog.

Wittgenstein observes that Saint Augustine's account of how he learned his (first) language "describes the learning of human language as if the child came into a strange country and did not understand the language of the country; that is, as if he already had a language, only not this one."[22] A German arriving in the United States, knowing no English, already has distinguished dogs from cows and cats—we can say that she already has the concept of a dog. All she has to learn is that the thing she calls "hund" is what we call "dog."

It is important to stress here that Wittgenstein is not denying that objects are real, and so exist quite apart from language. Of course, those two things that wake me up in the morning by jumping on my bed and licking me are real apart from any language. But our language groups these things together under the same concept—"Boxers." Learning to use the word "Boxer" is to learn what things are included and what are not; and when one has learned that, one has learned a good deal of the concept of a "Boxer." It is important to note here that different languages may group things together in different ways, reflecting different interests and concerns. Whereas, for example, we have one word for "snow," Eskimo languages have a variety of different words that pick out different types of snow—falling snow, packed snow, frozen snow, and so on—which are identified as different things, reflecting the importance snow has in the lives of Eskimos.[23]

Naming Versus Language Games

Recall again our builders' language. Suppose the assistant, having mastered the art of pointing, has learned the concept of slab to the extent that he can correctly identify the things in the world that the word links up with. Even in this ridiculously simple language, "slab!" is not just a name for a thing; to grasp the meaning of "slab!" the assistant must not only know what one *is*, but what to *do* when the master builder says, "Slab!" If, when the master builder said, "Slab!," the assistant went to a slab and danced a jig on it or broke it with a sledge hammer, he still would not know what "slab!" meant. Throughout his later work, Wittgenstein insists that language is not simply—indeed, not primarily—about *naming* things, but about *doing* things.

The key idea here is that of a "language game." The builder and his assistant are weaving together words and actions[24]: to know the meaning of a word is not simply to know what things it picks out in the world, but to know what to do with it—how it fits into our activities and relations with others. The idea of a "game" suggests a key feature of our language; it is about rules that govern the moves we can sensibly make. Think, for example, of the rules of chess: they tell us what constitutes a "move" and how we can respond to the moves of others. To know, for example, what is a queen is not to know simply (1) the name of a certain chess piece, but to know also (2) the rules that govern its movements. Someone who only can pick out the queen in a box of chess pieces has not really mastered the concept of a "queen," for she has not mastered the rules that govern its use in the game. This would become clear if she proclaimed that she knew what a queen was, picked out the queen, and used it to crush the other queen, declaring, "My queen beat yours, I'm the winner!"

If to master a word (or conceptual term) is to master its use or function, we might want to press Wittgenstein to tell us what, after all, is *the* function of language. But this is to ask the wrong question, for there is no single function that all words perform: "Think of the tools in a tool-box: there is a hammer, pliers, a saw, a screw-driver, a rule, a glue-pot, glue, nails, and screws.—The function of words are as diverse as the function of these objects."[25] Consider the number of different language games:

Giving orders, and obeying them
Describing the appearance of an object, or giving its measurements
Constructing an object from a description (a drawing)
Reporting an event
Speculating about an event

Forming and testing hypotheses
Making up a story, and reading it
Play acting
Making a joke, and telling it
Asking, thanking, cursing, greeting, praying[26]

Forms of Life and the Public Character of Language

One of the characteristics of most games is that those with whom we are playing also understand themselves to be playing the game. The players have a shared understanding of the rules and similar expectations about what sorts of responses are appropriate and which are not. In our builders' language game, the builder expects the assistant to bring a slab when he says, "Slab!" and the assistant expects the builder to use the slab to build with rather than, say, attack the assistant with it. They thus share an understanding of what this activity is and what their roles are in it. Their understanding of the language is thus embedded in what Wittgenstein calls a "form of life."[27] A language is part of living; to understand the words of that language one must understand the ways of living of which that language is a part.

Because language is a game—or rather, many different types of games—that is an element of a form of life, language is inherently public and shared. To understand a word (or a conceptual term), Wittgenstein argues, is necessarily a social act: one can only understand a word insofar as one is a member of a linguistic community. This idea leads Wittgenstein into complex investigations into just what is meant by "understanding" and what is involved in following the rules of a language game. We need not go into these complex matters here.[28] For us, the important point is that Wittgenstein adamantly denies that one can have private meanings for terms that are simply in one's head. Wittgenstein asks, "Can I say 'bububu' and mean 'If it doesn't rain, I shall go for a walk'?"[29] The answer, Wittgenstein believes, is no, because meanings are part of a language, which reflects the common interpretations and expectations that constitute a form of life. Because of this, he insists, it makes no sense to appeal to private meanings—what *you* (idiosyncratically) mean by a word.

1.4 Wittgenstein and Conceptual Investigations

What Do We Mean?

This last point is important. In response to Socrates's question, "What is justice?" people often reply with something like, "Well, what *I* mean by justice is . . ." In response to our deep disagreements about justice, it is tempting to resort to private meanings or definitions. It is, after all, much easier to answer, "What do I mean by 'justice'?" than "What is justice?" Indeed, it seems that you cannot be wrong about what you mean—it is simply a matter of reporting what is in *your* head when *you* talk about justice. Moreover, this may seem more tolerant; rather than proclaiming what justice *is,* you content yourself with explaining your meaning, allowing that others may mean something entirely different. As Wittgenstein sees it, however, to say, "This is what *I* mean by 'justice,' though no one agrees with me or uses the word that way" makes no more sense than to proclaim, "When I say 'bububu,' it means 'If it doesn't rain, I shall go for a walk.'" If language is inherently public and shared, conceptual investigation cannot be about individual reports of private meanings.

Recall again Socrates's question, and the answers given by Cephalus and Polemarchus (Section 1.1). Cephalus, having spent an honorable life in business, tells Socrates that justice is paying one's debts and keeping one's word. Socrates finds that this definition does not explain the injustice of returning a weapon to a mad friend, so Polemarchus replies with a more general definition, that justice consists in doing good to one's friends and harm to one's enemies. This, as I pointed out, was a traditional Athenian view. Wittgenstein's later philosophy suggests that Cephalus and Polemarchus are on the right track: they seek to explain what "we" (Athenians) mean by justice. Of course, they do not explain all of the "justice language game," but they appear to have the right idea. To explicate justice is to explain the way justice enters into the Athenian form of life. If doing good to one's friends and harming one's enemies is fundamental to Athenian justice, then Cephalus and Polemarchus provide the right sort of answer to Socrates's questions. From this perspective, even Thrasymacus makes a valuable contribution. Although he is no doubt wrong that "justice" *means* "in the interests of the stronger"—in this respect he is not really answering Socrates's question[30]—he does shed light on one function of justice talk. As Karl Marx pointed out (see Section 9.1), talk about justice can be employed as an instrument of the powerful to protect their own interests. If our interest is in understanding our language games (which, it will be recalled, includes the role or function they play), Cephalus, Polemarchus, and Thrasymacus all make important observations.

Two Errors of Socrates

If one takes seriously Wittgenstein's later view of language, Socrates seems the most confused of the discussants. Socrates's criticisms are based on three convictions, all of which Wittgenstein disputes.

First, Socrates is convinced that "justice" names a thing, and that the aim of conceptual inquiry is to discover the nature of that thing. As we have seen (Section 1.3), in many ways the guiding aim of Wittgenstein's later philosophy is to show the inadequacy of this naming theory of language.

Second, Socrates's criticisms of Cephalus, Polemarchus, and Thrasymachus all aim to show that they have not *defined* justice, in the senses of identifying the necessary and sufficient conditions for properly calling something "just" (Section 1.2). Socrates—and I have suggested that many of us concur—wants a definition in the sense of identifying that trait that every just thing has and that, if anything has it, makes that thing just. That is, he seeks a definition that identifies the essence of justice: that common thing all cases of justice share, and by virtue of sharing it are cases of justice. Socrates is convinced that if one does not know the essence, one can never know whether one is correctly ascribing justice in particular cases. If one does not know what makes something just, how can one justify a claim that "Socrates is a just man" or "Athens is a just city"? Thus, although he admits that his interlocutors plausibly identify some cases of justice, he insists that they fall far short of knowing what justice is (and so they cannot really be sure about their cases).

Wittgenstein, however, tells us that it is misguided to search for a definition that provides the essence of a concept:

> Consider for example the proceedings that we call "games." I mean board-games, card-games, Olympic games, and so on. What is common to them all?—Don't say: There *must* be something common, or that they would not be called "'games'"—but *look and see* whether there is anything common to all.—For if you look at them you will not see something that is common to *all*, but similarities, relationships. And a whole series of them at that. To repeat: don't think, look![31]

It might seem that all games involve a winner and loser. But what about solitaire? Perhaps all games are amusing—but war games are not at all amusing. Do all games involves rules—what of a child throwing his ball at the wall and then catching it again? What we see is "a complicated network of similarities overlapping and criss-crossing."[32] Wittgenstein calls these relations "family resemblances." We can identify members of the same family because they are united by a variety of crisscrossing traits. There is a "Gaus nose," but not all Gauses have it; there are "Gaus ears," shared by many, but not all Gauses—and similar things can be said about complexion, height, and the shape of the Gaus face. Wittgenstein's point is that none of these family traits are likely to be shared by each and every Gaus; one may have the Gaus height, nose, and ears; another the nose, complexion, and face; a third the face, nose, and height; and yet a fourth the face and complexion. In this list, the first and last share no common traits, yet it still may be quite obvious that they are members of the same family (once we consider their relations to the others). Wittgenstein sometimes uses another metaphor: that of a thread or a rope. No single fiber runs through the entire rope, yet we do not question the unity of the rope. Rather, the rope is composed of overlapping threads (traits).

If the unity of our concepts is best explained by family resemblances, the search for essentialist definitions is doomed to failure. Socrates's own attempts to formulate such definitions seem testimony to this. We already have seen that he defines shape as that which always follows color; after a long analysis in the *Republic* he seems to suggest several formulations of the concept of justice. Socrates defines justice as a proper ordering, in which each part performs its appropriate task; justice in a man is a just ordering of the parts of his soul, whereas a just city is one in which each class performs its appropriate function.[33] One can see how Socrates is led to these formalistic and highly abstract definitions, for he seeks what is common to all cases. But the very abstractness and formality of his proposals lead us to question whether the search for essences is really what we are interested in when we ask, "What is justice?"

If we take Wittgenstein's later philosophy seriously, we will understand our concepts as parts of language games—constellations of actions and utterances related in complicated and crisscrossing ways. The interest in conceptual investigations is not to see what all the members of this constellation share, but to chart out the relationships among them and to see precisely how the constellation hangs together to form our concept of justice. This looks much more promising than the search for the sorts of formal, shared essences that are the focus of Socratic philosophy; we shall develop this idea in the next chapter.

What to Do About Conceptual Confusion?

Wittgenstein's Approach to Confusion. The first two criticisms that Wittgenstein might make of Socrates seem sound and promise a much more fruitful path when analyzing political concepts: our task is not to find the "thing" to which the conceptual term refers, and we should not be seeking a shared essence of all appropriate uses of the conceptual term. Wittgenstein, however, suggests a third criticism of the Socratic approach that calls for closer examination.

More basic than conceptual realism and the search for definitions is Socrates's conviction that our actual practices are confused and contradictory, and the aim of philosophy must be to make them rational and consistent. Cephalus, Polemarchus, and Thrasymacus are all criticized because their proposals end up in contradictions or confusions: they assert that justice is one thing (for example, giving back what is owed) but then deny it (it is unjust to return a madman's weapon). Socrates takes it as manifest that insofar as our actual practices are confused or contradictory, they must be erroneous; and insofar as they are erroneous they cannot guide the actions of rational agents. As rational people, we want our actions and beliefs to make sense, and to act on inconsistent or erroneous views cannot make sense. Thus, Socrates takes it as given that when we show the confusions and inconsistencies of our actual views and language games, we show them to be defective, and so in need of revision. That, indeed, is the task of the philosopher.

Wittgenstein suggests a different understanding of philosophy. Because language games are to be understood in terms of the functions they serve, the very inconsistency or incoherence of a language game may help it serve its function. Consider, once again, our notion of justice.[34] Philosophers have long disagreed about the relation of justice to the social good or overall welfare of society. Some philosophers, especially those in the utilitarian tradition,[35] have insisted that "justice" picks out those things that are crucial for advancing the social good; justice is thus always a way to promote the social good or the welfare of society.[36] But as we shall see in Chapter 8, others have insisted that the demands of justice are constraints on promoting the social good: John Rawls, for example, famously proclaimed that "each member of society has an inviolability founded on justice which even the welfare of everyone cannot override."[37] If so, rather than deriving from our commitment to advancing social welfare, justice is independent of social welfare and, crucially, limits what can be done to advance it. Even if it would advance the social good, we cannot justly sacrifice some people to make others better off.

Now, it cannot be the case both (1) that justice derives from our commitment to social welfare and (2) that it is independent of our commitment to social welfare. A theory that asserted both would be inconsistent; to accept such a view of justice requires having inconsistent beliefs about justice. Socrates, of course, could not accept such a theory: we must either embrace (1) or (2) or try to show how to reasonably reconcile them (perhaps by showing that in some ways justice derives from the social good and in other ways it does not). Wittgenstein, however, suggests that the aim of conceptual investigation should not be to ensure our conceptual commitments are consistent, but to explain why our language games appeal to inconsistent beliefs. For example, a philosopher inspired by Wittgenstein might suggest that the job of individual rights—a crucial element of justice—(see Section 8.1)—is to ensure that people will, in a predictable way, be left to enjoy their life, liberty, and property as they see fit, at least within wide limits. People, we thus say, have rights to life, liberty, and property, and these cannot be taken away even if it would advance the welfare of society to, say, deprive some intensely disliked minority of their liberty and property. If justice is to perform this job of blocking appeals to social welfare, we must view it as independent of social welfare. How could justice effectively block proposals to advance the social welfare if everyone saw justice as deriving from the social welfare? So, to do its job, the Wittgensteinian might say, we must understand justice as quite independent of the social good, and so give it the standing to effectively block that good. Yet, the same Wittgensteinian may insist, for justice to be widely supported and endorsed, it generally must be consistent with the welfare of society: if justice really made society worse off, people would not be committed to it. Who would support justice if it was believed that it stood in the way of what is good for society? Individual rights must thus be seen as a way to advance the social welfare. To ensure commitment to justice, we need to believe that justice is good for society. Thus, for justice to effectively perform its function of securing certain sorts of treatment for individuals, it is *useful to think and say contradictory things about it*. Once we understand this character of justice—as simultaneously blocking and deriving from the social welfare—we can understand why philosophers have long defended these incompatible theories of justice. But having thus explained our concept of justice, there is nothing left for the Wittgensteinian philosopher to do. It is, our Wittgensteinian would say, a sign of philosophic confusion to then go on to ask, "Is justice *really* derivative of social welfare or independent of it?" We have seen how it both is and is not derivative, and why both ways of seeing it are crucial for it to effectively function: that is all there is to say about it. It is not the proper task of philosophers to "fix" our language for us.

Why We Need to Try to Clear Up Confusions.   Although it is enlightening to see why we are confused, and why some confusions persist and are even useful, Socrates's basic conviction is right. As rational believers, we cannot rest content with the thought that we entertain inconsistent beliefs about justice. We employ notions of justice to change our society, to punish, to reward, to justify interference or refraining from interfering with the lives of others, to tax, to educate, to guide voting and public policy, and sometimes to decide on life and death. If our beliefs about justice are confused and contradictory, then they cannot serve as an effective guide to action. Consider, for example, the case of Allied statesmen in World War II. The British held Russian and Ukrainian prisoners of war, some, but not all of whom, had fought in support of the Germans. Josef Stalin, the Soviet dictator, demanded that the prisoners be returned to the Soviet Union; it was widely believed that they would be sent to camps and killed if returned. The Americans, however, were convinced that the prospects for world peace after the war depended on securing the friendship of Stalin, and so, despite the manifest injustice to these prisoners, pressured the British to return to them to Stalin. The British acceded to the pressure, and the prisoners were returned and executed.[38] Both British and American statesmen were caught in a conflict between the demands of justice and the ability to secure social and world good by bringing about peace. They had to make a decision. Now, in making this decision, the relation between justice and the social good was crucially important. To the extent that justice serves the social good, the statesmen would have far more reason to sacrifice some for the sake of such a great good as world peace; to the extent that justice is independent of the social good, and blocks attempts to secure the good of many at a cost to the few, they had strong reasons to resist the temptation to accede to Stalin's demands. To tell them that justice both is and is not derivative of the social good does not assist them in making the right decision.

As Socrates realized, we seek to understand justice because we want to do the right thing and we wish to have a just society. Because we wish not only to understand the way concepts are used but to employ them to guide our own decisions and actions, we need to go beyond understanding confusions; we must try to clear them up. And as soon as we seek to clear up conceptual confusion, we encounter conceptual disputes: competing proposals as to the best way to clear up our concepts. We turn to such disputes in the next chapter.

1.5 Summary

In this chapter, I have explored three approaches to the analysis of political concepts. I began Section 1.1 with a discussion of Plato's *Republic*, in which Socrates is searching for a definition of justice; we saw that Socrates thinks that most people's ideas about justice are partly right, but deeply confused; Socrates is searching for a definition that shows what all cases of justice have in common. Socrates and Plato ultimately hold that notions such as "justice" refer to a realm of "forms" in which pure cases of the concepts exist; the examples of justice we see in the world in some way relate to or instantiate these concepts. More generally, Platonic *conceptual realism* makes sense of three common convictions about language and concepts: (1) words such as "justice" make sense and are important; (2) if a word makes sense we should be able to give a definition of it that reveals the essence of the idea to which the word refers; and (3) if a term makes sense and is important, and is not about fiction or fantasy, it must at least purport to refer to something real.

Although it makes sense of these three key convictions, Platonic conceptual realism strikes many as implausible. And though many are reluctant to accept Plato's theory of forms, they are also reluctant to abandon convictions (2) and (3). As we saw in Section 1.2, Wittgenstein's early work in the *Tractatus*, and the logical positivists, retain (2) and (3): they insist that words can be defined in terms of the objects to which they refer and that meaningful sentences seek to somehow picture or describe the world. But rejecting the idea that concepts such as justice are part of the world, they ultimately reject conviction (1): that such concepts are meaningful and important. The logical positivists hold that these concepts are neither meaningful nor important; Wittgenstein thinks they are important, but in a mystical way that transcends meaning. Neither leaves any room for rational analysis of our most important political concepts.

Last, in Sections 1.3 and 1.4, I turned to the later work of Wittgenstein in his *Philosophical Investigations*. Here he gives up both convictions (2) and (3). Words cannot be defined, and most language is not about naming objects. Language provides a wide range of functions; naming is one, but so are commanding, asking questions, telling jokes, making complaints, praying, and poetry. To understand a term is not to grasp what it names, but how it is used in a form of life. Conceptual investigation, then, seeks to understand the uses of a term—why we use it in different ways in different contexts to perform different functions. Although this view rescues our political concepts from the charge of senselessness—without resorting to any sort of conceptual realism—and in that respect is a great advance on the first two views we considered, it seems to have strayed too far from Socrates's (and our) interest in understanding political concepts. We do not wish to simply know how "justice" is used and to understand the ways in which it functions in diverse settings. We want to know what is just; we want a well-supported and coherent concept of justice to guide our deliberation and action.

Notes

1. Socrates (470–399 B.C.) was the first great Western philosopher. He did not leave any writings, but his philosophical views are reported—albeit in an edited and modified form—by his student, Plato (ca 428–347 B.C.). It is thus impossible fully to disentangle the views of Socrates and Plato, as the main evidence we have for Socrates's positions are the dialogues written by Plato.

2. Hans Kelsen, *What is Justice?* (Berkeley: University of California Press, 1957), p. 1.

3. Plato, *The Republic*, Francis MacDonald Cornford, ed. and trans. (Oxford: Oxford University Press, 1945), pp. 13–14 [I, 334–335].

4. Ibid., p. 20 [I, 340–341].

5. Socrates makes this point even clearer in another dialogue, the *Meno*, in which he is searching for a definition of virtue. Meno keeps giving Socrates examples of virtues, but Socrates seeks the common element that "permeates each of them" and explains why each is an example of virtue. See Plato, *Protagoras* and *Meno*, W.K.C. Guthrie, trans. (Harmondsworth, UK: Penguin, 1956), p. 119 [74 A].

6. Plato, *Meno*, p. 221 [75 B].

7. Plato's views about the forms seemed to undergo change. For more classic statements, see the *Meno* and the *Republic*; he seems more skeptical in the *Parmenides*.

8. See, for example, Felix Oppenheim, *Political Concepts: A Reconstruction* (Oxford: Basil Blackwell, 1981), pp. 177–178.

9. This movement was important in the years between the First and Second World Wars and in the 1950s. The British philosopher A. J. Ayer (1910–1989) was one of the leading logical positivists.

10. See Ludwig Wittgenstein, *Tractatus Logico-Philosophicus*, D. F. Pears and B. F. McGuinness, trans. (London: Routledge and Kegan Paul, 1961).

11. For a very helpful account, see K. T. Fann, *Wittgenstein's Conception of Philosophy* (Berkeley: University of California Press, 1969), esp. p. 20.

12. Wittgenstein, *Tractatus*, sect. 2.14.

13. Ibid., sect. 2.21.

14. Ibid., sect. 2.23.

15. Ibid., sect. 2.224.

16. See Hans Sluga, "Ludwig Wittgenstein: Life and Work," in Hans Sluga and David G. Stern, eds., *The Cambridge Companion to Wittgenstein* (Cambridge: Cambridge University Press, 1996), pp. 14–15.

17. Wittgenstein, *Tractatus*, sect. 6.622. See also Hannah Pitkin, *Wittgenstein and Justice* (Berkeley: University of California Press, 1972), chap. 2.

18. See Oppenheim, *Political Concepts*, chaps. 8–9. For a criticism, see William E. Connolly, *The Terms of Political Discourse*, 2nd ed. (Princeton: Princeton University Press, 1983), pp. 22ff.

19. Saint Augustine, as quoted in Ludwig Wittgenstein, *Philosophical Investigations*, 3rd ed., G.E.M. Anscombe, trans. (New York: Macmillan, 1958), note to sect. 1.

20. Ibid., sect. 1.

21. Ibid., sect. 2.

22. Ibid., sect. 32.

23. See Pitkin, *Wittgenstein and Justice*, pp. 102–103.

24. Wittgenstein, *Philosophical Investigations*, sect. 7.

25. Ibid., sect. 11.

26. Ibid., sect. 23.

27. Ibid., sects. 19, 23.

28. For useful discussions, see Fann, *Wittgenstein's Conception of Philosophy*, chap. 8; Pitkin, *Wittgenstein and Justice*, chap. 4

29. Wittgenstein, *Philosophical Investigations*, p. 18n.

30. See Pitkin, *Wittgenstein and Justice*, chap. 8.

31. Wittgenstein, *Philosophical Investigations*, sect. 66.

32. Ibid.

33. See, for example, Plato, *The Republic*, pp. 128–143 [IV, 433–444], pp. 298–315 [IX, 572–587].

34. Hannah Pitkin makes the same point with a different example—knowledge. See her *Wittgenstein and Justice*, pp. 85ff.

35. "The creed which accepts as the foundation of morals 'utility' or the 'greatest happiness principle' holds that actions are right in proportion as they tend to promote happiness; wrong as they tend to produce the reverse of happiness" (John Stuart Mill, *Utilitarianism*, in John Gray, ed., *On Liberty and Other Essays* [New York: Oxford University Press, 1991], chap. 2, para. 2). See my *Social Philosophy* (Armonk, NY: M. E. Sharpe, 1999), chap. 4.

36. See Mill, *Utilitarianism*, chap. 5.

37. John Rawls, *A Theory of Justice* (Cambridge, MA: Harvard University Press, 1971), p. 3.

38. See S. I. Benn, "Public and Private Morality: Clean Living and Dirty Hands," in S. I. Benn and G. F. Gaus, eds., *Public and Private in Social Life* (New York: St. Martin's Press, 1983), chap. 7.

2
CONCEPTUAL DISPUTES

2.1 Essentially Contested Concepts

The Politics of Political Concepts

I argued in the first chapter that not only do we need to understand our conceptual confusions, but we need to try to clear them up. This process of "clearing up" inevitably involves decisions about which uses—parts of the concept—we will stress and continue to affirm, and which we will revise or reject. To return to our example of justice and the social good (Section 1.4), if it cannot be the case that justice is both (1) entirely independent of considerations of social welfare and (2) simply a way to promote the social good, then we must in some way revise our understanding of justice. Thus, utilitarian philosophers such as John Stuart Mill (1806–1873) have tried to show how justice derives from considerations of social welfare, and is *not* something independent of it, whereas others have sought to demonstrate how social justice is entirely distinct from social welfare, and cannot be derived from it. As rational agents, we employ concepts to make sense of, and to change, our social life—we cannot remain content with contradictory and confused ideas.

Socrates understood this and was constantly seeking to get beyond the confusions of our normal ways of thinking. Philosophical reflection, he believed, could clear up these conceptual confusions. And many contemporary philosophers agree: philosophical investigation, they insist, can clarify and systematize our concepts.[1] Yet, when we examine disputes about the best way to interpret a political concept, we typically do not find dispassionate philosophers engaged in a disinterested pursuit of the truth, but partisan and charged conflicts, with all participants often denying that their opponents even make sense. Consider, for example, the notion of social (or distributive) justice that has been described as the "obsession of our time."[2] To many philosophers, especially socialists and defenders of the contemporary welfare state, social or distributive justice is a fundamental moral imperative:

> To have an understanding of the moral language-game, to have an understanding of what morality requires, we need to understand that we cannot be indifferent to the suffering of others. Are we justified in holding onto even a *minuscule* bit of our property, say food which could be shared with a starving person, when sharing it could be done without any serious inconvenience to ourselves? . . . Sometimes we are morally compelled to redistribute. . . . It is not so much demands placed on individuals within an unjust system that are crucial but a commitment on the part of individuals to alter the social system. . . . What needs to be altered is the social system. . . . Morally speaking, there has to be redistribution.[3]

In contrast, F. A. Hayek (1899–1992), a Noble prize–winning economist, defender of markets and opponent of economic planning, insists that "social justice" is an "abuse" of the word "justice":

> It is perhaps not surprising that men should have applied to the joint effects of the actions of many people, even where these were never foreseen or intended, the conception of justice which they had developed with respect to the conduct of individuals towards each other. "Social" justice (or sometimes "economic" justice) came to be regarded as an attribute which the "actions" of society, or the "treatment" of individuals and groups by society, ought to possess. As primitive thinking usually does when first noticing some regular process, the results of the spontaneous ordering of the market were interpreted as if some thinking being deliberately directed them, or as if the particular benefits or harm different persons derived from the market were determined by particular acts of the will, and could therefore be guided by moral rules. This conception of "social" justice is thus a direct consequence of that anthropomorphism or personification by which naïve thinking tries to account for the self-ordering process. It is a sign of the immaturity of our minds that we have not yet outgrown these primitive concepts and still demand from an impersonal process . . . that it conform to the moral precepts men have evolved for the guidance of individual actions.[4]

Thus, whereas the socialist, Kai Nielsen, insists that given the moral language game, social justice requires that the social system distribute goods in the way required by morality, Hayek maintains that this is to personify society, treating it as if it were an individual that could act, and so could violate rules of morality. Since society is the realm of impersonal forces, Hayek concludes, it is an abuse of language to talk about whether it is just. Nielsen is aware of, but rejects, Hayek's dismissal of social justice.[5]

In many ways, this dispute seems intractable: Nielsen believes that Hayek's view is based on a misunderstanding of the moral language game, whereas Hayek insists that Nielsen's socialism misunderstands the concept of justice. Rather than being an impartial dispute about the best way to clear up our confused thinking, the conflict is more akin to a political dispute, in which each side steadfastly upholds its interpretation. Why do our conceptual disputes about justice—and liberty, equality, and so on—take on this political character?

Gallie's Championship

In an important essay titled "Essentially Contested Concepts," W. B. Gallie tries to explain the intractable nature of disputes about political concepts.[6] Gallie explains his idea of an "essentially contested concept" through the example of championship. As Gallie points out, we are all familiar with the idea of a championship, or "the champions" in a sport. Typically, there is an annual competition, and the person or team selected by the rules is designated the "champion" for that year, and generally remains the champion until the next season's competition is concluded. Gallie, however, considers a different sort of competition, with some unusual features:

(1) Each team has a distinctive style of play; some teams specialize in speed, others in power or strategy.
(2) The championship is not awarded according to some settled and agreed-upon body of rules, but rather in virtue of the style and level of play. Everyone agrees, though, that the champion is the team that "plays the best."
(3) There is no one point at which a team becomes the champion, nor does it retain the title for a fixed period. Since there are continuous games, a team can be the champion today and dethroned tomorrow.
(4) The competition has no official judges. Each side has its devoted supporters, as well as less loyal "floating" fans, who endorse the team as "the best."
(5) Every team's supporters insist that it is the champion, or the "true" or the "real" champion. Even if one team tends to win the most, the supporters of other teams will insist that their team is the true champion, because their team excels in the style of play that is most important.

Each team stresses some aspect of the game—speed, power, strategy—and is supported by its fans, who insist that this is the truly crucial aspect of the game. So each side sees its team as the best because it expresses that part of the game that, they claim, is the most important.

Gallie's point, of course, is that such a competition would be characterized by constant, intractable dispute about who is the champion. Clearly, we would never expect the dispute to be settled: who was champion would always be *contested*. More important, though, it seems in principle impossible to resolve the dispute, for it seems impossible to show what aspect of the game is truly the most important, and so which team is truly the champion. In this sense, the championship is *essentially* contested.

Based on this model of the championship, Gallie lists the conditions a concept must fulfill to be essentially contested:

(I) The concept must be evaluative or "appraisive": it must indicate or signify something that is valuable, good, right, worthy, and so on. Each team wants to claim the title of "champion." No party to the dispute would be willing to let another team decide on how "champion" is to be used.

(II) The nature of the concept must be complex, so that different aspects of it can be stressed.

(III) Just why the achievement or condition signified by the complex concept is good, right, worthy, and so on is not manifest; its goodness, rightness, and so on can be explained in different ways, depending on which aspect of the complex concept a supporter focuses.

(IV) The concept is open to new interpretations.

(V) Parties to the dispute recognize that their own use is disputed, and each party has some understanding and appreciation of opposing uses and the aspects of the concept on which they are based.

Because of (V), all contestants must maintain their own use of the concept in the face of other uses; all must defend their claim that the aspect (or aspects) of the concept on which they focus is the most important and try to argue against those who stress other aspects.

An Example: Social Justice

Gallie provides several examples of essentially contested concepts, one of which is the concept of social justice, "or of the general principles that should govern the distribution of goods in a civilised and humane society."[7] There are, Gallie claims, two rival interpretations of social justice, one liberal or individualist, the other socialist or collectivist. The liberal conception builds on the idea of fair dealings between individuals and stresses that just rewards should reflect merit or contribution (see Sections 8.2, 8.3). The central case for this view is fair market relations: in fair transactions people are rewarded differently, and this reflects the merits of the individuals and the products they offer. "In fine," says Gallie, "from the liberal or individualistic standpoint, social justice consists of those arrangements whereby the meritorious individual shall receive back, for his products or services, his . . . due."[8] This has sometimes been called *commutative justice*—its model is a free and fair individual contract, in which both sides honor their commitments and provide a proportionate service to the other. Cephalus (Section 1.1) focused on commutative justice.

In contrast, Gallie tells us, the socialist or collectivist insists that justice is not so much about fair dealings between free individuals (though, of course, that is one aspect of justice), but about the best way for society to distribute its goods to help humans live the best lives possible (see Sections 8.3, 8.4, 9.1). "Social justice, from this standpoint, does not rest on any claims that individual or groups have ever made on one another in respect of fair rewards and returns for work done: rather it is an idea— one aspect of an ideal picture of human living."[9] Social justice looks at the justice or fairness of the overall distribution of goods in a society, not the fairness of individual transactions. Importantly, these two ideas of justice can conflict. Suppose that meritorious individuals make free and fair contracts in which they serve each other's interest, and that they are honest and always keep their contracts. Commutative justice is achieved. In such a condition, however, the skilled and industrious may accumulate great wealth while the unskilled or unindustrious may be left behind. Nielsen, of course, would insist that the resulting distribution of income would be unjust. Thus, a society that focuses on commutative justice may not achieve distributive justice.

Because the idea of justice is so complex, and because both commutative and distributive notions of justice are intelligible uses of the term "justice," it is hard to accept Hayek's claim that the socialist-collectivist is misusing the term or abusing the concept, just as it seems wrong to say that accepting only commutative justice is based on a (clear) misunderstanding of the moral language game. Commutative and distributive justice are, as Gallie notes, "conflicting facets of any advanced social morality."[10] But which is most important? To be sure, to most it would be desirable to achieve both, but if we cannot have both, does the "truly just society" (the "real champion") stress the commutative or the distributive aspect of the "justice game"? Just as we cannot see how the different teams could ever resolve their dispute about who is the champion, Gallie holds that liberals and socialists will not be able to resolve their differences over social justice.

Concepts and Conceptions

Gallie considers the possibility that, perhaps, there is no real disagreement about such concepts. Perhaps the contending parties are not really talking about the same thing at all. If we were more careful, we might say that one team's supporters maintain that it is the "speed champion," another team's declare it is the "power champion," and a third group supports its team as the "strategy champion." Or, in the case of justice, we might say that individualists are the advocates of commutative justice, whereas collectivists are the advocates of distributive justice. But if that is so, there really is no disagreement. The liberal and socialist thought they were arguing about justice, but it turned out that they were simply using the same word to describe different things. But that seems wrong. To claim that, in the end, the liberal and the socialist do not really disagree about justice because they are using the same word (j-u-s-t-i-c-e) to mean different things implies that these central political disputes are simply confusions based on ambiguous words; when once the confusions are exposed, we will see that the liberal and the socialist do not really disagree about the demands of justice. Yet nothing seems clearer than the fundamental difference between liberals and socialists about the demands of justice. We want to understand this dispute—we want to understand precisely what liberals and socialists are disagreeing about when they dispute the true meaning of justice.

To show that liberals and socialists are really disagreeing, Gallie provides two more conditions for essential contestability. According to condition VI, the conflicting parties agree on an "exemplar"—a sort of perfect case—that embodies all the important features of the concept. In the championship example, we might think of some past team that everyone agrees is the best team ever—the one that perfectly exemplifies all the aspects of the sport. Each team's supporters, then, claim that their team is closest to the exemplar. Furthermore, according to Gallie's seventh (VII) condition, each team's supporters claim that their team is the true inheritor of the exemplar's achievement and is developing that achievement in the best way.

Conditions VI and VII ensure that the disputants are really disagreeing: Accepting the same exemplar, all claim that their team is closest to it and develops it in the ways truest to why everyone values the exemplar. Thus, the supporters of the speed team claim that though speed, power, and strategy were all characteristics of the exemplar team, it was its speed that was crucial to its greatness, and that is why the speed team is the true inheritor of the exemplar's achievements. The power and strategy teams, of course, will stress that it was other elements of the exemplar that made for its greatness. In the case of social justice, both liberals and socialists typically accept that justice concerns the fair treatment of individuals, and that in a just society individuals would receive their fair share of the social resources. The idea of a society in which each person is always treated fairly is an ideal shared by a wide range of liberals and socialists; their debate is about how that ideal is best actualized in our world.

One way to understand Gallie's point is to distinguish between a *concept* and various *conceptions* of it.[11] The characteristics of the exemplar constitute the core of the concept: unless one explains this core, and can show that in some way one's account is the best interpretation of this core, one cannot be said to have provided an account of that concept. "Contests . . . are after all, contests over something: essentially contested concepts must have some common core; otherwise how could we justifiably claim that the contests were about the same concept?"[12] A team that ignored the qualities of the exemplar, but still insisted that it was the champion, would not be part of the competition, for the competition is about the best analysis of, and development of, the exemplar. We can call each of these interpretations of the concept a conception of it. Gallie's analysis suggests, then, that we understand each conception as providing an interpretation and development of the core—the concept.

But Gallie's claim that all the disputants accept a common exemplar, and the related idea that all the competing conceptions embrace a common core, falls into the same error as did Socrates: the assumption that there must be an essential common core to all the uses of a concept *C*, by virtue of which we see each of those uses as an instance of *C*. Recall Wittgenstein's directive from Section 1.4: "Don't say: There *must* be something common . . . but *look and see* whether there is anything common to all." We need not posit a common core that is shared by all the uses of a concept such as justice (or liberty or equality), which every conception must seek to explain and develop. Instead of understanding various conceptions as all developing a common core, it is better to see them as providing different accounts of a constellation or cluster[13] of the ideas, beliefs, and actions that make up the area of conceptual dispute. There may be no one element of the constellation that all agree is a part of the concept, but insofar as each conception provides an interpretation of the complex of values, beliefs, and actions (related by family resemblance), it competes with other conceptions.

A conception, then, identifies some parts of the cluster (or language game) as crucial to understanding the concept, while insisting that other elements of the cluster are of less importance, and some perhaps should be eliminated. We might say, then, that a conception *organizes the cluster of beliefs, values and activity, showing which are most important, and how they are all related to one another*. To employ a metaphor, we can think of a conception as a sort of map of the terrain covered by the concept. A good map tells us how to move around the terrain, identifying the crucial landmarks and showing how they all relate to each other.

2.2 Political Ideologies

Ideologies as Systems of Conceptions

Gallie believes that political concepts are essentially contested. A concept such as social justice, he claims, has multiple facets, which allow us to formulate different, essentially contested, conceptions of it. Insofar as Gallie shows how disputes about political concepts can themselves become political disputes, his essential contestability proposal has much to recommend it. But although Gallie does a lot to help explain *how* conceptual disputes arise, he is less clear why we fight so hard about political concepts and why we are so averse to adopting our opponent's conception. His main thought seems to be that because a concept such as justice is apprasive it is somehow a valuable weapon or trophy in our political battles and can be used aggressively against our political opponents. Surely there is more behind our disputes than that. Gallie's individualist liberals and collectivist socialists believe that it is vitally important to understand justice in their preferred ways. In this regard, the championship example seems to mislead us. A team's fans support a team as champion just because it is *their team*. It seems odd to think of people coming to reasoned conclusions about what team they will be a fan of. In an important sense, the choice of one's favorite team is just a preference, like a taste for ice cream or pizza. Liberals and socialists, however, do not typically see their disputes like this; they see themselves as engaged in a deeply important dispute, one in which getting the answer wrong leads to all sorts of problems. Why do they see their conceptual disputes in this way?

Michael Freeden goes far toward explaining the nature of our disputes about "essentially contested concepts." Our political conceptions, Freeden points out, are the basic building blocks of our thinking about politics.[14] What is constructed from these building blocks—conceptions of liberty, power, equality, justice, authority, and so on—are what Freeden classes as "ideologies," comprehensive systems of ideas that provide the basis for explanation and criticism of political life. Thus, on his view, liberalism, socialism, and conservatism are all ideologies built up from an interrelated series of interpretations of political concepts. Liberalism, then, constitutes a *system of conceptions*, centered on a certain conception of liberty, with an allied understanding of equality and justice, supporting a distinctively liberal understanding of authority and democracy.[15] It is important to stress that on Freeden's view liberalism (and the same can be said about other ideologies) is not simply a group of political conceptions: it is a system of interpretation of political concepts; the case for, say, its interpretation of liberty supports, and is supported by, its interpretation of equality, justice, and authority. For example, in examining the theory of John Stuart Mill, the great nineteenth-century liberal, Freeden uncovers

> a mutually sustaining core structure of political concepts that holds Mill's ideology together. It is a core structure in a dual sense: the removal of any one of the concepts would change the peculiar pattern created by their joint intermeshing, causing the core to collapse; and a further range of adjacent and peripheral concepts derives from, and is in a slightly looser sense dependent on, that core. If Mill is a typical liberal, liberal ideology places the protection of individual capacities at the core of its programmatic concerns and its arrangements are primarily geared to ensuring that free individuals will be able to develop their rational and sociable attributes. A diffused, responsible, and limited use of political power is the chief institutional corollary of liberty; it complements Mill's specific conception of liberty, of achieving non-constraint through space for individual expression. It also complements the avoidance of sectional privileges and, with the adjacent concept of democracy that attaches itself to limited power, the accountable and educated exercise of political choices and decisions.[16]

My concern at present is not the accuracy of Freeden's specific analysis of the system of conceptions that constitutes liberalism, but his idea that political ideologies are systems of interpretations of concepts. If we understand political views in this way, we can see why, for example, disputes between liberals and socialists have two key features. First, these disputes run deep. A socialist's devotion to her favored account of social justice is not at all like a devotion to a sports team; it follows from everything else she believes about equality, liberty, and the point of political life. To challenge her views on social justice is not simply to challenge this one political concept, but her system of conceptions—her entire ideology. Because, as Freeden argues, the interpretation of one concept affects the interpretation of others, if (to revert to Gallie's example; Section 2.1) the liberal individualist could convince her that the commutative notion was superior to distributive justice, this would challenge her notions of equality, liberty, and political life, and so undermine her entire socialist ideology. In disputes about social justice, it is not simply one's views about social justice that are being challenged, but ultimately one's overall understanding of political, and perhaps nonpolitical, life.

Second, if our view about one political concept is greatly influenced by our views on others, it should be no surprise that these debates seem so intractable. Running so deep, and involving so much of our overall view of politics and society, our arguments about justice lead us to further disagreements about the nature of liberty, power, equality, and authority. Just because the debates cover so much ground, we must expect that it will be very hard to make headway. In the face of your good reasons for questioning another's view of justice, she replies with an argument that relies on her theory of equality, which you do not share and which you then proceed to criticize. Hence the familiar feeling that our disagreements not only go around in circles, but are continually leading to new disagreements rather than producing agreement.

Reason and Ideology

Freeden's notion of an ideology as a "combination of political concepts organized in a particular way"[17] helps us to explain the nature of our disputes about political concepts. We need to be clearer, however, as to precisely what he means by ways of organizing the interpretations. Freeden emphasizes three main ways that political concepts are linked.

(1) Freeden allows that reason, or what he often calls "logic," organizes our beliefs. This, of course, is the heart of Socrates's method, and indeed all of philosophy. As Socrates reminds Cephalus (Section 1.2), one's beliefs must be consistent; if one accepts that (a) it is always right to do justice and (b) it is wrong to keep one's promise to return a weapon to a madman, then one must reject (c) the claim that justice always requires keeping one's word, including one's promise to return what one has borrowed. A rational person's beliefs must be consistent—more generally, we can say that a rational person's beliefs hang together in a coherent way. As a whole, the beliefs of a rational person make sense, and they support each other to form a sensible and coherent view of the world.

(2) Freeden stresses, however, that ideologies are not simply organized by reason. Because "ideologies have to deliver conceptual social maps and political decisions, and they have to do so in language accessible to the masses as well as intellectuals, to amateur as well as professional thinkers," they freely mix appeals to reason and emotion.[18] An ideology may be organized in a way that is rationally flawed, but emotionally appealing. An emotionally appealing ideology may entertain inconsistent beliefs. Fascism, for instance, seemed to simultaneously maintain that all individuals should be subservient to the collective group and that some individuals were superior and should lead and shape the collectivity. On the face of it, these are inconsistent beliefs; but if they are emotionally appealing—say, to the masses who desire to be led by their superiors and yet yearn for equality—they both may be important parts of an ideology.

(3) More generally, Freeden emphasizes that ideologies are shaped by culture and history. What combinations of interpretations are accepted as "going together" in such a way as to form an ideology is as much a matter of history and culture as it is of reason. Ideologies, on his view, are attached to social groups and shaped by political and social conflicts about

power, and their character is dependent on the requirements of these conflicts as well as the relations between ideas. Because ideologies "perform a range of services, such as legitimation, ordering, simplification, and action-orientation," the configurations of concepts they produce are ones that have arisen because they serve these purposes.[19]

The upshot of Freeden's analysis is that the student of ideologies should not engage in a "quest for a good usage of a concept."[20] We can try to *understand* ideologies—to understand how they organize political conceptions in a particular way—but it seems illegitimate to try to "clear up" the interpretations. After all, reason is not the sole, perhaps not even the primary, organizing principle of an ideology. To revise an ideology's interpretation of a concept by making it better conform to reason, or by abandoning some parts of it that do not fit with the others, is to ignore that the glue holding an ideology together is an emotive-political-cultural-rational mix. Given this, it seems that "there are no correct ways of defining concepts."[21]

Gallie arrived at if not the same then at least a broadly similar conclusion. Gallie believed that recognizing "a given concept as essentially contested implies recognition of rival uses of it (such as oneself repudiates) as not only logically possible and humanly 'likely,' but as of permanent critical value to one's own use or interpretation of the concept in question."[22] As Gallie perceives it, the various contenders all have value—all articulate elements of the concept, albeit in differing ways. Thus, Gallie too seems suspicious of those who would dismiss rival uses as wrong and who claim that they alone have the correct interpretation. And he seems suspicious because he apparently doubts that there is such a thing as *the correct* interpretation of an essentially contested concept.

2.3 Political Philosophy and Political Theories

Ideology Versus Political Theory: The Example of Public and Private

Freeden is certainly correct that liberalism, socialism, and conservatism can be viewed as systems of conceptions organized on partly rational, but also emotive, cultural, and historical grounds. And thus it may well be that an ideology will not be fully consistent, but nevertheless (indeed, perhaps because of that inconsistency) it can serve to legitimate and organize political movements. For students of political thinking, it will be important and interesting if, say, the political movement known as "liberalism" should turn out to be in some way rationally flawed. Consider, for example, Stanley Benn and my work on the liberal conception of the public and private. For the most part, we argued, the liberal conception of the private and the public presupposes an individualist theory of social life:

society can be reduced to individuals (see Section 3.4). On this view, "*Public*, as opposed to *private*, is that which has no immediate relation to any specified person or persons, but may directly concern any member or members of the community, without distinction."[23] In contrast, what is private is that which can be assigned to a specific person or group. So, we might say, in the basically liberal individualist world, the idea of the private focuses on specific, assignable individuals, whereas the public centers on general classes and can refer to *anyone* or *everyone* in that class. A library is public because it is open to any member of the class of residents, whereas a private house is only open to the *specific* individuals owning it or invited into it. Both these conceptions—of the public and private—make perfect sense in a world composed simply of individuals, however.

But as Jeremy Bentham (1748–1832) recognized, this purely individualist way of looking at society makes less sense of other ideas, such as the public interest:

> The interest of individuals, it is said, ought to yield to the public interest. But what does this mean? Is not one individual as much a part of the public as another? This public interest, which you introduce as a person, is only an abstract term; it represents nothing but the mass of individual interests. It is necessary to take them all into account, instead of considering some as all, and others as nothing. . . . In a word, the interest of everybody is sacred, or the interest of nobody.
>
> Individual interests are the only real interests.[24]

In Bentham's thoroughly individualistic world, the only sensible meaning of the "public interest" would be the "interest of everyone." Yet Bentham is quite right that political discourse often treats "the public" as a sort of giant person: the public interest is not the interest of everyone, but the interest of "the community," considered as an entity in its own right, and one that cannot be reduced simply to a collection of individuals. After all, very few of our appeals to the public interest really are appeals to the interests of absolutely each and every person in the community, but neither do they reduce to appeals to the interests of the mere majority. Rather, one who speaks of the public interest typically has in mind some notion of the interest of the community as a whole, or the society as such. Although, as Bentham recognized, this idea does not fit into an individualist understanding of society, liberals often make appeals to the public interest or the public good.

Now, as *outsiders* trying to understand liberal ideology, we find this an enlightening insight: we find that the power and persuasiveness of liberalism may result from its ability to switch from its predominant individualist theory to a nonindividualist view of community when making certain sorts of political appeals. Consider, however, what a liberal—someone who accepted liberal ideas and conceptions as her guide in politics—would make of this. From the *inside*—from within liberalism—could one reasonably continue to affirm this doctrine knowing that one was appealing to inconsistent views of society? It seems not. The analysis of the liberal conception of the public and private implies that the liberal conception is rationally flawed: it cannot be sound, because it supposes an impossibility—that society both is, and is not, simply composed of individuals. The liberal conception of the public and private thus cannot be justified, and it certainly cannot in any sense be correct. To continue adherence to the liberal conception of the public and private would be an act of faith, as some Roman Catholics accept the mystery of the Trinity (but, unlike the Catholic, the liberal could not have faith that this mystery will be resolved in an afterlife). As rational agents, however, we seek beliefs that make sense of the world, and inconsistent beliefs cannot help us do that.

If liberalism is not simply an *ideology*—a social or political phenomenon that merits study—but a *political theory* that contends for our allegiance and that seeks to guide our actions, it must be plausible; and to be plausible, it must be internally consistent. Should a liberal confront the sort of inconsistency revealed in liberal conceptions of the public and private, the rational liberal must either abandon liberalism or reconstruct it so as to make it consistent. And of course, the same can be said of conservatism, socialism, and so on.

Consider again the metaphor of a map. Freeden and others have compared systems of political conceptions to maps (Sections 2.1, 2.2): they help us navigate around the political world by highlighting some features and showing how one feature is related to others. Now, one thing a rational agent wants is a consistent map. Imagine that you are visiting Australia, and you wish to drive from Sydney to Melbourne. After nine hours, you stop to consult your map to see just where you are. Unfortunately, your map has two different, inconsistent parts; if you look at the first sheet you are almost in Melbourne, but if you check the second, you have gone entirely in the wrong direction and will soon be in Brisbane. Where are you, and in which direction should you go? Clearly, an inconsistent map is no help at all. Until the entire map makes sense and all its directions are consistent with each other, it does not even begin to help you make sense of your (conceptual) world. Of course, even such inconsistent maps may have their uses: if Australia was invaded by a foreign power, this would be the prefect map for Australians to give to their invaders! One thing such a map will not do, however, is to help people make sense of the locations of Australian cities.

Justificatory Political Theories

We can think of a political theory (as opposed to an ideology) as seeking to *justify* a specific organization of different interpretations of political concepts. A political theory will provide linked arguments for conceptions of liberty, power, equality, justice, authority, democracy, and so on. It will justify each interpretation of the chief political concepts by appeal to other interpretations, as well as other fundamental values and claims (for example, individualism or collectivism; see Section 3.4). Furthermore, the justifications offered by the political theory will place some political ideas at the core of its concerns, while putting others in a secondary position, and pushing yet others to a marginal place or even entirely rejecting them.

To say that a political theory justifies a particular conception involves four important claims. (1) A justification does not seek simply to convince or persuade: it provides *reasons*. A justification, then, does not appeal to mere emotions or prejudices. Because political theories seek to justify rather than merely persuade, they are bound by reason to respect consistency and logicality. No matter how persuasive, an appeal to contradictory considerations cannot count as a justification.

It may be useful here to distinguish *justification* from *legitimation*. A political view is justified if it is supported by good reasons, is free from internal inconsistency, is consistent with known facts, and so on. Justification is a matter of sound belief. Rational adherents of a political theory must suppose that the view is justified; if it is not supported by good reasons, then adherence to it is not rational. Although related, the idea of legitimation is distinct. A political ideology may legitimize a conception of, say, justice, for its adherents insofar as the ideology advances considerations that lead its adherents to approve or accept that conception. The considerations advanced by the legitimizing ideology may be good reasons, but they also may be emotional appeals, ungrounded cultural prejudices, and inconsistent doctrines: what matters is that the package of considerations advanced by the ideology actually induces people to accept or approve of its conception of justice. If the package of considerations actually produces widespread support for the conception or provides considerations that lead people to conclude that it is the best conception, the ideology has legitimized the conception. People view it as legitimate. Viewed from the inside, then, the ideology seeks to legitimize certain conceptions, social arrangements, and policies for its adherents: it seeks to induce them to accept or approve of the conceptions and arrangements. But insofar as the package of considerations involves unreasoned emotional appeals or relies on inconsistent claims or false or weakly grounded theories, the package fails to justify the arrangement.

Thus, if liberalism is an inconsistent or confused political doctrine it can still legitimize (and so may be a perfectly good ideology) but it cannot justify (and so is inadequate as a political theory). [25] Now, interestingly, insofar as you and I are rational agents, we must suppose that the political doctrine that guides us is not merely a legitimizing ideology but a justificatory political theory. A rational adherent of liberalism (or socialism or conservatism) must see it as more than a way to legitimize certain social arrangements—as a way to induce people to approve of those social arrangements. The rational adherent must suppose that liberalism is a justified political theory; that is, it provides good reasons to adopt the liberal view of politics.

(2) To say that political theories justify an interpretation of a political concept is different from saying that a theory "chooses," "adopts," or "prefers" a specific conception. This is an important point. Conceptual analysis is not about "choosing" how to "clear up" our inconsistent or confused concepts, nor is it a decision to "stand by" one interpretation rather than another. Justifying a specific conception is, in the end, not at all like becoming the fan of a sports team. A political theory identifies some considerations as important, and having done that, it is led to seeing some aspects of, for example, justice or liberty as more important than others. As a contemporary political philosopher observes, our arguments—our justifications—"are our connection with the considerations that ultimately matter to us," and it is those considerations that lead us to favor one way of seeing justice or liberty rather than another.[26] We cannot answer Socrates's question—"What is justice?"—until we know the things that really matter to us, and the way in which we understand society. Thus, only within a political theory can we justify one conception of, say, justice, rather than another.

(3) This explains the intractable nature of political disputes to which Gallie has called our attention. If we can only justify a conception within the framework of a political theory, we will find that our justifications—however convincing they are to us—will not move those who are employing a competing political theory. From their point of view, our conception will not seem justified, for the considerations that matter to us will not necessarily be compelling in their competing political theory. Hence we may well find that even our very best arguments do not move those with whom we disagree. And because our conceptions follow from the other things we see as important, we are not apt to compromise or back down in these political disputes, for that would be to give up much of what we hold important.

(4) In contrast to Freeden and Gallie's view (Section 2.2), however, it does not follow from this that none of the parties is correct and there is no correct answer to conceptual disputes. It is certainly true that given the

limits of time, and our ability to think things through, we cannot resolve the differences between the major political theories. We cannot know in advance, however, whether this is because none of the theories is better than all the others or because we have not yet carried on the argument far enough and thoroughly enough to discover which theory is the best. In the end, both Freeden and Gallie claim that they know what the result would be if we carried out a rational dialogue to its completion—they know that in the end no theory can be shown to be the best. But how can we *know that?* All we can say right now is that given the imperfect and limited reasoners we are, we disagree about which conception of liberty, justice, or equality is best.

The question, then, is, which should we assume: (a) that no theory can ever lay claim to being the best, or (b) that some theory could perhaps make out such a claim if we thought long enough and hard enough? Gallie seems to think that (a) is the superior assumption. As he sees it, the assumption that there is no single correct answer induces a tolerance of the views of others:

> Recognition of a given concept as essentially contested implies recognition of the rival uses of it (such as oneself repudiates) as not only logically possible and humanly "likely," but as of permanent critical value to one's own use or interpretation of the concept in question; whereas to regard any rival use as anathema, perverse, bestial or lunatic means, in many cases, to submit oneself to the chronic human peril of underestimating, or completely ignoring, the value of one's opponents' positions.[27]

Recognition that there is no uniquely correct answer, Gallie believes, will tend to undermine an intolerant fanatical belief that one's political opponents have nothing worthwhile to say, while encouraging an appreciation that one's opponents also see an aspect of the concept, and so have a valuable critical contribution to make to the debate. Because your favored conception of an essentially contested concept cannot be shown to be the uniquely correct one, Gallie believes that recognition of the essentially contested nature of political concepts leads you to be more tolerant and appreciate of other conceptions.

If, however, we know in advance that no position can be shown to be superior to the others, what is the point of argument? We might hope to win converts, but to do that emotive appeals are likely to be more effective than arguments about "What is liberty?" or "What is justice?" If we know there could never be a correct answer, why waste the time arguing and debating? Rather than promoting a tolerant debate, accepting that there can be no correct or best answer makes rational defense of one's position and critique of the other's position pointless. Why argue when no one can be right? Perhaps *some* point remains: even if there is no correct answer, there might be some that are thoroughly wrongheaded—perhaps debate is simply about showing that your position is not one of the wrong ones.[28] But there is still no point arguing with the good alternatives to your view—and it would seem that it is precisely those that we most want to confront and question.

Of course, fanaticism and intolerance are to be avoided. The spirit of tolerant debate, however, is not fostered by a conviction that there is no right answer to be had (for that undermines the spirit of debate) but by a recognition of our own *fallibility*—recognition that we all easily fall into error and we can never be certain that we possess the truth and others are in the grip of error. Recognition of our fallibility leads us to appreciate the potential value in the conflicting opinions of others and to constructively engage them rather than repress or ignore them. And given the complexity of the issues, involving as they do entire systems of concepts, it would be a foolish person indeed who did not appreciate her own fallibility. In contrast, Gallie's position suggests a *skepticism* that there is any correct answer to be had. Although the fallibilist believes that there is a best answer but is always aware that her own position may be wrong, the skeptic questions whether there is a best answer.

It is clear why the fallibilist sees potential value in the competing positions of others: perhaps they have the best answer, and it is the best answer the fallibilist seeks. Thus, the fallibilist will not wish to silence opposing views. As John Stuart Mill argued, we should not seek to repress a view that competes with our own because it

> may possibly be true. Those who desire to suppress it, of course deny its truth; but they are not infallible. They have no authority to decide the question for all mankind, and exclude every other person from the means of judging. To refuse a hearing to an opinion, because they are sure that it is false, is to assume that their certainty is the same thing as absolute certainty. All silencing of discussion is an assumption of infallibility.[29]

It is far less clear why skepticism would lead to toleration of competing views. True, a skeptic cannot claim that competing views are false or wrong, but neither can the skeptic hope to learn the truth from his opponent (because, says the skeptic, "there are no correct ways of defining concepts"). If part of the skeptic's ideology is that those who disagree with him are a menace (not because they are wrong, just because they disagree) and so should be silenced, his skeptical view of political concepts provides him with no reason to refrain from silencing others. Why should he not stand up for his intolerant ideology? It is, after all, no less correct than other, more tolerant, views.

2.4 Summary

This chapter has considered several explanations of the nature of conceptual disputes and the reasons why they run so deep and are so difficult to resolve. In Section 2.1, I examined Gallie's essential contestability thesis, according to which parties to a conceptual debate favor conceptions that place importance on different aspects of a complex concept. In some sense, Gallie seems to be arguing, the different conceptions each stress a different, but valuable and important, aspect of the concept, and there is no way to adjudicate which is the superior. In Section 2.2, I inquired into why the participants in these conceptual debates are so wedded to their positions. I argued that a person's favored conception of, say, liberty is not freestanding, but linked to her favored conceptions of equality, justice, and so on. Consequently, debates about one political concept lead to our interpretations of others; to give way to our opponent on one concept may lead to undermining our entire political outlook. If, then, one wants to understand a particular political conception, one must place it in a political theory—a system of such conceptions.

The chapter concluded with a contrast between two ways of understanding political theories: as ideologies and as justificatory. If we follow Freeden, we shall understand these systems of conceptions as held together not only by reasons, values, and claims about society, but by emotional and cultural appeals that may lead to inconsistent yet engaging political views. In contrast, for political theories to be understood as genuinely justificatory, they must make sense by providing a reasoned and coherent view of the world. We saw that although a student looking at a political view from the "outside" can see it as an ideology, those who accept it and use it to make sense of the world and organize their political action must see it as justificatory.

Justificatory political theories, I argued, make claims that they are in some way correct. As we saw in Section 2.1, liberals and socialists disagree about the nature of justice: each not only favors her own view, she thinks it the best view. Both Gallie and Freeden suggest that this is a mistake—there really is no true or correct conception. "The language of ideologies," says Freeden, "is couched in terms of truth-assertions, but ideologies . . . do not attain truth-value status."[30] I concluded the chapter by considering whether tolerant debate is best supported by the assumption that (1) none of our views can possibly be the correct or best view, or (2) although there may well be a best answer to our disputes, because they are so complex, and we are so apt to error, we should not suppose we are certainly right and our opponents wrong beyond a doubt. The second assumption, I argued, gives us reasons both to pursue debate and to conduct it in a tolerant way.

Notes

1. See Felix Oppenheim, *Political Concepts: A Reconstruction* (Oxford: Basil Blackwell, 1981), chap. 9.

2. By the French political philosopher, Bertrand de Jouvenel, *Sovereignty: An Inquiry into the Political Good,* J. F. Huntington, trans. (Cambridge: Cambridge University Press, 1956), p. 317.

3. Kai Nielsen, *Equality and Liberty: A Defense of Radical Egalitarianism* (Totowa, NJ: Rowman and Allenheld, 1985), p. 70.

4. F. A. Hayek, *Law, Legislation and Liberty,* vol. 2, *The Mirage of Social Justice* (London: Routledge, 1982), p. 62.

5. Nielsen, *Equality and Liberty,* for example, p. 197.

6. W. B. Gallie, "Essentially Contested Concepts," in his *Philosophy and the Historical Understanding,* 2nd ed. (New York: Shocken Books, 1968), pp. 157–191. For discussions of this idea, see Christine Swanton, *Freedom: A Coherence Theory* (Indianapolis, IN: Hackett, 1992), chap. 1; John Gray, "On the Contestability of Social and Political Concepts," *Political Theory,* vol. 5 (August 1977), pp. 331–348.

7. Gallie, "Essentially Contested Concepts," p. 181.

8. Ibid.

9. Ibid., p. 182.

10. Ibid.

11. For a very helpful analysis, see Swanton, *Freedom: A Coherence Theory,* chap. 1.

12. Steven Lukes, *Power: A Radical View* (New York: Macmillan, 1974), p. 187.

13. On the idea of a "cluster concept," see William E. Connolly, *The Terms of Political Discourse,* 2nd ed. (Princeton: Princeton University Press, 1983), chap. 1.

14. Michael Freeden, *Ideologies and Political Theory: A Conceptual Approach* (Oxford: Clarendon Press, 1996), p. 2.

15. See ibid., chap. 4.

16. Ibid., pp. 153–154.

17. Ibid., p. 75.

18. Ibid., p. 30.

19. Ibid., p. 22.

20. Ibid., p. 53.

21. Ibid.

22. Gallie, "Essentially Contested Concepts," p. 188.

23. Sir George Cornewall Lewis, quoted in Stanley I. Benn and Gerald F. Gaus, "The Liberal Conception of the Public and Private" in Benn and Gaus, eds., *Public and Private in Social Life* (New York: St. Martin's Press, 1983), p. 32.

24. Jeremy Bentham, *The Theory of Legislation,* 2nd ed. (London: Trübner, 1871), p. 144.

25. I argue in my "Liberalism at the End of the Century," *Journal of Political Ideologies,* vol. 5 (2000), pp. 45–65, that the incoherence of liberal ideology may well account for its wide appeal.

26. Jeremy Waldron, *The Right to Private Property* (Oxford: Clarendon Press, 1988), p. 433.

27. Gallie, "Essentially Contested Concepts," pp. 187–188.

28. See here Swanton, *Freedom: A Coherence Theory*, chap. 1.

29. John Stuart Mill, *On Liberty*, in John Gray, ed., *On Liberty and Other Essays* (New York: Oxford University Press, 1991), chap. 2, para. 3.

30. Freeden, *Ideologies and Political Theory*, p. 94.

3

POLITICAL THEORIES: CONCEPTUAL STRUCTURES AND ENDURING TYPES

3.1 Liberalism, Socialism, and Conservatism

Enduring Types

In the last chapter, I argued that political theories involve systems of interpretations of political concepts. A political theory will, for example, advance a certain conception of liberty, which helps justify a view of equality, which in turn supports (and is supported by) a conception of justice and authority. And as Freeden rightly contends (Section 2.2), the political theory will order these concepts—some will be given pride of place, whereas others will be accorded supporting roles or a peripheral status in the overall scheme.

The construction of such a system of concepts will often involve creativity, producing novel combinations of interpretations. Political theorizing is an ongoing enterprise, and one aspect of that enterprise is drawing new conceptual maps, which logically relate political concepts in hitherto unthought-of ways. There is no formula for the creation of a political theory. That said, the history of political theory reveals enduring types: systems of interpretations that traditions of thinkers have embraced and, within limits, have sought to improve and modify. These enduring types unite conceptions of liberty, power, equality, justice, and political authority, appealing to values and visions of society that produce a coherent and compelling view of these fundamental political concepts. These enduring political theories are by no means the only reasonable ways to arrange political conceptions, but their appeal over hundreds of years to sizable groups of thinkers and citizens makes them of special importance in our debates about political concepts.

When describing political theories as systems of political conceptions, we must always remember Wittgenstein's insight that language is not merely about words, but about actions and practices (Section 1.3). To understand liberty, power, equality, justice, rights, and authority in certain ways is not just to *think* and *talk* in certain ways, but to *do* certain things: to work for certain sorts of just arrangements, opposing some sorts of governmental actions while supporting others, and so on. Like language itself, political theories are complexes of words and actions.

The focus of this book will be on liberalism, socialism, and conservatism—three enduring political theories and arguably the three most important of the past two hundred years. We shall see that these are by no means monolithic views: within each there are varieties, which arrange political concepts in different ways. Also, as we proceed we will have occasion to contrast these three enduring theories to other political theories.

Liberalism

"By definition," it has been said, "a liberal is a man who believes in liberty."[1] All liberal theories, regardless of their disagreements, place individual liberty (or freedom) at the heart of politics[2]; indeed, so important is liberty to liberals that, to a large degree, debates about the nature of liberty are debates within the liberal tradition. We shall see that liberal devotion to freedom leads to a view of justice that gives pride of place to expansive liberty rights while making equality a more limited, secondary, notion. Justice focuses on equal liberty rights. Because liberals typically see the authority of government as a limitation of freedom, they are usually suspicious of it.

The liberal tradition and its debates about the nature of liberty approximates one aspect of Gallie's description of an essentially contested concept. It will be recalled from Section 2.1 that, according to Gallie's condition VI, the conflicting parties agree on an "exemplar"—a sort of perfect case—that perfectly embodies the concept. In his championship example, it was perhaps some past team that everyone agrees is the best team ever—the one that perfectly exemplifies all aspects of the sport. Now, in the liberal tradition John Stuart Mill's *On Liberty* (1859) approximates the status of an exemplar. Although a few liberals are highly critical of *On Liberty*, to an amazing extent it is seen as the quintessential liberal text. In what is perhaps the most famous paragraph in the liberal tradition, Mill explains the aim of *On Liberty:*

The object of this Essay is to assert one very simple principle, as entitled to govern absolutely the dealings of society with the individual in the way of compulsion and control, whether the means used be physical force in the form of legal penalties, or the moral coercion of public opinion. That principle is, that the sole end for which mankind are warranted, individually or collectively, in interfering with the liberty of action of any of their number, is self-protection. That the only purpose for which power can be rightfully exercised over any member of a civilized community, against his will, is to prevent harm to others. His own good, either physical or moral, is not a sufficient warrant. He cannot rightfully be compelled to do or forbear because it will be better for him to do so, because it will make him happier, because, in the opinions of others, to do so would be wise, or even right. These are good reasons for remonstrating with him, or reasoning with him, or persuading him, or entreating him, but not for compelling him, or visiting him with any evil, in case he do otherwise. To justify that, the conduct from which it is desired to deter him must be calculated to produce evil to some one else. The only part of the conduct of any one, for which he is amenable to society, is that which concerns others. In the part which merely concerns himself, his independence is, of right, absolute. Over himself, over his own body and mind, the individual is sovereign.[3]

As Mill says in another work, the proper role of coercion—of employing threats to get people to do what you want them to do (see Section 4.1)—"is to enforce upon everyone the conduct necessary to give all other persons their fair chance: conduct which chiefly consists in not doing them harm, and not impeding them in anything which without harming others does good to themselves." And Mill adds, "Demanding no more than this, society, in any tolerable circumstances, obtains much more: for the natural activity of human nature, shut out from all noxious directions, will expand itself in useful ones."[4]

These passages express fundamental liberal themes. First, Mill defends one's sovereignty over one's own life—the freedom to lead one's own life in a way that one sees fit. Yet, though liberals insist on the primacy of freedom, they recognize the necessity of limits on freedom. My freedom may be limited if I use it in a way that harms others. Mill is explicit that my freedom cannot be limited to protect *me* from *my own* choices: what I do with my life is up to me *except* insofar as it harms *others*. Because Mill places so much value on the individual's sovereignty over her own life, he places severe limits on the authority of others, including government, over the individuals. And although Mill was a proponent of democratic government, he was always worried that democratic majorities may tyrannize over the individual, wrongfully limiting her liberty. (Compare Freeden's description of the Millian conceptual map in Section 2.2.)

Toward the end of the nineteenth century, liberal theory split into two camps. What are often called "classical" liberals followed Mill in insisting on the central role of freedom, and the necessity, in the interests of freedom, to drastically limit coercion or force, including the force of government. For classical liberals, both freedom and justice are closely bound to the protection of the market order and private property rights. Hence classical liberals have been advocates of limited government and free markets. Being wary of all government, they are cautious advocates of democracy. Insofar as democracy protects liberty, they support it, but, again following Mill, they oppose democracies that overly restrict the freedom of some of their citizens. F. A. Hayek, one of the preeminent classical liberals of the twentieth century, writes of democracy that it "is an ideal worth fighting for to the utmost, because it is our only protection . . . against tyranny. Though democracy itself is not freedom . . . it is one of the most important safeguards of freedom."[5] In all this, Hayek sees himself developing Mill's liberalism. Although critical of some of Mill's specific views, Hayek concludes one of his most important works with the same quote with which Mill introduced *On Liberty*: "The grand, the leading principle, towards which every argument unfolded in these pages directly converges, is the absolutely and essential importance of human development in its richest diversity."[6]

Contrasting to the classical liberals are "revisionist" or "new liberals," who sought to move liberalism closer to socialism. L. T. Hobhouse (1864–1929), a leading new liberal, went so far as to advocate a "Liberal Socialism."[7] Hobhouse also saw himself as developing Mill's doctrine: "The teaching of Mill brings us close to the heart of Liberalism."[8] Hobhouse and his fellow revisionist liberals reinterpret liberty, distancing it from private property and moving it closer to a full embrace of the democratic welfare state. Though individual liberty remains at the core, their favored conception of liberty harmonizes with an extensive democratic welfare state pursuing social justice and regulating market relations.

Because liberals have developed Mill's exemplar in such profoundly different ways, I will distinguish throughout between classical and revisionist liberalism. We shall see that classical and revisionist liberals defend markedly different conceptions of liberty, equality, and justice, yet their common stress on liberty and their Millian heritage firmly identify them both as parts of the liberal tradition.

Socialism

As Freeden notes, "All socialisms assert the equality of human beings,"[9] placing strong ideals of equality at the core of their political outlooks, which in turn provides the basis for strongly egalitarian conceptions of social justice and democracy. It has often been said that one of the great debates in political theory is between proponents of liberty and of equality. Now, since liberals place liberty in a supreme position, relegating equality to secondary status, it may seem that as standard bearers of equality, socialists would simply reverse this priority, upholding equality over liberty. Although this may well have been a characteristic of early socialist theories, it is not a feature of recent socialism. Indeed, according to one contemporary socialist, "Liberty deserves almost fanatic support from democratic socialists."[10] Fundamental to most recent socialisms is the claim that given the proper interpretations, liberty and equality are mutually supporting. Liberty, says an important contemporary socialist philosopher, "requires equality,"[11] in particular, an equality of power. In a similar vein, another contemporary socialist insists that "freedom and equality, far from being opposed ideals, actually coincide."[12] In arguing for a coincidence of liberty and equality, socialists pave the way for claims that strongly egalitarian democratic governments enhance freedom. In contrast, they insist, private property–based markets—perhaps all markets—are the enemy of freedom, producing inegalitarian concentrations of property and power.

Again, although some simplification is helpful in understanding complex political theories, we must be careful not to be too simplistic. Socialists, like liberals, disagree on important issues. One such disagreement, which we will consider in Section 10.4, occurred between democratic socialists and the followers of Vladimir Ilich Lenin (1870–1924) as to whether a nondemocratic state, controlled by a socialist elite, could be a justified means to socialist egalitarian values. Could the values of social and economic equality justify an authoritarian state that was devoted to those socialist aims? And what feature of the socialist conceptual map could lead an otherwise egalitarian political theory to endorse a highly inegalitarian view of political authority?

Conservatism

One recent political theorist has characterized conservatism as "a philosophy of imperfection, committed to the idea of limits, and directed towards the defense of a limited style of politics."[13] At the core of conservatism is a conception of politics as a limited and difficult activity—one that is typically misunderstood. Conservatism arose as a reaction to the grand political projects of first liberals and then socialists to bring about revolutionary changes in support of their key political values: liberty and equality. The French Revolution of 1789 was the spur for the greatest of all conservative works, Edmund Burke's (1729–1797) *Reflections on the Revolution in France* (1790). Because of the complexity of society and the limits of our reason, the conservative stresses that politics cannot bring about great, beneficial, revolutionary changes. Attempts at such revolutionary change almost always bring about disasters—witness, says the conservative, the great liberal and socialist revolutions, France in 1789 and Russia in 1917. As Burke saw it, "A man full of warm speculative benevolence may wish his society otherwise constituted than he finds it; but a good patriot, and a true politician, always considers how he shall make the most of the existing material of his country. A disposition to preserve, and an ability to improve, would be my standard of a statesman."[14]

As we shall see, the conservative typically stresses that politics is a practical and complex activity. Indeed, says the conservative—and Plato has been the inspiration of many conservatives on this point—it is the art of governing people and running a state. The main justification for some rather than others possessing this authority is that some, and not others, have practical knowledge of the art of politics. Ruling, like medicine or carpentry, is an art. It requires a proper knowledge of the techniques of the art, its tools and its aims. And like any art, it should be performed by those who are best equipped to participate. If one would not trust one's body to a doctor who has no practical knowledge of medicine, but only has read a book, why would one trust one's society to a group that has no practical knowledge of politics? Because the conservative insists that most do not understand the limited possibilities of the art of politics, conservatives offer a view of political authority that stresses the importance of expertise, and so is critical of egalitarian (democratic) values. The attitude toward liberty is more complex—it is not so much a rejection of the idea as an attempt to control and limit its revolutionary potential, stressing not a general, expansive notion of liberty, but a defined enumeration of important traditional political liberties. And it is clear that the conservative rejects the socialist's attempt to reconcile liberty and equality: "There is no principle more basic in the conservative philosophy than that of the inherent and absolute incompatibility between liberty and equality."[15]

Again, within the conservative tradition there is variety and subtlety. Some conservatives stress the limits of politics, whereas others grant great political authority to political experts, and yet others give government the role of enforcing traditional virtue and morality. One of our aims will be to discover what parts of the conservative system of ideas justify these different understandings of justice and authority.

Three Enduring Political Issues

Although political theories are systems of mutually supporting interpretations of political concepts, our enduring political theories have other elements as well. As we have just seen in our sketch of conservative political thinking, one of its roots is a skepticism about the powers of human reason to understand and control society. Liberalism, for example, can be understood as having positions on the nature of knowledge, human society and psychology, reason, and ideals of life.[16] A liberal's position on these matters helps justify her interpretations of political concepts and the policy proposals that follow from them. An entire political theory, then, is a highly complex structure, involving claims about morality, the nature of society and persons, reason, liberty, equality, justice, and so on.

To fully grasp the justification for a liberal, conservative, or socialist analysis of a political concept, we would have to take account of the relevance of the political theorist's positions on all these other matters. That, though, would be a daunting undertaking, and one outside the scope of the book. Although we cannot consider all these other elements, we can identify three crucial issues on which liberals, socialists, and conservatives have long disagreed and that are crucial to understanding their disagreements about political concepts: (1) rationalism/antirationalism, (2) theories of human nature, and (3) individualism/collectivism. Again, these three issues are by no means the only relevant ones; but they are fundamental, and they explain a great deal of the differences in the socialist, liberal, and conservative outlooks. Throughout this book, we shall see that differences on these three basic issues often result in very different interpretations of our main political concepts.

3.2 Rationalism/Antirationalism

Rationalism

An enduring issue in political theory is the role of reason in human affairs. A rationalist is one who stresses the power of human reason to understand society, to enlighten us about what is good and right, and guide society along the best path. The rationalist is generally suspicious of custom and tradition, for people follow them without knowing why they do so or whether the actions dictated by custom and tradition are the best options open to us. When confronted with a customary practice, the rationalist analyzes and questions it: does reason point toward a better way of doing things? A rationalist is thus apt to look to science rather than tradition for guidance, for science is the systematic effort to apply reason to understand nature and society. For similar reasons, rationalists are apt to be suspicious of religion insofar as it asks us to accept beliefs on faith rather than reason.

Oakeshott on Rationalism

Fundamental to most conservative political theory is a criticism of rationalism in politics. Michael Oakeshott (1901–1990), the foremost recent conservative political philosopher, tells us that a rationalist in politics is characterized by the following traits:[17]

(1) A rationalist believes that thought should be free from any obligation to any authority and should follow the dictates of reason alone.

(2) A rationalist is the enemy of tradition, authority, custom, and prejudice.

(3) A rationalist feels herself free to question any opinion, belief, or habit.

(4) A rationalist trusts the power of reason to determine truth and value.

(5) A rationalist believes that the power of reason is common to all humans.

(6) A rationalist finds it hard to believe that others who think about a problem in a clear and honest way will arrive at an answer that differs from her own.

(7) A rationalist does not pay enough attention to experience; he always wants to rely on his own reason and begin afresh the solution to every problem.

(8) When a rationalist does learn from experience, he wants to transform its lesson into a rational formula that can be conveyed to all.

(9) A rationalist does not grasp the mysteries of life.

(10) A rationalist uses theories to understand events; hence she only recognizes the large outline of experience.

As Oakeshott sees it, this sort of thinking has characterized much of modern life, and especially political theory since the Middle Ages. Liberalism and socialism, with their strong declarations of political values around which politics should be organized, are, in Oakeshott's eyes, manifestations of the rationalism that has characterized modern European politics.[18] These rationalistic theories ignore experience and seek to regulate the life of complex societies by abstract concepts invented by political thinkers. Oakeshott does not claim that such theories are useless. But, he insists, they capture only a part of the truth. The rationalist, though, does not see this; she mistakes part of the truth for the whole truth.

Oakeshott builds his case around two types of knowledge: what he calls "technical knowledge" and "practical knowledge." The first— technical knowledge—involves knowledge of technique:

In every art and science, and in every practical activity, a technique is involved. In many activities this technical knowledge is formulated into rules which are, or may be, deliberately learned, remembered, and, as we say, put into practice; but whether or not it is, or has been, precisely formulated, its chief characteristic is that it is susceptible of precise formulation, although special skill and insight may be required to give it that formulation. The technique (or part of it) of driving a motor car on English roads is to be found in the Highway Code, the technique of cookery is contained in the cookery book, and the technique of discovery in natural science or in history is in their rules of research, observation and verification.[19]

Oakeshott contrasts this sort of knowledge to practical knowledge, which cannot be formulated into rules. It is knowledge one gains through actual experience, as a cook knows many things that are not written in cookbooks, but can only be learned by being a cook. As Oakeshott puts it, technical knowledge will tell a person *what* to do, but practical knowledge will tell him *how* to do it.[20]

Technical knowledge can be written down. It can be codified or put in the form of rules. Practical knowledge, Oakeshott believes, cannot be. This does not mean that practical knowledge cannot be taught; a master craftsman teaches his apprentice his skills. But all that he teaches cannot be reduced to rules and put down in some book. The typical expression of such practical knowledge, Oakeshott writes,

is in a customary or traditional way of doing things, or, simply, in practice. And this gives it the appearance of imprecision and consequently of uncertainty, of being a matter of opinion, of probability rather than truth. It is, indeed, a knowledge that is expressed in taste or connoisseurship, lacking rigidity and ready for the impress of the mind of the learner.[21]

Now, says Oakeshott, "Rationalism is the assertion that what I have called practical knowledge is not knowledge at all, the assertion that, properly speaking, there is no knowledge that is not technical knowledge."[22] That is, Oakeshott thinks that rationalism equates knowledge with what can be systematized, cast in the form of a general theory, and written down in books. "The sovereignty of 'reason,' for the Rationalist, means the sovereignty of technique."[23]

It would appear that both liberal and socialist thinking are rationalist insofar as they are attempts to rethink the nature of political life from the beginning and aim to codify all this into neat, logical systems of thought. In place of the practical knowledge that one needs to engage in politics—knowledge that can only be gained through experience—the liberal and the socialist give us the equivalent of political "cookbooks"—"how to" books that simplify politics by reducing it to technical knowledge. Thus, to Oakeshott, the great works of the liberal and socialist traditions—for example, Mill's *On Liberty* and the writings of Karl Marx (1818–1883) and

Friedrich Engels (1820–1895)—manifest the rationalist urge to equate all political knowledge with technical knowledge that can be written down for all to read.[24] Both liberalism and socialism, he suggests, arose as guides for a politically inexperienced class that was coming to power. These new classes—first the middle class and later the workers—gained power, but were without the necessary practical political knowledge. So they sought political "cribs": they needed a book to tell them what to do. As he sees them, liberal and socialist political theories might be aptly subtitled "political rule made easy" or "a layman's guide to politics." If all political knowledge is reduced to technical knowledge, it can be taught to the inexperienced.

Burke's Attack on Rationalism

Burke's attack on the French Revolution shares much with Oakeshott's criticism of rationalism. Throughout the *Reflections*, Burke calls attention to the way in which the French Revolution was being guided by "metaphysics" and "philosophy."[25] "They [the French Assembly] commit the whole to the mercy of untried speculations; they abandon the dearest interests of the public to those loose theories, to which none of them would chuse [sic] to trust the slightest of his private concerns."[26] What so appalls Burke—and every other conservative who has followed him—is the way in which the revolutionaries in France sought to create a whole new social and political order based on the abstract theory of the rights of man. In place of the political traditions of France—traditions that had grown and developed over many generations—the leaders of the French Revolution sought to remold French society and politics on the basis of a philosophic theory of natural rights (see Sections 8.1, 8.2). As Burke sees it, this view of politics places far too much faith in the powers of human reason to understand society. Writing to a supporter of the French Revolution, Burke writes, in defense of the English,

> You see, Sir, that in this enlightened age I am bold enough to confess, that we [in England] are generally men of untaught feelings; that instead of casting away all our old prejudices, we cherish them to a very considerable degree, and, to take more shame to ourselves, we cherish them because they are prejudices; and the longer they have prevailed, the more we cherish them. We are afraid to put men to live and trade each upon his own private stock of reason; because we suspect that this stock in each man is small, and that the individuals would do better to avail themselves of the general bank and capital of nations, and of ages. Many of our men of speculation, instead of exploding general prejudices, employ their sagacity to discover the latent wisdom which prevails in them.[27]

Thus, whereas the rationalist grounds her theory in the power of reason in each individual, the conservative places his faith in the accumulated practical knowledge embedded in custom and tradition. Thus, to Burke, the rationalist "science" that would attempt to destroy all tradition and start afresh is no more than a "presumptuous ignorance."[28]

Socialism and Rationalism

The conservative characterization of rationalism seeks to show it in a negative light—in Burke's words, as a "presumptuous ignorance." We should not expect that any liberal or socialist would concur with *that* characterization of their doctrine. Nevertheless, it seems generally correct that liberalism sometimes, and socialism usually, tends toward something akin to Oakeshott's notion of rationalism.

Especially since the writings of Marx and Engels, socialism has tended to stress the powers of human reason, the accomplishments of sciences in understanding humans and society, and the ability of rational people to control their societies. For Friedrich Engels, Marx's collaborator, the great triumph of Marxism was to transform socialism into a science.[29] According-ing to a contemporary socialist, rationalism is one of the basic tendencies of socialism:

> The human race, rationalism maintains, has now grown up and at last has freed itself from the age-old yokes of ignorance and superstition. We have in our possession "science," the rational, ordered knowledge of the laws of na-ture: we can progressively domesticate, mould nature as to make it serve our own ends, and we can apply this knowledge to human society. Since it is primarily material wealth (objects gained through the process of subjugat-ing nature) that conduces to our happiness, we should organize our lives, our relationships as to secure the maximum technical, economic and admin-istrative efficiency in all our social activities. The rationalistic critique of cap-italism, therefore, decries most of the *chaos* and *waste* involved in capitalist production, and its continued enthronement of ignorance and supersti-tion. . . . Socialism, the rational organization of society, it holds to be the self-evident crowning of the values and aspirations of the Enlightenment: it needs only common sense and the right kind of education to make people accept it and work towards its realization.[30]

Liberalism's Complex Relation to Rationalism

Liberal Rationalism.   Like socialism, liberalism has its roots in the intellec-tual period known as the Enlightenment. This era—the heart of which was in the seventeenth and eighteenth centuries in France, England, Scotland, and America—insisted on the power of individual reason. Reason, insisted the philosophers of the Enlightenment such as Voltaire (1694–1778) and Denis Diderot (1713–1784), was the key to progress and scientific discovery, whereas custom codified superstition and error.[31] From this followed the supreme importance of individual freedom, especially freedom of thought. John Stuart Mill was to make this a key theme of *On Liberty*. Mill repeatedly criticized "the despotism of custom . . . the standing hindrance to human advancement, being in unceasing antagonism to that disposition to aim at something better than customary, which is called, according to circumstances, the spirit of liberty, or that of progress or improvement."[32] As Mill saw it, improvement in human affairs depended on the free exercise of human reason, which is always questioning tradition and custom; to insist that we follow custom is to stifle liberty, reason, and progress. Liberalism thus asserts the primacy of reason in conducting human affairs. As the great classical liberal Ludwig von Mises (1881–1973) argued, "All that man is and all that raises him above animals he owes to his reason. Why should he forgo the use of his reason . . . in the sphere of social policy and trust to vague and obscure feelings and impulses?"[33]

Liberal Antirationalism: Value Pluralism.   As one contemporary liberal has pointed out, not only are liberals identified with rationalism, but its critics often associate them with "hyperrationalism":

> Rationalists are said to believe that human reason is powerful enough to construct a workable blueprint for the best possible social order and that people can be led by rational argument to accept this blueprint. The critics of such hyperrationalism argue that reason is too feeble for such a task, given the complexity of social life.[34]

Liberals seldom embrace hyperrationalism. Although drawing on the Enlightenment's faith in reason, liberalism also displays skepticism about—or at least a cautious attitude toward—the powers of human reason.[35] Von Mises asserts not only the importance of being guided by reason, but its limits: "Our powers of comprehension are limited. We cannot hope ever to discover the ultimate and most profound secrets of the universe."[36] Indeed, one of the most famous liberal works of the twentieth century, Karl Popper's (1902–1994) *The Open Society and Its Enemies*, was, first and foremost, a criticism of the highly rationalistic philosophies of, among others, Plato and Marx. The most famous liberal criticism of rationalism was advanced by Isaiah Berlin (1909–1997). According to Berlin,

One belief, more than any other, is responsible for the slaughter of individuals on the alters of the great historical ideas—justice or progress or the happiness of future generations, or the sacred mission or emancipation of a
nation or race or class, or even liberty itself, which demands the sacrifice of
individuals for the freedom of society. This is the [rationalistic] belief that
somewhere, in the past or the future, in divine revelation or in the mind of
an individual thinker, in the pronouncements of history or science, or in the
simple heart of an uncorrupted good man, there is a final solution.[37]

For Berlin, the rationalists of the Enlightenment believed that, ultimately,
the use of human reason would reveal the best way to live; it would
show us what values we all should follow, and how those values should
be ordered in our lives. They were convinced that application of human
reason would, in the end, tell us how to live and what to strive for. As
Berlin sees it, the error of rationalism is its failure to grasp that there is no
final answer to the questions, "What is best in life?" or "Which is the
most worthy end for our society to pursue?" The rationalist seeks to answer a question that cannot be answered; and her effort to mold society
to conform to her answer is no more than someone trying to live out an
illusion, albeit at great costs to others.

   Berlin, drawing on the tradition of antirationalist thinkers, advocates
"value pluralism"—the doctrine that there are many values or good
things in life, and there is no rational basis for concluding that one is best,
or that some combination is best. Says Berlin,

The world that we encounter in ordinary experience is one in which we are
faced with choices between ends equally ultimate, and claims equally absolute, the realization of some of which must inevitably involve the sacrifice
of others. . . . If, as I believe, the ends of men are many, and not all of them
are in principle compatible with each other, then the possibility of conflict—
and of tragedy—can never wholly be eliminated from human life, either
personal or social. The necessity of choosing between absolute claims is then
an inescapable characteristic of the human condition.[38]

Berlin thus contrasts his notion of *pluralism* (according to which there is
no rational answer about how to resolve basic conflicts of values) to
monism, a rationalistic doctrine that insists that a rationally correct answer to value disputes can be discovered, and there is, in principle, a rationally best way for us all to live. On Berlin's view, true liberalism rests
on pluralism: because there is no single correct answer as to how each
should live, it is essential to ensure each has liberty to arrive at her own
answer. In contrast, Berlin insists, socialism, and much of revisionist liberalism, are informed by a monistic understanding of life: the application

of human reason, these theorists believe, can show us how all our important and cherished ideals can be had simultaneously, eliminating the need to sacrifice some good and important things so as to achieve others.

Liberal Antirationalism: Anticonstructivism.   Liberals have defended two opposing views of the liberal order—one stressing the spontaneous, unplanned order of a market society, the other stressing intentional design. The former has been of fundamental importance to classical liberalism. As Lord Robbins observed,

> The essence of Classical Liberalism was the belief that, within a suitable system of general rules and institutions, there will arise spontaneous relationships also deserving the name "order" but which are self-sustaining and, within the limits prescribed by the rules, need no detailed and specific regulation.[39]

The most sophisticated articulation of this conception of liberal society and institutions is to be found in the work of Hayek, who contrasts two "ways of looking at the pattern of human activities which lead to very different conclusions concerning both its explanation and the possibilities of deliberately altering it."

> The first [that is, constructivist] view holds that human institutions will serve human purposes only if they have been deliberately designed for these purposes, often also that the fact that an institution exists is evidence of its having been created for a purpose, and always that we should so redesign society and its institutions that all our actions will be wholly guided by known purposes. . . .
>
>   The other view, which has slowly and gradually advanced since antiquity but for a time was almost entirely overwhelmed by the more glamorous constructivist view, was that the orderliness of society which greatly increased the effectiveness of individual action was not due solely to institutions and practices which has been invented or designed for that purpose but was largely due to a process described as "growth" and later as "evolution."[40]

On the first view of society—implicit in the writings of revisionist liberals such as John Dewey (1859–1952)—human reason can grasp the purposes of society and plan society so as to fulfill this purpose; indeed, on this view, conscious planning is the only way social order can be achieved. This constructivist theory of society is thus highly rationalistic: the application of the powers of human reason is what allows for ordered social life. On the alternative, anticonstructivist view characteristic of much classical liberal thought, the social order is so complex that human reason cannot grasp it—it cannot understand and control society.

Rationalism and Political Theories.   Socialism, then, is committed to strong forms of rationalism. Socialists, we will see, closely link freedom with reason and insist that, properly understood, freedom and equality are consistent. Conservatives typically strongly disagree, insisting that reason cannot show us how to avoid conflicts between commitments to liberty and the promotion of equality. Nor do they believe that politics is properly understood as the attempt to rationally reconstruct society. Liberals, we have seen, are profoundly divided on rationalism in politics. Although all liberals believe that we should seek to apply our reason to better understand society and reform it, they fundamentally disagree as to the limits of this rationalistic endeavor. Although many revisionist liberals have believed that reason can reveal the true good for humankind and the best sort of society (see Section 4.3) that unites freedom with equality, those such as Berlin insist that reason can never tell us the one best way to live or harmonize liberty and equality. And although revisionist liberals such as John Dewey have endorsed the power of reason to understand and plan society, classical liberals such as Hayek insist that no such comprehensive planning is possible. As we shall see throughout this book, because liberals disagree on the basic issue of the place of reason in politics, liberalism fractures into divergent political doctrines and interpretations of political concepts.

3.3 Theories of Human Nature

Human Nature and Political Theory

The notion of "human nature" has been used in narrower and wider senses. In its narrower sense, human nature is about human "instincts" or "drives." In the wider sense, "human nature" is much the same as "psychology"—explanations of human behavior and characteristics. When the term is used in the narrower sense, many dispute whether there is really such a thing as human nature, since many doubt whether we have natural instincts or drives. Indeed, as we will see, the claim that humans are moved by powerful instincts can be understood as one view of human nature—a view rejected by many. In the wider sense, however, it seems that any political theory must include some picture of human nature. Insofar as a theory of human nature tries to tell us what humans are *really* like,[41] this will be of obvious relevance to questions such as, "Why do we value liberty?" "Are we suited to an egalitarian society?" and "How much can justice demand of people?" Let us briefly consider four theories of human nature that have played important roles in liberal, socialist, or conservative theories.

Self-Interest

According to one familiar view of human nature, people are basically self-interested—if not in all aspects of their lives, certainly in politics. David Hume (1711–1776) famously argued that it is "a just political maxim, that every man must be supposed a knave,"[42] that is, that people will always act to promote their own self-interest. Jeremy Bentham went a good deal further, arguing that in all areas of life each person pursues her own pleasures and avoids her own pains:

> Nature has placed mankind under the governance of two sovereign masters, pain and pleasure. It is for them alone to point out what we ought to do, as well as to determine what we shall do. . . . They govern us in all we do, in all we say, in all we think: every effort we can make to throw off our subjection, will serve but to demonstrate and confirm it.[43]

This conception of human nature has had great influence in economics. In many ways, the notion of *Homo economicus*—economic man—can be traced back to Bentham; economic man acts to pursue his own interests and plans and is not directly concerned with advancing the goals and interests of others. Because of the close tie between classical liberalism and economics, this self-interested theory of human action has had great influence in classical liberal thought. James Buchanan, another Noble Prize–winning classical liberal economist, has repeatedly argued that *Homo economicus* explains political as well as economic behavior.[44] This theory also has been a favorite target of criticism by revisionist liberals, conservatives, and socialists who have strenuously argued that the flaw in classical liberal capitalism is its view of humans as self-interested consumers with infinite appetites.[45]

Self-Development

The divide between classical and revisionist liberals is nowhere sharper than concerning their views of human nature. In the place of the basically (if not entirely) self-interested conception of persons that dominated classical liberal economic thinking, liberals in the late nineteenth and twentieth centuries embraced a view of humans as self-developers, focused not on promoting their interests but on developing their capacities, talents, and abilities. Again, Mill is the critical figure. In *On Liberty*, Mill argues that freedom is necessary for individual self-development and growth;

only if a person is allowed great scope for choosing a life of her own will she find a life that suits her talents, abilities, and interests. Later liberals such as T. H. Green (1836–1882), L. T. Hobhouse, Bernard Bosanquet (1848–1923), and John Dewey developed this idea. In his analysis of the "Heart of Liberalism," Hobhouse insisted, "The foundation of liberty is the idea of growth."[46] Although this view of humans is by no means absent from classical liberal theory,[47] it dominates revisionist liberalism.

Individuals, says the revisionist liberal, are not moved simply to advance their interests and consume or satisfy their appetites, but to develop and refine their capacities and talents. Moreover, according to revisionist liberals, self-development is a cooperative activity: only by participating in a community of self-developers can one best develop one's talents. The development of others stimulates and completes one's own: one cannot be a developed, realized individual in a world of undeveloped, stunted people. Consequently, we have an interest in each other's development. This idea was crucial to T. H. Green's notion of the common good; according to Green, "Man cannot contemplate himself as in a better state, or on the way to the best, without contemplating others, not merely as a means to that better state, but as sharing it with him."[48] Thus, revisionist liberalism comes to advocate a cooperative and sociable view of human beings as partners in each other's self-development.

The ideal of self-development, central to revisionist liberalism, has also been influential in socialist thought. C. B. Macpherson (1911–1987)—a Marxist philosopher and a harsh critic of the self-interested conception of human nature that looms large in classical liberalism—was much more sympathetic to the revisionist liberal view of the human being "as exerter and enjoyer of his own powers."[49] The problem for revisionist liberalism, Macpherson repeatedly insisted, was that liberal capitalism did not allow people to direct and develop their powers and capacities, requiring instead that workers must sell their labor to the capitalist so that he could use their powers and abilities for his own purposes. This criticism can be found in the early works of Karl Marx, in which he developed his theory of alienation, maintaining that under capitalism workers were alienated from their work—they saw their work as controlling them rather than as their own creation. A worker's labor is not a way for her to express her humanity; it is the way for the capitalist to make the worker reflect his aims. Work, as Marx saw it, becomes under capitalism simply a means to meet one's most basic needs. Rather than the expression of the distinctively human capacities, work is reduced to being a mere means for animal subsistence. The worker works in order to eat: "It is . . . not the satisfaction of a need [that is, the human need to express oneself by changing the world], it is merely a *means* to satisfy needs external to it."[50] Moreover, far from developing the distinctively human capacities of the worker, labor under capitalism destroys those capacities. Capitalists do not employ machinery to lighten the load of workers, but to get more out of them. Consequently, Marx argued, work under capitalism is dehumanizing in the sense that it starves higher human capacities and molds humans in the image of machines.

Social Environmentalism

Although the self-developmental ideal looms large in both revisionist liberal and socialist theories, in socialist theories it is very nearly always complemented by a conception of human nature that lays great stress on the ways in which our environment shapes our personalities. A *social environmentalist* conception of human nature stresses that people's characters are largely produced by the culture in which they live.[51] One's culture provides the roles, categories, and symbols by which one defines oneself and generates what we think of as "personality." On this view, people are formed by their history and culture—the characteristics of people in one country or epoch will differ fundamentally from those of others. The personality of an American living at the beginning of the twenty-first century will be radically different from that of a Greek in the third century B.C.

Now, although socialists have emphasized the individual's capacity for self-development, they have also put great stress on the malleability of human nature. Socialists have long maintained that the selfishness of humans in capitalist society is the creation of capitalist society: a changed society will produce radically different types of people with radically different concerns and motivations. Thus, for example, Marx believed that in a communist society that does away with private property and the market, individuals will no longer see work as drudgery that they only perform if rewarded.

> In a higher phase of communist society, after the enslaving subordination of the individual to the division of labor, and therewith also the antithesis between mental and physical labor, has vanished; after labor has become not only a means of life but life's prime want; after the productive forces have also increased with the all-round development of the individual, and all the springs of cooperative wealth flow abundantly—only then can the narrow horizon of bourgeois right be crossed in its entirety and society inscribe on its banner: From each according to his ability, to each according to his needs.[52]

Marx's point was that this transformation in our understanding of justice, and the sort of people who would embrace this new conception of justice, would only arise after the corrupting influences of capitalist culture had been eliminated. Thus, the antisocialist claim that people are too self-interested to embrace communist society fails to appreciate that selfishness is not a trait of humans as such, but of humans under capitalism. Because socialism insists that many of the traits of "capitalist man" will not be traits of "socialist man," it emphasizes the ways in which our society shapes our personality.

Interestingly, on this point conservatives tend to agree with socialists. Conservatives too see humans as essentially beings of a particular time and place, and so "their nature" is to a large extent a product of society and its tradition. What a person is depends very much on her history, the traditions in which she has been brought up, her affections, and her attachments. Simply put, humans are essentially historical creatures: to be a person is to be an Englishman of a certain locality at a certain time or an American at the turn of the twenty-first century, but it is not simply to be "a human." For the conservative, our traditions constitute our nature: what we are is to a large extent determined by our customs, traditional ways of doing things, traditional religious beliefs, traditional political arrangements, and so on. To take these away—to embark on the rationalist project of starting out from scratch—is to attack the basis of our personalities. Oakeshott makes this point in an essay entitled "On Being Conservative":

> Change is a threat to identity, and every change is an emblem of extinction. But a man's identity (or that of a community) is nothing more than an unbroken rehearsal of contingencies, each at the mercy of circumstances and each significant in proportion to its familiarity. It is not a fortress into which we may retire, and the only means of defending it (that is, ourselves) against hostile forces of change is in the open field of our experience; by throwing our weight upon the foot which for the time being is most firmly placed, by cleaving to whatever familiarities are not immediately threatened and thus assimilating what is new without becoming unrecognizable to ourselves. The Masai, when they were moved from their old country to the present Masai reserve in Kenya, took with them the names of their hills and plains and rivers and gave them to the hills and plains and rivers of the new country. And it is by such subterfuge of conservatism that every man or people compelled to suffer a notable change avoids the shame of extinction.[53]

Thus, the conservative view of humans as essentially constituted by their history and tradition leads to the conservative's deep concern about change: change undermines our very identity. We are creatures embedded in a particular time and a particular place, and that is why the conservative so stresses tradition and locality.

We are confronted with a puzzle. It would seem that the socialist is attracted to a social environmentalist view of human nature because she supports and welcomes great changes. Because she can look forward to new sorts of people in the new society, the motives and shortcomings of people under liberal capitalism need not carry over into socialist society. But the conservative fears change just because our personalities are shaped by our historical and cultural heritage. How can the same theory of human nature be employed to welcome and discourage change? We must recall that whereas conservatives are antirationalist, socialists are rationalist. Socialists have faith in our ability to control changes and through reasoned planning produce the sort of society that will create desirable human beings. In general, for the socialist, that our character is shaped by our society is an opportunity to bring about the right sort of character in the right sort of society. We have seen, however, that conservatives such as Oakeshott and Burke deny that we can have such knowledge about, and control of, our society and how it can be altered. For the conservative, great change is a leap into the dark, where we will become, in ways we cannot even guess, different sorts of people.

Instinctivism

We saw that Marxian socialism (and it is not at all unique in this regard) combines a self-developmental with a social environmentalist view of human nature. Conservatives such as Burke combine social environmentalism with what can be called an *instinctivist* theory of human nature. According to one of the most famous instinctivist psychologists, "The human mind has certain innate or inherited tendencies which are the essential springs or motive powers of all thought and action." And these innate tendencies are the basis of the "character and will of individuals and of nations"; thus the characteristics of people from one era to the next are largely unchanging, since these instincts have a "stable and unchanging character."[54] Instincts, then, are innate propensities for humans to behave in certain ways, propensities that are relatively constant in all times and cultures.

Although, as I have said, conservatism stresses the way in which humans are the product of their history and culture, it also has an instinctivist strain. Conservatives such as Burke and Oakeshott insist that we are inherently passionate creatures. According to Burke,

> Society requires . . . that the passions of individuals should be subjected . . . the inclinations of men should frequently be thwarted, their will controlled, their passions brought into subjection. This can only be done *by a power out of themselves*; and not, in the exercise of its function, subject to that will and to those passions which it is its office to bridle and subdue.[55]

And to Oakeshott, a man of conservative "disposition understands it to be the business of government not to inflame passion and give it new objects to feed upon, but to inject into the activities of already too passionate men an ingredient of moderation; to restrain, to deflate, to pacify and to reconcile; not to stoke the fires of desire, but to damp them down."[56]

The tie between conservative and Christian thinking is evident in their shared conception of humans as passionate, flawed creatures, who cannot obtain perfection on this earth.[57] Thus, in contrast to the socialist, who envisages grand projects to reconstruct humans and society to achieve a community in which all cooperate and thrive, for the conservative the possibilities of politics are much more limited. Although it would, no doubt, be going too far to say that conservatives adopt Saint Augustine's characterization of the political role as one of jailer to sinful creatures, the inherently passionate and flawed nature of human beings puts severe constraints on what politics can achieve. These constraints were emphasized by the psychologist Sigmund Freud (1856–1939). Although Freud is not typically associated with conservatism, his book *Civilization and its Discontents*—written late in his life (1930)—paints a deeply pessimistic picture of what can be achieved by civilization. As Freud understood it, our death instinct—our destructive and aggressive nature—is always threatening to undermine civilization. Thus, rather than being devoted to the perfection of humans, politics is properly focused on controlling their destructive urges.

3.4 Individualism/Collectivism

In Section 2.1, we examined one of Gallie's examples of an essentially contested concept: social justice. It will be recalled that Gallie argued that liberals and socialists advanced competing conceptions because they have different ideas about the relation of individuals to society: liberals, Gallie argued, favor an "individualist" view, whereas socialists understand society in a "collectivistic" way. Now, although, of course, this is far too simple, and although political theorists have often meant very different things by "individualism" and "collectivism," Gallie nevertheless is right that debates about the proper interpretation of concepts such as liberty, equality, and justice inevitably involve debates about persons and society. Indeed, according to Bernard Bosanquet—an important revisionist liberal—"the relation of the individual to society is the root of every social problem."[58]

A number of different senses of individualism and collectivism can be distinguished.[59] We have already considered one in our examination of human nature: is human personality largely the result of cultural and social influences (as the social environmentalist maintains) or the consequence of factors arising out of individuals (as, for example, in the self-interest or instinctivist views)? Two additional individualism/collectivism disputes should be briefly mentioned: (1) the *methodological* dispute about the best way to understand humans-in-society, and (2) the *moral* dispute about the relative moral claims of the individual and community.

Methodological Individualism/Collectivism

A methodological individualist believes that people's actions, social customs, and institutions are ultimately best explained in terms of the characteristics of individuals—their beliefs, desires, actions, and effects on each other. In contrast, a methodological collectivist believes that not only the workings of society and its institutions, but the beliefs, actions, and other characteristics of individuals, are to be explained by the social system in which people find themselves.[60] Often, this comes down to a simple question: what is more basic—the individual or society?

Jeremy Bentham (Section 2.3) had no doubts: "The community is a fictitious *body,* composed of the individual persons who are considered as constituting as it were its *members.*"[61] For an individualist such as Bentham, the "community" is simply a name we use to describe the actions, traits, and interactions of individuals, who are real. Any useful account of social life has to start off from what is real—individuals. During the nineteenth century, however, a wide variety of political thinkers—including many conservatives, socialists, and revisionist liberals—began to question this individualist understanding of society. Although a "first look" may seem to reveal independent individuals living next to each other in society, a deeper understanding would show the extent to which individuals are expressions of their society and their place in it.[62] Following the French political philosopher Jean-Jacques Rousseau (1712–1778), many of these political philosophers insisted that individuals in society share a common life, culture, and will. Individuals are a reflection of this common life and culture: "Every mind is a mirror or impression of the whole community."[63] Individuals are thus held to be reflections or expressions of the essence of their social order. They do not just live next to each other—society is not simply an aggregation or "heap of individuals."[64] Rather, says the collectivist, a "society," "nation," or "people" is much more than a group of individuals: it has a culture and customs that shape the individuals born into it. Whereas as "aggregation" is simply a collection of particulars, a society is a system of organized life. The collectivist believes that it is generally far more fruitful to explain facts about individuals by appeal to more basic facts about their society. If one wants to explain the hopes, fears, and dreams of the average American citizen, one must first understand the nature of America and its life, customs, and traditions.

Moral Individualism/Collectivism

To a *moral collectivist*, morality "consists in the social purpose working by its own force on the individual will."[65] Since individuals are expressions of their societies, morality is the expression of social purposes in individual lives. Bernard Bosanquet, a revisionist liberal collectivist, explicitly contrasted this "socialistic" conception of morality, which firmly focuses morality on social purposes and the social good, with an individualist conception of morality that stresses only what is good for individuals. Thus, as a moral collectivist, Bosanquet maintains that the individual's life expresses the common will of society, and in extreme cases may have to be sacrificed for the good of her society. In contrast, moral individualists such as John Rawls put at the very center of their political theory the principle that "each person possesses an inviolability founded on justice that even the welfare of the whole society cannot override."[66]

Of course, we are not confronted with simply the stark alternatives of radical individualism (of either the methodological or moral sort) or radical collectivism (of either sort). Political theorists have sought to articulate intermediate positions, giving weight to both individual and social factors. Rather than two stark alternatives, it is more enlightening to think of a continuum of positions, from radical individualism at one end to radical collectivism at the other. Nevertheless, disputes between individualists and collectivists—whether individuals are or are not more basic than society, or whether individual persons do or do not have moral priority over social purposes and the good of society—have been at the core of political theorizing for the past two hundred years. As we shall see in the following chapters, socialists, and in general conservatives too, have been attracted to positions toward the collectivist end of our continuum (though, as always, there are exceptions—some socialists have embraced forms of individualism).[67] Typically, conservatives as well as socialists have been critical of what has been described as "liberal," "capitalistic," or "bourgeois" individualism. As Marx wrote,

> The further back we go into history, the more the individual, and, therefore, the producing individual, seems to depend on and constitute a part of a larger social whole. . . . It is but in the eighteenth century, in "bourgeois society," that the different forms of social union confront the individual as mere means to his private ends, as an outward necessity. . . . Man is in the most literal sense of the word a *zoon politikon* [political animal] not only a social animal, but an animal that can only develop into an individual in society. Pro-

duction by isolated individuals outside of society . . . is as great an absurdity as the idea of development of a language without individuals living together and talking to one another.[68]

Interestingly, although liberalism has often been equated with individualism, liberals themselves have been deeply divided about the merits of various forms of individualism and collectivism. Revisionist liberals explicitly sought to bring collectivism—both methodological and moral—into liberalism. As we saw above, liberals such as Bosanquet insisted that the classical liberals had an overly individualistic view of humans and society, in both the methodological and moral senses. Since the nineteenth century—and right up until today—there have been persistent attempts to move liberalism away from stronger forms of individualism to the middle of the individualist-collectivist continuum, or even toward the collectivist end.[69] As Gallie indicates, this has had significant impact on the ways concepts such as justice are understood by, on the one hand, classical liberals and, on the other, more collectivist views such as socialism and much revisionist liberalism.

Communitarianism

The past two decades have witnessed a renewed interest in collectivist analyses of society—though the term "collectivist" is abjured in favor of "communitarian." Writing in 1985, Amy Gutmann observed, "We are witnessing a revival of communitarian criticisms of liberal political theory. Like the critics of the 1960s, those of the 1980s fault liberalism for being mistakenly and irreparably individualistic."[70] A number of critics have insisted that liberalism is too individualistic; it puts too much weight on individual choice, individual self-interest, and individual moral rights and pays too little attention to the ways in which individuals are members of a community and how group, cultural, and ethnic identities shape individuals. A political doctrine—or rather, a loose group of diverse political views—known as "communitarianism" has thus arisen as a challenge to what is seen as the overly individualistic nature of liberal political theory. Some observers maintain that communitarianism is a distinct and important view, taking its place next to liberalism, conservatism, and socialism as an enduring political theory. Should we add it as a fourth enduring political theory?

I think not. Debates about the relations of individuals to their societies are indeed fundamental to political theory. Whether individual personalities are in some basic way shaped by society, whether individual facts can be best explained in terms of social facts, and whether the moral claims of the community are in some way superior to those of the individual are, without doubt, enduring political questions. Alone, however, answers to these questions do not constitute a political theory—they are simply one type of issue with which a comprehensive political theory must deal. Communitarian convictions in themselves have no clear political implications; only when embedded in a system of interlocking theories and interpretations of political concepts does communitarianism yield a political doctrine. Communitarianism as part of a socialistic rationalism, which stresses humans' ability to plan and control their society and the importance of equality for a healthy community, is vastly different from conservative communitarianism, which stresses the importance of traditions and habits in the life of a community, and the way this endorses an inegalitarian social order (see Sections 9.2, 9.3, 10.1, 10.4). Communitarianism alone is no more of a political theory than is rationalism alone or a theory of human nature alone. We shall see, however, that it is a crucial element of socialism and conservatism (as well as much revisionist liberalism); it will thus loom large in the analysis of this book.

3.5 Summary

In this chapter, I have considered three enduring political theories, liberalism (in both its classical and revisionist versions), socialism, and conservatism. Of course, all three enduring political theories are complex families of doctrines; I have tried to draw attention to important differences within each. Nevertheless, these families do have their internal resemblances that distinguish them from the others. In Section 2.1, we saw that each has a distinctive conceptual structure; liberalism puts individual liberty in the pride of place, limiting the importance of equality and tying justice closely to the protection of liberty. Socialists, in contrast, almost always insist that liberty and equality are consistent and mutually reinforcing; justice is tied very closely to equality, and democracy is close to the heart of most socialisms. Conservatives are deeply skeptical of equality, insisting that it is at odds with individual liberties; conservative justice, we shall see, tends to stress the inequality of rights and duties in a well-ordered society. Political authority is a core idea of most conservative accounts of politics.

Although our three enduring political theories have different conceptual structures, their justifications of these different structures depend significantly on their positions in three enduring debates in political theory: the role of reason in politics, human nature, and the relation of individuals to society. In Sections 3.2 to 3.4, we examined these three debates and the positions on each that liberals, socialists, and conservatives tend to take. Again, it is important to be aware that within each tradition there are disputes and diversity. Because there is no essential core to liberalism, socialism, or conservatism, we shall encounter versions of conservatism that embrace a type of rationalism, socialisms that advocate inequality, and liberalisms that are collectivist. Nevertheless, in the course of our analysis the family resemblance (Section 1.4) within each type of theory should reveal itself.

Notes

This chapter draws on the work of John W. Chapman, "Political Theory: Logical Structure and Enduring Types" in *L'idée de philosophie politique: Annales de philosophie* (Paris: Presses Universitaires de France, 1965), pp. 57–96.

1. Maurice Cranston, "Liberalism," in Paul Edwards, ed., *The Encyclopedia of Philosophy* (New York: Macmillan and the Free Press, 1967).
2. See Michael Freeden, *Ideologies and Political Theory* (Oxford: Clarendon Press, 1996), chaps. 4 and 5.
3. John Stuart Mill, *On Liberty*, in John Gray, ed., *On Liberty and Other Essays* (New York: Oxford University Press, 1991), chap. 1, para. 9.
4. John Stuart Mill, *Auguste Comte and Positivism*, in J. M. Robson, ed., *The Collected Works of John Stuart Mill* (Toronto: University of Toronto Press, 1963), vol. 10, p. 339.
5. F. A. Hayek, *Law, Legislation and Liberty*, vol. 3: *The Political Order of a Free People* (London: Routledge and Kegan Paul, 1979), p. 5.
6. Wilhelm von Humboldt, quoted in F. A. Hayek, *The Constitution of Liberty* (London: Routledge and Kegan Paul, 1960), p. 394.
7. L. T. Hobhouse, *Liberalism* (New York: Oxford University Press, 1964), p. 87.
8. Ibid., p. 62.
9. Freeden, *Ideologies and Political Theory*, p. 430.
10. Bernard Crick, *Socialism* (Milton Keynes, UK: Open University Press, 1987), p. 84.
11. Kai Nielsen, *Equality and Liberty: A Defense of Radical Egalitarianism* (Totowa, NJ: Rowman and Allenheld, 1985), p. 201.
12. Richard Norman, *Free and Equal: A Philosophical Examination of Political Values* (Oxford: Oxford University Press, 1987), p. 133.
13. Noël O'Sullivan, *Conservatism* (London: Dent, 1976), p. 12.
14. Edmund Burke, *Reflections on the Revolution in France* (Harmondsworth, UK: Penguin, 1968), p. 267.
15. Robert Nisbet, *Conservatism* (Milton Keynes, UK: Open University Press, 1986), p. 47. Compare Freeden, *Ideologies and Political Theory*, p. 397.
16. See, for example, my essay on "Liberalism," in Edward N. Zalta, ed., *The Stanford Encyclopedia of Philosophy* [online at http://plato.stanford.edu].
17. This list is given by Kirk F. Koerner in *Liberalism and its Critics* (London: Croom Helm, 1985), p. 272.
18. Michael Oakeshott, *Rationalism in Politics*, expanded ed. (Indianapolis, IN: Liberty Press, 1991), pp. 5–42.
19. Ibid., p. 12.

20. Ibid., p. 13.

21. Ibid., p. 15.

22. Ibid., p. 16.

23. Ibid.

24. Ibid., pp. 29–30.

25. See, for example, pp. 153, 171, 185, 237, 244 of Burke's *Reflections on the Revolution in France*.

26. Ibid., p. 277.

27. Ibid., p. 183.

28. Ibid., p. 174.

29. Frederick Engels, "Socialism: Utopian and Scientific," in Robert C. Tucker, ed., *The Marx-Engels Reader*, 2nd ed. (New York: Norton, 1978), p. 700.

30. R. N. Berki, *Socialism* (London: Dent, 1975), pp. 27–28.

31. For more on the influence of the Enlightenment on liberal thinking, see John Gray, *Liberalism* (Milton Keynes, UK: Open University Press, 1986), chap. 3.

32. Mill, *On Liberty*, chap. 3, para. 17.

33. Ludwig von Mises, *Liberalism in the Classical Tradition* (San Francisco: Cobden Press, 1985), p. 7.

34. Stephen Holmes, *The Anatomy of Antiliberalism* (Cambridge, MA: Harvard University Press, 1993), p. 247.

35. This aspect of the liberal tradition is stressed by D. J. Manning, *Liberalism* (London: Dent, 1976), pp. 43–50.

36. Von Mises, *Liberalism in the Classical Tradition*, p. 7.

37. Isaiah Berlin, "Two Concepts of Liberty," in his *Four Essays on Liberty* (Oxford: Oxford University Press, 1969), p. 167.

38. Ibid. pp. 168–169. For a good account of the antirationalist roots of Berlin's pluralism see John Gray, *Isaiah Berlin* (Princeton: Princeton University Press, 1996), chap. 5.

39. Lord Robbins, *Political Economy: Past and Present* (London: Macmillan, 1977), p. 9.

40. F. A. Hayek, *Law, Legislation and Liberty: A New Statement of the Liberal Principles of Justice and Political Economy*, vol. 3: *Rules and Order* (Chicago: University of Chicago Press, 1973), pp. 8–9.

41. Alan Ryan, "The Nature of Human Nature in Hobbes and Rousseau," in Jonathan Benthall, ed., *The Limits of Human Nature* (New York: E. P. Dutton, 1974), p. 4.

42. David Hume, "Of the Independency of Parliament," in his *Essays, Moral, Political and Literary* (Oxford: Oxford University Press, 1963), pp. 42–43.

43. Jeremy Bentham, *Introduction to the Principles of Morals and Legislation*, in Alan Ryan, ed., *Utilitarianism and Other Essays* (Harmondsworth, UK: Penguin, 1987), p. 65.

44. See James Buchanan, *The Limits of Liberty* (Chicago: University of Chicago Press, 1975).

45. C. B. Macpherson, *The Political Theory of Possessive Individualism* (Oxford: Clarendon Press, 1962).

46. Hobhouse, *Liberalism*, p. 66. I have explored this theory in my *Modern Liberal Theory of Man* (New York: St. Martin's Press, 1983).

47. See, for example, Tibor Machan, *Individuals and their Rights* (La Salle, IL: Open Court, 1989).

48. T. H. Green, *Prolegomena to Ethics*, A. C. Bradley, ed. (Oxford: Clarendon Press, 1890), p. 210.

49. C. B. Macpherson, *Democratic Theory: Essays in Retrieval* (Oxford: Clarendon Press, 1973), p. 33. See also his *Life and Times of Liberal Democracy* (Oxford: Oxford University Press, 1977).

50. Karl Marx, *Economic and Philosophic Manuscripts of 1844*, Martin Milligan, trans. (New York: International Publishers, 1964), p. 111. For an analysis of Marx's theory of alienation, see Bertil Ollman, *Alienation: Marx's Conception of Man in Capitalist Society* (Cambridge: Cambridge University Press, 1971).

51. This term derives from Maurice Mandelbaum, *History, Man and Reason* (Baltimore: Johns Hopkins University Press, 1971), pp. 142ff.

52. Karl Marx, "Critique of the Gotha Program," in the *Marx-Engels Reader*, p. 531.

53. Michael Oakeshott, "On Being a Conservative," in his *Rationalism in Politics*, p. 410.

54. William McDougall, *An Introduction to Social Psychology* (London: Methuen, 1931), pp. 17–18.

55. Burke, *Reflections on the Revolution in France*, p. 151.

56. Oakeshott, "On Being a Conservative," p. 432.

57. On Christianity's doubts about perfection, see John Passmore, *The Perfectibility of Man* (London: Duckworth, 1970), chap. 4.

58. Bernard Bosanquet, *The Philosophical Theory of the State*, in Gerald F. Gaus and William Sweet, eds., *The Philosophical Theory of the State and Related Essays* (Indianapolis, IN: St. Augustine Press, 2000), p. 79.

59. For very useful overviews, see J. Roland Pennock, *Democratic Political Theory* (Princeton: Princeton University Press, 1979), chap. 3; Steven Lukes, *Individualism* (Oxford: Basil Blackwell, 1973).

60. For a useful introduction, see Jon Elster, *An Introduction to Karl Marx* (Cambridge: Cambridge University Press, 1986), chap. 2.

61. Jeremy Bentham, *Introduction to the Principles of Morals and Legislation*, chap. 1, sect. 4.

62. Bosanquet, *The Philosophical Theory of the State*, p. 106.

63. Ibid., p. 51.

64. See D. G. Ritchie, *The Principles of State Interference* (London: George Allen, 1912), p. 13.

65. Bosanquet, "The Antithesis of Individualism and Socialism, Philosophically Considered," in *The Philosophical Theory of the State and Related Essays*, p. 329.

66. John Rawls, *A Theory of Justice* (Cambridge, MA: Harvard University Press, 1971), p. 3. See Section 1.4 above.

67. Jon Elster, for example, is a methodological individualist and a Marxist. But his is a fairly new, and somewhat unorthodox, socialist approach. See his *Introduction to Karl Marx*.

68. Karl Marx, *Introduction to the Critique of Political Economy*, quoted in D.F.B. Tucker, *Marxism and Individualism* (Oxford: Blackwell, 1980), p. 2.

69. See Alan Ryan, "The Liberal Community," in John W. Chapman and Ian Shapiro, eds., *NOMOS XXXXV: Democratic Community* (New York: New York University Press, 1993), pp. 91–114.

70. Amy Gutmann, "Communitarian Critics of Liberalism," *Philosophy & Public Affairs*, vol. 14 (1985), p. 308.

PART TWO

POLITICAL CONCEPTS

4

NEGATIVE AND POSITIVE LIBERTY

4.1 Negative Liberty: Some Ordinary Language Considerations

Freedom as the Absence of Obstacles[1]

Let us begin by focusing on a simple case:

> *Case 1:* Alf is a political dissident and has been jailed by the government and locked in a cell. He shakes the bars but cannot get out.

If we ask why Alf is unfree, the simplest answer is that he is locked in a cell and *cannot* leave it. For Thomas Hobbes (1588–1679), "Liberty is the absence of . . . impediments to action."[2] As Hobbes understood it, something that is not prevented from moving by an external obstacle is free: if something stops it from moving it is unfree. A ball moves freely down a hill until something stops it; Alf moves freely across his cell until the locked cell door stops him.

We immediately come to a crucial question: do all external impediments to action or obstacles involve a loss of freedom? Consider the following cases:

> *Case 2:* Alf is hiking across the Rocky Mountains and encounters an avalanche that blocks his way. The avalanche occurred naturally.

> *Case 3:* Alf is hiking across the Rocky Mountains and encounters an avalanche that blocks his way. Betty wanted to get across first, so she used dynamite to cause the avalanche.

In each case, Alf meets an obstacle that prevents him from going further, and so would seem unfree in Hobbes's sense. Yet, many have been reluctant to depict Case 2 as a limitation of Alf's liberty. According to Isaiah Berlin, one of the most famous of modern philosophers of freedom, "You lack political liberty or freedom only if you are prevented from attaining a goal by other human beings."[3] Thus, even though gravity is an obstacle to your jumping higher than ten feet in the air, says Berlin, that does not make you unfree, since no human created the obstacle. We may dispute this; after all, it is not senseless to say that people are not free to jump more than ten feet in the air. But insofar as our interest is political and moral discourse—those moral and political language games that focus on people's complaints and challenges to one person creating obstacles in the path of others—it does indeed seem that what Berlin calls "political liberty" involves humanly created (or, perhaps, maintained) obstacles. Thus, even modern followers of Hobbes are more likely to adopt the view that "broadly speaking, . . . a person is unfree to do an action if, and only if, his doing that action is rendered impossible *by the action of another person*."[4] Case 3 is clear: not only does Alf confront an obstacle, but it is one that was created by another person, Betty. What, however, about

Case 4: Alf is hiking across the Rocky Mountains and encounters an avalanche that blocks his way. The avalanche was accidentally caused by Betty, who was skiing in the higher reaches of the mountain.

Berlin, at least sometimes, indicates that Case 4 would not involve a lack of freedom. To constitute a limitation of freedom, Berlin suggests in his famous essay, "Two Concepts of Liberty," the obstacle must not only be created by humans, but it must be a deliberate or intentional obstacle to a person's activity. Liberty talk, on Berlin's view, is not simply about one person accidentally getting in the way of another, but deliberate interventions in another's life. If someone gets in my way, I may point out to her that she is blocking me, but I am not likely to complain that she is limiting my freedom until I see her as deliberately or knowingly blocking me. If someone accidentally parks her car in front of your driveway, it is true that you are not free to drive away, but it would be somewhat odd to appeal to the value of freedom in your complaint against your neighbor; the most likely and appropriate complaint would be that she is inconsiderate or thoughtless.[5] On the other hand, if she deliberately blocked your path, then a complaint about limiting your freedom would be perfectly sensible and not at all odd.

In another essay, however, Berlin suggests a different understanding of what sorts of obstacles are relevant to freedom. Here Berlin seems to argue that if (1) Alf is blocked by an obstacle that (2) could be removed by someone (3) who fails to do so, then (4) Alf's freedom is limited.[6] On this view, it would seem that Alf's freedom is limited in

> Case 5: Alf is hiking across the Rocky Mountains and encounters an avalanche that blocks his way. The avalanche was natural and was no one's fault. Betty, however, sees him stuck in the snow, but passes by without helping.

On Berlin's alternative conception, Betty limits Alf's freedom in Case 5. If we adopt this notion of freedom, it seems that we are never really free. After all, if enough money was spent, the obstacles that stop me from going to the moon could be overcome (by supplying me with a spaceship). So if my freedom is limited every time I confront an obstacle that *could* be removed by humans, my freedom is now drastically limited. If we take a more moderate view, and say that one's freedom is limited wherever one confronts an obstacle that could *feasibly* be removed by others, things become more manageable, but now we confront deep problems with explaining what we mean by "feasible."[7] If other people did not want BMWs and beach houses, the obstacle to me living the life of ease and pleasure—lack of money—could easily be overcome: they could pay for my pleasures. Does this mean that I am unfree?

Coercion and the Ineligibility of Options

Thus far we have been exploring Hobbes's idea that one is free unless an obstacle prevents one from acting. Consider, though,

> Case 6: Alf is hiking through the Rocky Mountains and comes upon Betty, a thief who wants his new hiking boots. She says, "Give me your boots or I'll break your arm! But I'm not a murderer, so that's all I'll do. You choose." Alf likes the boots, but not *that* much, so he hands them over.

Betty did not *prevent* Alf from walking by with his boots; he *could have* chosen to do that, though the cost would have been a broken arm. Since she did not prevent Alf from continuing, according to Hobbes Alf is still free. After all, he can choose whether to keep his boots or have a broken arm, and if he can choose what to do, it would seem that he is free. As Hobbes sees it, one is free unless an obstacle renders the action *impossible*. And since it is not impossible for Alf to keep his boots, he is free to do so (though the cost will be a broken arm). Of course, it is now impossible for Alf to perform the complex action of continuing-walking-with-his-boots-

and-not-having-a-broken-arm.[8] Before Betty arrived, Alf had a possible
complex action—his preferred action—of keeping his boots *and* keeping
his arm in one piece. Betty has provided an obstacle that has rendered
that action impossible.

Still, it seems that although Alf is not completely unfree to choose to
keep his boots (and have a broken arm)—it is, after all, *possible* to choose
that option—neither is he perfectly free to choose to keep his boots. Most
of us would say that his freedom has been limited by Betty's threat. Most
philosophers have thus rejected Hobbes's claim that you are free to do
what no obstacle prevents you from doing; rather, most have argued that
coercion—threats to do you harm—limit your freedom. As F. A. Hayek
says, "Coercion implies that I still choose but that my mind is made
someone's else's tool, because the alternatives before me have been so
manipulated that the conduct the coercer wants me to choose becomes
for me the least painful one. Although coerced, it is still I who decide
which is the least evil under the circumstances."[9]

We might say that although coercion does not entirely block off an option (for example, "Alf keeps his boots"), it makes the option "less eligible" for choice—it renders an option not a real option by attaching a
severe penalty (for example, Alf's arm is broken) to choosing it.[10] According to this *ineligibility view of freedom*, Alf's freedom is infringed if either
(1) another person has intentionally blocked off an option or (2) another
person has employed coercion against Alf to render an option ineligible.[11] Although this seems to accord much better with ordinary usage
than does Hobbes's simple impossibility view, it raises a number of additional problems. Most important, a threat that renders an option ineligible to Alf may not have the same effect on Charlie. Consider, for instance,

Case 7: Betty is a mild-mannered bank robber. She passes Alf, the
teller, a note, "Give me all the money or I will call you a nasty
name!" Alf hates to be called names, so concludes that Betty's threat
has rendered the option "don't turn over the money" ineligible for
choice—the costs are just too high. So he hands over the money.
When he explains what happened to Charlie the police officer, Charlie arrests Alf, insisting that the threat was not sufficiently great as to
render the option ineligible.

Alf may be telling the truth, in which case it does seem that perhaps his
freedom was limited. But if we accept that conclusion, we will not be able
to say when a person's freedom is limited without knowing a great deal
about that person, such as what sorts of things he really fears. Advocates
of the ineligibility view have been reluctant to take this path, and generally have argued that judgments about freedom should be guided by
how a *normal* or *typical* person would view the threat, and whether such a

normal or typical person would see the threat as sufficiently severe as to render the option ineligible. It is important to observe in Case 7 that everyone would agree that Betty's threat made the option "don't hand over the money" *less attractive* or *less eligible*, but simply making an option somewhat less attractive is not enough to render you (as Hayek says) "someone else's tool" and so unfree.

There has been considerable debate among philosophers whether *offers* as well as *threats* can be coercive, and so limit freedom. Consider an example from J. G. Murphey:

> *Case 8:* Suppose I own the only water well within a two-hundred-mile radius of desert. A man, nearly dead from thirst, drags himself to my well and begs for water. Realizing (a) that the well is lawfully owned by me and that I am entitled to all its water, and (b) that the thirsty man's predicament is no fault of mine . . . I say "I will sell you a glass of water only if you sign over to me all your worldly goods."[12]

This is an offer. Unlike a threat—in which someone says that he is going to inflict pain on you, or take away something that is yours, or somehow make you worse off than you now are—an offer gives you the opportunity to get something you need or want. But many have believed that an offer can be coercive if (1) it allows you to get something at a terribly high cost, but because of your circumstance (2) you cannot afford to turn the offer down. In such a case, many have believed that the option of rejecting the offer is ineligible: "You have no choice." On the other hand, it seems hard to see how the offer *restricts* your options: it seems that all offers *expand* your options. Even though it is not a desirable offer, it gives you an additional option. Those who believe that offers can be coercive typically argue that they should be compared to the "standard" options that a person would normally expect in this situation. In Case 8, a standard option might be that a person in desperate need can expect help from others at no or minimal costs. If we accept this as a standard option—part of the normal background—we might say that the person making the coercive offer not only is making an offer, but at the same time is blocking that standard option ("low-cost help"), offering instead *only* high-cost help, thus decreasing our options.[13] To apply this notion of freedom, however, we need an account of what are one's "standard options," something that would seem to differ by locality, economic prosperity, culture, tastes, and so on.

Negative Freedom as an Opportunity Concept

Thus far we have been considering Alf unfree when he confronts an obstacle to what he wants to do or when someone renders ineligible an option of his. This, then, is a *negative conception of liberty*: liberty consists in the absence of obstacles to, or interference with, action. But consider,

> *Case 9:* Alf is in jail. He is tied to the wall and has duct tape over his mouth so that he cannot talk. Alf, however, is a strange fellow. He thinks, "What luck, this is what I've always wanted!"

Berlin, the preeminent theorist of negative liberty, would insist that Alf is not free; freedom, he tells us, is "the absence of obstacles to *possible* choices and activities—absence of obstructions on roads which a man *can* decide to walk."[14] Alf is not free to take many roads—there is not much he *can* do, though in fact he is doing everything he *wants to do*. He is contented, but not free. In this sense, slaves, even happy, contented, slaves who cherish their chains, are not free: there are many obstacles placed in the path of possible choices.

We may say, then, that negative liberty is an *opportunity* concept: one's freedom depends on what one has an opportunity to do, not what one actually does.[15] A person who does little, but who has few paths rendered ineligible by others, is free, even if she does little. Think about

> *Case 10:* Betty is not in jail. In fact, Betty really has no significant restraints on her. Well, there is one. Betty is a thrill seeker: she likes driving without a seat belt. Unfortunately, she lives in a state with only one law: mandatory seat belts. You can do anything you want, as long as you wear your seat belt. Alas, this prohibits the thing Betty most wants to do. In fact, she dislikes this prohibition more than any other one she can imagine.

Proponents of negative liberty such as Berlin maintain that Betty is much freer than is Alf in Case 9, even though in Case 9 Alf is doing what he wants to do, whereas in Case 10 Betty cannot do what she really wants to do. As we are about to see, proponents of what has been called "positive freedom" seek a much more intimate tie between Betty being free and doing what she wants to do.

4.2 Positive Freedom

T. H. Green and Liberty as Autonomy

In a famous lecture, "On the Different Senses of 'Freedom' as Applied to the Will and the Moral Progress of Man,"[16] the English liberal T. H. Green developed a conception of liberty that closely links being free to doing what one truly desires. Green begins his famous lecture by acknowledging that, in a sense, the negative conception of political liberty is basic to our understanding of freedom. As he says, "It must be of course admitted that every usage of the term [that is, freedom] to express anything but a social and political relation of one man to another involves a metaphor. . . . It always implies . . . some exemption from compulsion by another."[17] But Green wants to explore an extension of this usage, one that centers on the idea of *a free person*.

We all agree that an unfree person is one who is in some sense in bondage: he is a slave and cannot do as he wishes. Now, Green acknowledges that this is certainly true if others are preventing him from acting, and advocates of negative liberty are right about that. But Green wants to explore another case: where one is unfree because one is subject to an impulse or craving. A person who is subject to some impulse or craving that he cannot control, Green said, is "in the condition of a bondsman who is carrying out the will of another, not his own."[18] Green is suggesting here that the basic model of negative liberty—the relation between an actor and someone trying to make him or her a "tool"—can be applied within the individual psychology of a person. Assume that we identify a person's basic personality—the sort of things a person likes to do, what she cares for, her long-term plans and goals, and so on. Now, further assume that a person has an addiction, say, to narcotics, which impels her to satisfy her craving regardless of the harm it does to all the other things she cares for. Green believes that she is not free: she is a slave to her addiction. The real, basic personality cannot express itself: the foreign impulse takes over.

To grasp the crux of Green's proposal, suppose that a person can sometimes be considered as being split into two parts. One part is sometimes called her "real self"—those values, interests, and plans that really make up this person. The second part can be an intrusive impulse or addiction that sets itself up in opposition to the real self. Now, if we view the self in this way, we can consider the "real self" as being enslaved by the impulse. The person in such a condition is not really free: she is a slave of her impulse. A free person, then, is one *who does what she really wants to do*—what her real self wants—and so the free person does not wish to give in to the impulse. On this view, then, a free person is what is often called an *autonomous* person: someone who can decide for herself what to do and is not the slave of impulses, ignorance, error, past conditioning, or addiction. She is, literally, self *(auto)* ruled *(nomos)*.[19]

Autonomy can be limited both by *internal* and *external* restraints or obstacles. Advocates of negative liberty are sensitive to the importance of external restraints: you cannot be your own master if others are interfering with your actions and restraining you. But also, you cannot be your own master if there are internal restraints: these too prevent you from being a free person—from leading a self-directed or autonomous life. We see here, then, that in contrast to negative liberty, which makes liberty an opportunity concept, the positive conception sees liberty as an *exercise* concept: one is free when one exercises one's capacities for self-control and self-direction and so does what one really wants to do. Under the influence of this way of thinking, the idea of freedom moves away from a focus on interpersonal relations—who is blocking or controlling whom?— to a character ideal. A free person is a self-controlled, self-directed person who is not under the sway of external or internal compulsions.

Other Senses of Autonomy

Green provided a classic case for freedom as a self-ruled life. But in developing this general idea, philosophers have come to distinguish a number of different senses in which one can be self-ruled; indeed, even in Green's writings we can discern more than one notion of being self-ruled.

Autonomy as Development of One's Capacities.   Green, we have seen, described the life of freedom as one in which one's real self ruled over impulses and passions. In addition, he believed that, given human nature, this involved a life in which one developed one's capacities (Section 3.3). The only satisfying life for humans is a life in which one's distinctly human capabilities are developed, and so that is the only life a free person will live. A person pursuing a life that cannot satisfy his capacities, wrote Green,

> is not free, because the objects to which his actions are directed are objects in which, according to the law of his own being, satisfaction of himself is not to be found. His will to arrive at self-satisfaction not being adjusted to the law which determines where this self-satisfaction is to be found, he may be considered in the condition of a bondsman who is carrying out the will of another, not his own. From this bondage he emerges into real freedom, not by overcoming the law of his being . . . but by making its fulfillment the object of his will; by seeking the satisfaction of himself in objects in which he believes it *should* be found, and seeking it in them *because* he believes it should be found in them.[20]

Autonomy as a Self-Chosen Life.   Some advocates of autonomy reject Green's claim that only a life devoted to the realization of one's capacities is truly free. According to Joseph Raz, whereas "self-realization consists in the development to their fullest extent of all, or all the valuable capacities a person possesses . . . the autonomous person is one who makes his own life and he may choose the path of self-realization or reject it."[21] The basic thought is that according to the ideal of autonomy, it is not crucial that a person develops her capacities, but that she *decides whether* to develop her capacities and, more generally, how to live her life. The fully autonomous person is one who leads a life of her own choosing—who makes decisions about her life on the basis of the things to which she is committed.

The worry about this notion of autonomy, however, is whether anyone really ever chooses his life. Our personalities and choices are deeply influenced by our natural talents and propensities, our culture and our upbringing. By the time a person reaches adulthood, many of his desires, goals, ends, and aims have been learned from parents, friends, and teachers. Given this, in what sense can one say that one creates oneself? Even if one decides to reject some of one's cultural and intellectual heritage, one will make that decision because of other things one believes and values— but those too almost surely have been learned from someone. If one is raised a Catholic and rejects that life because of one's commitment to humanistic philosophy, where did one get that humanistic commitment? No matter where one turns, it seems one's deliberations and decisions draw on aspects of oneself that one did not create.

Autonomy as the Life of Reason. Perhaps an autonomous person is not necessarily one who creates her life, values, and commitments, but who subjects all aspects of her life to critical scrutiny, and always acts according to her understanding of what she has the best reasons to do.[22] Thus, even if a person does not create her commitments, if she has thought through all of them, and deliberated about which seem well grounded and which ought to be rejected, and acts on those deliberations, her life is ruled by reason; she is not the slave of ignorance or past conditioning.

Autonomy as a Second-Order Desire. Contemporary philosophers are skeptical about Green's claim that a person can be divided into a "real self"—which concerns the person's true wants, goals, and so forth—and a nonreal, lower, or "actual" self that is ruled by impulses, passions, and ignorance (see Section 4.3). Although Green's idea is out of favor today, many proponents of autonomy have adopted a surprisingly similar division of the person, into "first-order" and "second-order" desires. A first-order desire is a desire the object of which is an action or event: a person desires to be rich or skinny, to eat, or to win the Nobel Prize. All these are first-order desires. A second-order desire is a desire the object of which is a first-order desire. A desire not to have the desire to be skinny is a second-order desire. Now, some advocates of autonomy have argued that an autonomous person is one who exercises her capacity to reflect on her first-order desires in terms of her second-order desires, and rejects or amends first-order desires in the light of her second-order desires.[23]

Thus, for example, a person may have a first-order desire to be skinny, but also think that this desire is silly and is interfering with her life. She is a healthy weight and enjoys eating; although she wants to lose more weight and become skinny, when she reflects on this, she sees that the best thing for her life would be to rid herself of the desire to be skinny. In Green's terms, she is seeking satisfaction where she does not think it can be found, and so is not free. Thus, on this view, an autonomous person seeks to make her first-order desires conform to her second-order desires.

*   *   *

Even this brief survey of different senses of autonomy demonstrates the relation between positive liberty and rationalism (Section 3.2): we can only achieve true freedom if we are rational. When we are acting on good reasons and are reflective, are not ruled by custom or tradition, and are not the subject of cravings or impulses or arbitrary interferences; when we reflect on our first-order desires; when we use our reason to choose our lives for ourselves, then we are truly free. The life of freedom is the life of reason.

4.3 Two Concepts of Liberty

Berlin's Attack on Positive Liberty

In his famous essay, "Two Concepts of Liberty," Isaiah Berlin attacks positive liberty and argues that it is fundamentally opposed to negative liberty. Three claims made by Berlin stand out.

(1) The pursuit of positive liberty can lead to infringing negative liberty. If we accept Green's view, it would seem that the ideal of positive liberty as autonomy is simply an elaboration, or at most an extension, of the case for negative liberty. Berlin, however, wants to show that far from being an *extension* of the case for negative liberty, the ideal of positive liberty *clashes* with the ideal of negative liberty. This clash comes out most clearly on the issue of *paternalism*. Legal paternalism involves the use of legal sanctions to make someone do what is good *for him* or prevent him from doing what is bad *for him*. Paternalism is, roughly, treating adults like children: it is forcing them to do things for *their own good*. That is just the sort of intervention that John Stuart Mill's Harm Principle prohibited: "The only purpose for which power can be rightfully exercised over any member of a civilized community, against his will, is to prevent harm to others. His own good, either physical or moral, is not a sufficient warrant" (see Section 3.1). Now, it would seem that Green's view of positive

liberty supports paternalism as a way to achieve fuller freedom. If I act in ways that make me less autonomous—if I act in ways that will make me ignorant or give into impulses—then if someone renders these autonomy-harming options ineligible for me (that is, he interferes with my negative liberty), this interference can promote my positive liberty. T. H. Green himself was deeply concerned with alcoholism among members of the working class in late-nineteenth-century Britain. As he saw it, this addiction was impeding their freedom; they were slaves to alcohol. Green would allow laws designed to limit or prohibit the consumption of alcohol, because doing so would promote positive freedom.

To Berlin, such paternalism is a great despotism: the state is interfering with your freedom to make you a better person. Other people are imposing some way of living on you; the liberal tradition from John Stuart Mill onward has opposed paternalism because liberalism rejects the legitimacy of one person or a group of people imposing their way of living on others. Moreover, Berlin argues, not only does Green's notion of positive freedom allow paternalism that limits freedom, it adds insult to injury by calling this interference "freedom"! Berlin depicts the argument for positive liberty in the following way:

> The dominant self is . . . identified with reason, with my "higher nature," with the self which calculates and aims at what will satisfy in the long run, with my "real," or "ideal," or "autonomous" self, or with my self "at its best"; which is then contrasted with irrational impulse, uncontrolled desires, my "lower" nature, the pursuit of immediate pleasures. My "empirical" or "heteronomous" self, swept by every gust of desire and passion, need[s] . . . to be rigidly disciplined if it is ever to rise to the full height of its "real" nature. . . . Once I take this view, I am in the position to ignore the actual wishes of men or societies, to bully, oppress, torture them in the name, and on the behalf, of their "real" selves, in the secure knowledge that whatever is the true goal of man (happiness, performance of duty, wisdom, a just society, self-fulfillment) must be identical with his freedom—the free choice of his "true," albeit often submerged and inarticulate, self.[24]

For one person to take charge of the life of another, arguing that the other is controlled by her own "false" or "lower" self instead of her "higher" self, attacks precisely the freedom that Berlin cherishes. And to make things worse, all this is done in the name of freedom!

(2) Positive liberty splits not only individuals but also societies into the higher and lower.   Berlin advances another criticism of positive liberty: its split between the "higher" and the "lower" self is often transferred to a division in society between those who are enlightened and those who are not:

The reason within me, if it is to triumph, must eliminate and suppress my "lower" instincts, my passions and desires, which render me a slave; similarly (the fatal transition from individual to social concepts is almost imperceptible) the higher elements in society—the better educated, the more rational, those who "possess the highest insight of their time and people"—may exercise compulsion to rationalize the irrational section of society. For . . . by obeying the rational man we obey ourselves: not indeed as we are, sunk in our ignorance and our passions, weak creatures afflicted by diseases that need a healer, wards who require a guardian, but as we could be if we were rational; as we could be now, if we would listen to the rational element which is, *ex hypothesi* [by hypothesis] within every human being who deserves the name.[25]

Thus, being subjected to the authority of another—the very essence of being restrained—is, Berlin argues, converted into a sort of freedom (see Sections 5.4, 10.1, 10.4). Because the "other"—the King, the Great Dictator, or the People—represents what is higher and rational, whereas what you want manifests the lower and irrational, to obey the higher and control the lower is freedom.

(3) The positive conception is not an extension of the negative conception, but undermines it.   Points (1) and (2) support Berlin's third, and in some ways most basic, claim: those who depict positive liberty as simply an extension of negative liberty are wrong. As (1) and (2) demonstrate, the proponent of positive liberty entertains a conception of liberty according to which the most basic feature of negative liberty—to be free from restraint in order to live your life as you see fit—is not only ignored, but is ignored in the name of liberty itself. Thus, Berlin concludes, "These are not two different interpretations of a single concept, but two profoundly divergent and irreconcilable attitudes to the ends of life."[26] Consider again Case 1 in Section 4.1. On the negative understanding of freedom, being locked in jail is a core and obvious case of unfreedom; some of our other cases may pose puzzles for negative liberty, but not Case 1. But on the positive conception, it may turn out that in Case 1 Alf is being forced to be free—perhaps he is in jail to stop him from getting drunk. Because positive freedom takes a basic case of (negative) unfreedom and turns it into a possible (positive) freedom-enhancing condition, it seems that these are two fundamentally opposed ways of looking at freedom.

Monism and Pluralism

To understand why Berlin insists on the fundamental opposition between negative and positive freedom, we have to go back to the contrast between *monism* and *pluralism* (Section 3.2). Value pluralism, it will be recalled, stresses the diversity of the ends of life. As a form of antirationalism, it insists that our reason cannot provide a single, agreed-upon, answer to the question, "What is the best way to live?" There are innumerable ways of living that appeal to each of us, but they conflict and we often cannot decide among them. As Berlin says, "That we cannot have everything is a necessary, not a contingent, truth."[27] *Monism,* in contrast, is a form of rationalism: our reason can be employed to reveal the one type of life, or the set of good lives, that best suits everyone—perhaps the one sort of life that combines, in just the right measure, all good things.

Berlin convincingly argues that a notion of positive liberty such as T. H. Green's is based on a rationalistic, monistic view of life: a developed, autonomous person is the true goal for everyone. Anyone who forsakes this goal and who lives a life that does not develop her capacity for choice is not seeking the one, true human end. In contrast, says Berlin, pluralism leads to understanding liberty as a negative concept. Guaranteeing each a measure of negative liberty is, Berlin argues, the most humane ideal, as it recognizes that "human goals are many," and no one can make a choice that is right for all people.[28] If you are to avoid being a despot (that is, someone who forces others to live *their* lives as *you* see fit), you must grant others freedom to make their own decisions. According to the value pluralist, just because reason cannot reveal what is the best way of living—just because there are so many human goals, so many things that are worth pursuing—it is necessary to ensure that no one needlessly raises obstacles to the possible choices of others.

Although I think Berlin is correct in arguing that a rationalistic monism informs the ideal of autonomy and, so, positive liberty, it is important not to push the point too far. The ideal of autonomy is certainly less monistic and rationalistic than, for example, some religious understandings of the good life. Basic to the ideal of autonomy is that one should choose the life that fits one's capacities and talents; and because our capacities and talents differ, the ideal of an autonomous life justifies each person living a different sort of life, stressing different values and interests. This is much more accommodating to pluralism than, say, a religious ideal according to which everyone, regardless of his or her capacities, must lead a specific sort of life, stressing simplicity, otherworldliness, and absolute obedience to God's will. Such a conception of the good life is much less open-ended than the ideal of autonomy. There are certainly degrees of rationalism and monism. Nevertheless, the ideal of autonomy points toward an ideal of a good life that can identify a "real self" that seeks the cultivation of its capacities and is "unfree" when the lower self pursues a life inconsistent with that ideal.

Berlin, then, believes that a commitment to monism supports positive liberty: those who exercise their will in such a way as to lead the truly human life are free. On the other hand, a pluralist, believing that there is no uniquely or truly human manner of living, will stress the way in which liberty provides opportunities for choice, and so be attracted to the negative concept. Many political theorists note Berlin's distinction between negative and positive liberty, but fail to grasp his broader point: that these two theories reflect opposing political theories and views of reason and values. One misses Berlin's message if one understands him as simply arguing for a certain negative conception of liberty. Rather, he is arguing for a certain sort of political theory, one devoted to pluralism: if we adopt this political theory, Berlin believes, we will also be committed to accepting the negative, and rejecting the positive, notion of liberty.

Liberty and Human Nature: Mill as an Exemplar

Not only does it seem that positive liberty draws on what Berlin calls monism, but it also is supported by what I described (Section 3.3) as the "self-developmental" theory of human nature. As I noted earlier (Sections 3.1, 3.3), John Stuart Mill's case for individual liberty was based on our capacity for growth and development. If each is guaranteed liberty to make his or her own choices, Mill believed, each person would exercise that freedom to find ways of life that suited his or her unique capacities and encouraged his or her growth and development. In *On Liberty*, Mill indicates that this supports negative freedom: he wished to show that we should not place needless obstacles in the paths of others, as this may limit their development. I also pointed out that classical liberals such as F. A. Hayek look back to Mill as an exemplar of the case for negative liberty (Section 3.1). But—consistent with the idea that Mill's *On Liberty* is something akin to Gallie's notion of an exemplar, accepted by proponents of competing conceptions of liberty (Section 3.1)—proponents of positive liberty have also looked to Mill as an inspiration. Mill's case for liberty depended on the desirability of autonomous people who thought for themselves and developed their natures and so were not ruled by custom or prejudice. If the development of such people is indeed a good thing, and if that is why negative liberty is a good thing, then, some philosophers have concluded, positive liberty must be a good thing too. Although Mill may not have realized it, say some advocates of positive liberty, not only was he presenting the case for negative liberty, but he was laying the foundations for development of the positive concept. If only fully developed people are free people, the positive conception of freedom can explain why this is so and, on that ground, seems superior.

Thus, according to one contemporary proponent of positive liberty, if we grasp why Mill valued freedom—why he thought it was something to be prized and cherished—we will be led to embrace positive freedom—freedom understood as the ability to make choices that develop one's nature.[29] To many advocates of positive freedom, Mill's stress on self-development and self-perfection supplies what is missing from theories of negative liberty: an answer to the questions, "Why do we value liberty?" and "What sort of liberty is most important to us?"[30] Thus, it has been argued,

(1) If we want to understand what freedom is, we have to understand why it is important.
(2) And Mill's answer to the question is, "Freedom is important because it promotes choice and self-development."
(3) But once we see that choice is at the heart of the value of freedom, then we will also see that negative freedom is not enough. And some negative freedoms, that is, those that interfere with development or are not necessary for development, may not even be very valuable.

So the answer Mill gives to the question, "Why is freedom important?" it has been argued, leads his theory beyond negative freedom to a fuller, positive ideal of freedom.

Liberty and Liberalisms

Liberty, I have said, is at the heart of all liberalisms (Section 3.1). We can now see, though, that different conceptions of liberty can lead to divergent understandings of liberalism. Classical liberalism is built on a negative conception of freedom.[31] A person, on the negative conception, is free when others are not erecting obstacles in his path or rendering some of his options ineligible. John Locke's *Second Treatise of Government* (1689) in many ways remains the clearest statement of the classical liberal's devotion to each individual's liberty (and property—see Section 5.3). According to Locke, the original condition of human beings is a "*State of perfect Freedom* to order their Actions, and dispose of their Possessions, and Persons as they think fit, within the bounds of the Law of Nature, without asking leave, or depending upon the Will of any other Man."[32] This notion of a person's natural freedom or liberty is fundamental to the classical liberal tradition. The natural condition of humans—in Locke's case, the condition in which God created humans—was one in which each has a claim to act as he chooses without interference from others, so long as he respects the freedom and property of others. An implication of this view is that social life, and life under government, is somehow artificial. The original, natural state of humans, the state that does not stand in need of any justification, is a state in which each is perfectly free to do as he wishes as long as he does not interfere with the liberty of others. And if the natural state is one of perfect freedom, any departure from this natural state, any loss of freedom, requires special justification.

The upshot of this is the doctrine that government is only legitimate if it is consented to by all citizens (Section 10.3). Government imposes *obstacles and restrictions* in the forms of laws, the collection of taxes, and so on. Thus, it limits freedom (notice, then, that the classical liberal sees freedom as the absence of restraints). But according to the classical liberal, no one has the right to interfere with the natural freedom of anyone else, and that includes government. Consequently, only if people consent to the creation of government, that is, only if they agree to its creation, can government be legitimate. A government that sought to impose its will on people without the consent of the people would be tyrannical. It would invade the natural liberty of the people.

But if government is a limitation on natural freedom, why would anyone ever consent to it? Why voluntarily limit your own negative freedom? Locke's answer, and this has been the general classical liberal answer, is that we accept the limits on freedom that government requires for the sake of better protecting our freedom itself. In the absence of government, we are always in danger of having our freedom limited by others. Even if others try to respect our freedom, disputes will arise, and unless some authority exists (see Section 10.3), there will be no easy way to resolve them. And of course, some people may not even try to respect the freedom of others, and so they pose a real threat to everyone else. Thus, the chief task of government, the job for which it was primarily designed, is the protection of individual liberty (and property). To use the phrase of Robert Nozick, a contemporary follower of Locke, the state is essentially a "protection agency."[33]

In the late nineteenth century, the "new liberalism," or "revisionist liberalism," arose to challenge this minimalist theory of government, and one of its pillars was T. H. Green's positive conception of liberty. T. H. Green was indeed himself active in the Liberal Party in the United Kingdom, and that was the party (at the time) urging reform. Now, it can be argued that those who are in extreme want—those unable to gain the basic necessities of food and shelter—are unfree in the positive sense of freedom. Under the burden of their circumstance, they are unable to develop into self-directing, autonomous individuals, being instead constantly concerned with obtaining the daily necessities of life. For similar reasons, Green was an educational reformer. If to be free people must be autonomous, they must be educated: education provides the basic tools necessary for people to act rationally and develop and understand their long-term plans and goals. Liberal education, then, aims to develop autonomous individuals—those capable of thinking for themselves and not tied to custom or prejudice. If the liberal state—the state devoted to liberty—was to do its job, it had to provide citizens with the conditions to achieve autonomy, including at least a primary education. So those liberals who came to embrace Green's positive conception of freedom began to see the task of protecting freedom as requiring wide-ranging positive state action.

These revisionist liberals agree that the liberal state is devoted to the protection of liberty and that the great classical liberals such as John Locke and John Stuart Mill were quite right about that. But given their more complicated notion of freedom, these revisionists insist that the protection of liberty is a more complicated job than the great early liberals thought. Yes, the liberal state must ensure noninterference, but it also must provide for the conditions necessary for the development of autonomous people. T. H. Green and his followers thus could argue that they were true to the traditional liberal doctrine of the functions of the state: the main job of government was to protect freedom. So in contrast to socialists and Marxists, these revisionist liberals were not advocating a nonliberal answer to the question, "What is the function of the state?" Instead, they agreed with the classical liberals that the main job of the state was to protect freedom, but now that freedom is understood in this positive, rather than a negative, way, the job of protecting freedom is a much more demanding one.

Once again, we need to be careful. I do not wish to imply that everyone who embraces negative liberty must be a classical liberal or all those who embrace positive liberty must embrace revisionist liberalism and some notion of a welfare state. We can find some Marxists who adopt negative liberty and some classical liberals who advocate a sort of positive liberty.[34] As I remarked earlier, constructing political theories is a complex and creative matter for which there are no formulas (Section 3.1). Nevertheless, (1) the endorsement of a self-developmental view of human nature, (2) a monistic view of values, (3) positive liberty, and (4) a supportive welfare state has been a coherent enduring political theory, and this has been the crux of the monistic revisionist liberal theories that arose in the United Kingdom and the United States at the end of the nineteenth century. In contrast, classical liberalism can be understood as an enduring theory based on (1) a Lockean moral individualism, (2) a pluralist theory about the values people pursue, and (3) a negative conception of liberty, all helping to justify (4) a state the most essential function of which is to protect individuals from interference by others.

4.4 Questioning the Positive/Negative Distinction

The Triadic Analysis

Thus far, I have followed Berlin, accepting that negative and positive liberty are two opposed understandings of freedom. Gerald C. MacCallum Jr., however, has questioned the distinction, insisting that all uses of liberty conform to the same schema. According to MacCallum,

> Whenever the freedom of some agent or agents is in question, it is always freedom from some constraint or restriction on, interference with, or barrier to doing, not doing, becoming, or not becoming something. Such freedom is thus always *of* something (an agent or agents), *from* something, *to* do, not do, become, or not become something. Taking the format "*x* is (is not) free from *y* to do (not do, become, not become) *z*", *x* ranges over agents, *y* ranges over such "preventing conditions" as constraints, restrictions, interferences, and barriers, and *z* ranges over actions or conditions of character or circumstance.[35]

To simplify, MacCallum's basic point is that all ascriptions of freedom always refer to three different elements: (1) an actor *(x)*, (2) some restraint *(y)*, and (3) some action *(z)*. So, we can say, "Person *x* is free/not free from restraint *y* to do/not do *z*." This has been called a triadic analysis of freedom: any intelligible use of "freedom" in political discourse always refers, explicitly or implicitly, to these three elements. For instance,

> Alf is free from Betty's handcuffs to run away.
> Betty is free from the constraint of too little money to attend a university.
> Charlie is free from his addiction to develop his capacities.

As MacCallum sees it, the debate between proponents of negative and positive liberty rests on a confusion. For example, Berlin tells us that negative liberty is "freedom from" restraints,[36] and this is to be contrasted with positive freedom that emphasizes "freedom to" do things or act in a certain rational way. MacCallum says this is a mistake. *All* ascriptions of freedom concern a claim that someone is *free both from* something and *to do* something.

Not only is it wrong, MacCallum argues, to say that "freedom from" and "freedom to" are distinct "concepts of liberty," but he holds that looking at liberty through the negative/positive distinction leads us to ignore the really important political issues. The fundamental questions that separate different political theories are how the three variables are identified. What sorts of entities are ascribed liberty *(x)*? What sorts of restraints are identified as politically most objectionable *(y)*? What sorts of actions does a political theory indicate that we should be free to do *(z)?* Looking at these differences, says MacCallum, will reveal the real basic differences in various defenses of liberty offered by political theories. He adds,

> The distinction between positive and negative freedom has, however, stood in the way of this approach. It has encouraged us to see differences in accounts of freedom as resulting from differences in concepts of freedom. This in turn has encouraged the wrong sorts of questions. We have been tempted to ask such questions as "well, who *is* right? Whose concept of freedom *is* the correct one?" or "Which *kind* of freedom do we really want after all?" Such questions will not help reveal the fundamental issues separating major writers on freedom from each other, no matter *how* the various writers are arranged into "camps." It would be far better to insist that the same concept of freedom is operating throughout, and that the differences, rather than being about what *freedom* is, are for example about what persons are, and about what can count as an obstacle to or interference with the freedom of persons so conceived.[37]

So MacCallum wants us to abandon talk about "negative" and "positive" freedom and instead focus debate on the ways various theories identify the elements of the triadic relation *(x, y, z)*.

Berlin replies to MacCallum, insisting that someone who is chained simply wants to be free *from* her chains: "A man struggling against his chains or a people against enslavement need not consciously aim at any definite further state. A man need not know how he will use his freedom; he just wants to remove the yoke."[38] As I understand Berlin, though, his main concern is not to provide an analysis of ordinary language and analyze the structure of freedom sentences. Berlin's crucial claim is that certain theories of liberty, which he identifies as "positive" conceptions, focus on the question, "Who governs me? A rational will or an irrational passion?" Berlin wants to impress on us that these are very different questions from those that move proponents of negative liberty: "How much am I governed? What do others stop me from doing?" One way to understand Berlin is that a theory of human liberty that begins with the first question will lead to policies and political programs that will be rejected—or, at least, seen as liberty infringing—by a theory that starts with the second question. Although many have thought that the positive conception is simply an extension of the negative conception, Berlin tells us that it is a very different approach to the analysis of liberty.

Bridging Negative and Positive Liberty?

We have seen that those advocating positive liberty tie freedom very close to reason; a free person must be a person who acts according to reason rather than through impulse, superstition, or custom or out of ignorance. In contrast, what has been called pure negative liberty seems to understand freedom without any reference to what it is rational for a person to do: it does not concern itself at all with why a person acts, only whether this act is obstructed.[39] Indeed, Hobbes's own account applies to the movement of natural objects as well as people: whatever moves unobstructed is free. Yet, even those attracted to negative freedom have thought that freedom involves something more than mere movement. In *On Liberty*, John Stuart Mill writes,

> If either a public officer or anyone else saw a person attempting to cross a bridge which had been ascertained to be unsafe, and there was no time to warn him of his danger, they may seize him and turn him back, without any real infringement of his liberty; for liberty consists in doing what one desires, and he does not desire to fall into the river.[40]

According to Mill, the man chose the action "cross the bridge." He cannot, however, perform that action: he is lacking crucial information that would show the impossibility of that act. The action open to him is "try to cross the bridge and end up falling into the water," and that is not an action he has chosen to perform. Since you are not stopping him from "crossing the bridge," you are not stopping him from doing anything that he has chosen to do. You are only stopping him from "trying to cross the bridge and instead falling into the river," something that he has not chosen. Because stopping him from walking on the bridge does not stop him from doing what he really wants to do, stopping him does not override any decision that he has made.

A free act must in some sense be chosen. To act freely, one must be capable of choice, or be a chooser, and one must exercise that capacity. Thus, if a person is sleepwalking, we do not consider it an interference with her liberty to stop her from crossing a busy street, because she has not chosen to cross the street. Free action, even in the negative sense of freedom, thus does, after all, presuppose the *exercise of a capacity*: the capacity for voluntary choice. To choose voluntarily,[41] (1) the person must not be so subject to cravings that she is literally compelled to act; (2) she must know what she is doing, in the sense that she intends to perform the act (for example, she is not sleepwalking); (3) she must not so misunderstand the context of her action that she does not know what she is really doing (as in Mill's bad bridge case); (4) she must not be so greatly influenced by drugs or psychological distortions that she does not know what she is doing or is unable to control herself; and (5) she must not have been conditioned by others to the extent that what she thinks of as her choices actually have been programmed into her (that is, she must not be "brainwashed").

These are all complex conditions and I have dealt with them in more length elsewhere.[42] The crucial point, though, is that insofar as negative liberty presupposes a minimally competent chooser, negative liberty begins to move in the direction of positive liberty. Thus, observes an advocate of positive liberty, Mill's claim that one does not infringe the liberty of a person crossing the bridge because the person does not wish to fall into the river is "in germ the doctrine of the 'real will.'"[43] As soon as an advocate of negative liberty acknowledges that a free person must be a chooser, the proponent of positive freedom can insist that a better chooser is freer than a worse chooser. Advocates of negative liberty, of course, do not accept this. They deny that a free person is inherently a good chooser, or one who follows her real, fully rational, will. A free person is a chooser whose opportunities for action are not made ineligible by others. Nevertheless, insofar as defenders of negative liberty are concerned about obstacles to *choice*, freedom cannot be understood purely in terms about external restraints. A person must have, if not a real will, a minimally effective will, allowing us to accurately describe what he does as his own choice. As one contemporary philosopher has put it, although negative freedom is by no means to be equated with autonomy, it does presuppose the exercise of a more modest capacity, *autarchy*, the capacity to choose.[44]

4.5 Summary

This chapter has focused on the distinction between negative and positive liberty. In Section 4.1, I considered a series of examples and tried to develop a conception of freedom on the basis of ordinary language. Beginning with the simple idea of freedom as movement that is not blocked, we saw that one's freedom can be limited when a possible course of action has been made ineligible by threats, even if it is still possible to perform the action. Not just force, but threats of force, limit freedom. I also considered whether offers can be coercive and limit freedom.

Section 4.2 turned to positive freedom, which T. H. Green believed was a development of the notion of negative freedom. A free person, on this view, is one guided by her real will—her settled aims, goals, and desires. For Green, such a person was necessarily concerned with the development of her capacities. Only a person guided by reason, on this view, can be free. Thus, although external obstacles can prevent one from being guided by reason, so too can internal obstacles. This idea is central to the various notions of an autonomous life that we examined.

Section 4.3 then examined Isaiah Berlin's analysis of the difference underlying positive and negative liberty. Positive liberty, Berlin argues, is grounded on monism—the belief that all values ultimately are harmonious and that a single answer can be uncovered to the question, "What makes life worth living?" In contrast, Berlin believes that negative liberty is supported by pluralism, a conviction that the ends in life are many and conflicting. Because there are many good things in life and we cannot have them all, we must choose, but it does not seem that any one choice is demanded by reason. Hence the importance of negative liberty. I extended Berlin's point, showing how positive liberty reflects rationalism and allegiance to a self-developmental view of human nature. This combination of rationalism and self-development views of human nature characterized much of the "new liberalism" that arose at the beginning of the twentieth century, thus helping to explain why new liberal theorists tended to adopt positive conceptions of liberty. In contrast, the classical liberal tradition has been far less prone to accept either rationalism or self-developmental views of human nature, and has tended to stress moral individualism and pluralism.

In Section 4.4, I examined two challenges to the stark contrast between negative and positive liberty. Gerald MacCallum tries to show that all freedom claims—negative as well as positive—have a three-part structure; he insists there is but one concept of liberty. Last, I argued that we should be careful not to overstate the differences between negative and positive liberty, since even advocates of negative liberty must concern themselves with the internal conditions for genuine choice. Only choosers can be denied political liberty. Nevertheless, although the distinction is not quite so stark as some have thought, it seems that Berlin has made out a powerful case that the different interpretations of liberty are grounded on different, indeed competing, understandings of value, reason, and human nature.

Notes

1. In this book, I follow normal philosophical practice in treating "liberty" and "freedom" as synonyms, though they have slightly different uses in English. A person, for instance, might be said to "take liberties" with the English language; he would not be said to "take freedoms" with it.

2. Thomas Hobbes, "Of Liberty and Necessity," in Sir William Molesworth, ed., *English Works [of Thomas Hobbes]*, vol. 4 (London, 1840), p. 273.

3. Isaiah Berlin, "Two Concepts of Liberty," in his *Four Essays on Liberty* (Oxford: Oxford University Press, 1969), p. 122.

4. Hillel Steiner, *An Essay on Rights* (Cambridge, MA: Blackwell, 1994), p. 8. Emphasis added.

5. For different analyses of cases such as these, which link interfering with freedom to moral responsibility for obstacles, see David Miller, "Constraints on Freedom," *Ethics*, vol. 94 (1983), pp. 66–86; Kristján Kristjánsson, *Social Freedom: The Responsibility View* (Cambridge: Cambridge University Press, 1996), chap. 2.

6. Isaiah Berlin, "Introduction," in his *Four Essays on Liberty*, pp. xxxix–xl.

7. See Kristjánsson, *Social Freedom*, pp. 68–69; William E. Connolly, *The Terms of Political Discourse*, 2nd ed. (Princeton: Princeton University Press, 1983), pp. 165ff.

8. See J. P. Day, "Threats, Offers, Law, Opinion and Liberty," *American Philosophical Quarterly*, vol. 14 (1977), p. 263.

9. F. A. Hayek, *The Constitution of Liberty* (London: Routledge and Kegan Paul, 1960), p. 133.

10. On the option view of freedom, see Joel Feinberg, *Rights, Justice and the Bounds of Liberty* (Princeton: Princeton University Press, 1980), p. 36.

11. See S. I. Benn and W. L. Weinstein, "Being Free to Act, and Being a Free Man," *Mind*, vol. 80 (1971), pp. 202–203; See Kristjánsson, *Social Freedom*, pp. 41ff.

12. Quoted in Joel Feinberg, *Harm to Self* (New York: Oxford University Press, 1986), p. 250.

13. For a good discussion, see Kristjánsson, *Social Freedom*, pp. 51ff. For doubts about the idea of coercive offers, see my *Social Philosophy* (Armonk, NY: M. E. Sharpe, 1999), pp. 209–210.

14. Berlin, "Introduction," p. xxxix. Emphasis added.

15. See Charles Taylor, "What's Wrong with Negative Liberty," in Alan Ryan, ed., *The Idea of Freedom* (Oxford: Clarendon Press, 1979), pp. 175–194.

16. This lecture has been reprinted in several places. For some useful selections, see John R. Rodman, ed., *T. H. Green: Political Theory* (New York: Appleton-Century-Crofts, 1964). For the full lecture, see Paul Harris and John Morrow, eds., *Green's Lectures on the Principles of Political Obligation* (Cambridge: Cambridge University Press, 1986). My references are to the latter.

17. Green, "On the Different Senses of Freedom," p. 229.

18. Ibid., p. 228.

19. For different views on the relation of positive freedom and autonomy, see Robert Young, *Personal Autonomy: Beyond Negative and Positive Liberty* (London: Croom Helm, 1986); Horacio Spector, *Autonomy and Rights: The Moral Foundations of Liberalism* (Oxford: Clarendon Press, 1992), pp. 94ff.

20. Green, "On the Different Senses of Freedom," p. 228.

21. Joseph Raz, *The Morality of Freedom* (Oxford: Clarendon Press, 1986), p. 375.

22. See S. I. Benn, *A Theory of Freedom* (Cambridge: Cambridge University Press, 1988), chap. 9; Thomas E. Hill Jr., *Autonomy and Self-Respect* (Cambridge: Cambridge University Press, 1991), pp. 35ff. Susan Wolf distinguishes freedom as following the real self from freedom as living according to reason in her *Freedom Within Reason* (Oxford: Oxford University Press, 1990).

23. See, for example, Gerald Dworkin, *The Theory and Practice of Autonomy* (Cambridge: Cambridge University Press, 1988), chap. 1.

24. Berlin, "Two Concepts," pp. 132–133.

25. Ibid., p. 150.

26. Ibid., p. 166.

27. Ibid., p. 170.

28. Ibid., p. 171.

29. Richard Norman, *Free and Equal: A Philosophical Examination of Political Values* (Oxford: Oxford University Press, 1987), pp. 36–37.

30. See Taylor, "What's Wrong with Negative Liberty."

31. See Jan Narveson, *The Libertarian Idea* (Philadelphia: Temple University Press, 1988).

32. John Locke, *Second Treatise of Government,* in Peter Laslett, ed., *Two Treatises of Government* (Cambridge: Cambridge University Press, 1960), sect. 4.

33. See Robert Nozick, *Anarchy, State and Utopia* (New York: Basic Books, 1974), Part 1, especially chap. 5.

34. See Kristjánsson, *Social Freedom,* p. 114; Spector, *Autonomy and Rights.*

35. Gerald C. MacCallum Jr., "Negative and Positive Freedom," in Peter Laslett, W. G. Runciman, and Quentin Skinner, eds., *Philosophy, Politics and Society,* 4th series (Oxford: Basil Blackwell, 1972), p. 176.

36. Berlin, "Two Concepts," p. 127.

37. MacCallum, "Negative and Positive Freedom," p. 181.

38. Berlin, *Four Essays on Liberty,* p. xliii, note.

39. See Richard E. Flathman, *The Philosophy and Politics of Freedom* (Chicago: University of Chicago Press, 1987), p. 32.

40. John Stuart Mill, *On Liberty,* in John Gray, ed., *On Liberty and Other Essays* (New York: Oxford University Press, 1991), chap. 5, para. 5.

41. I am following Joel Feinberg, *Harm to Self* (New York: Oxford University Press, 1986), p. 115; Benn, *A Theory of Freedom,* chap. 8.

42. See my *Social Philosophy,* pp. 202–205.

43. Bernard Bosanquet, *The Philosophical Theory of the State,* in Gerald F. Gaus and William Sweet, eds., *The Philosophical Theory of the State and Related Essays* (Indianapolis, IN: St. Augustine Press, 2000), p. 97.

44. Benn, *A Theory of Freedom,* chap. 8.

5

LIBERTY AND POWER

5.1. Positive Freedom as Power to Act

Freedom as Being Able to Do What One Desires

The previous chapter focused on the distinction between negative and positive liberty, the latter being understood as autonomous, rational, or self-controlled action. We now must consider a different conception of positive liberty—one that is often confused with freedom as autonomy—which I call *liberty as power to act*. Although distinct, freedom as power to act is conceptually tied to liberty as autonomy. T. H. Green (Section 4.2) was concerned with one's *power or ability to act*; someone under the influence of alcohol did not have the power to act according to her true preferences. At one point, Green actually defines man's freedom as "the power of acting according to his true will or preference."[1] Now, in Green's mind this idea is always linked to the concept of freedom as autonomous action, but later theorists develop a different conception of positive freedom. According to this second conception of positive freedom, someone is free to perform act Φ if she has the effective power to Φ. By "effective power," I mean skills, resources, or whatever one needs to perform Φ. This sort of positive formulation of freedom locates freedom in not simply the absence of impediments to action, but the ability to perform the actions a person's desires. In short, a free person can do what she desires to do. Or as the British socialist R. H. Tawney (1880–1962) put it, liberty implies "the ability to act."[2]

To see how freedom as power differs from negative liberty, consider the case of segregated universities and colleges in the United States. Through the 1950s, and well into the 1960s, universities and colleges in many southern states in the United States were legally segregated: blacks were legally barred from attending all-white universities. Such segregation was declared illegal by federal authorities and no longer is practiced today. Many blacks are still unable to attend these formerly all-white universities, however. Family incomes are lower among blacks, so they are less able to send their children to any university; and because black elementary and secondary schools are often poorly funded compared to the schools whites attend, blacks are often less well prepared for college. Now, our question is not whether this is just—that is a wider query that is relevant to Chapters 8 and 9—but whether blacks *are as free* as whites to attend universities. A liberal defender of negative freedom would agree that prior to the desegregation of southern colleges and universities, blacks were not free to attend schools like the University of Mississippi (Oxford). The option of attending was made ineligible; efforts by black students to attend would be, and were, blocked by threats and force. The question concerns the present: are blacks *now* free to attend these universities? Advocates of negative liberty maintain that as long as black students are not threatened for attending, or excluded by racist admissions policies, black students are free to attend these universities. To be sure, poorer black students—like poorer white students—*are not able to use this liberty,* but that does not mean they do not have it. In contrast, a proponent of freedom as power will insist that a person who is not able to go to a university simply is not free to do so. A poor person, on this view, is not free to go to a university, take the Concorde to Europe, or buy a Mercedes. What one is not able to do, one is not free to do.

Freedom and Material Well-Being

The debate between advocates of liberal, negative liberty and liberty as power is highlighted in the debate whether it makes sense to distinguish a person's liberty from the worth or value of that liberty. Liberals almost always insist that "poverty and ignorance, and a lack of means generally," are not constraints that limit one's freedom, but affect "the worth of liberty."[3] Not too surprising, socialist writers tend to reject this distinction.[4] For the socialist, human emancipation is inherently linked to material well-bring:

> In contemporary society . . . the most obvious example of the liberating character of material conditions is monetary wealth. If I inherit a fortune or win the pools or, less spectacularly, get a new job which will provide me with a larger income, new opportunities become available to me which were previously inaccessible: I can travel to different places, engage in different activities or pastimes—new worlds, geographically new or culturally new, are opened up for me. The connection with freedom lies not in the greater material comforts or enjoyments, but in the increase of possibilities—the greater scope for choice.[5]

To be free to do something, one needs both to be free from restraint *and* to have the resources to do the thing. Obviously, this conception of liberty tremendously increases the scope of state action required to ensure freedom. The task of ensuring freedom becomes the job of providing a multitude of resources: income, health care, education, housing, and so on. To make citizens free, the state must provide them with the resources necessary for action. So understood, the responsibilities of the freedom-enhancing state go far beyond even that of T. H. Green's autonomy-enhancing regime. For according to freedom as autonomy, a state devoted to freedom must provide the conditions for autonomy; and although this may include some provision of basic educational, cultural, and welfare goods, it does *not* imply that all resources increase freedom. According to freedom as power to act, however, every increase in material resources that increases your ability to pursue your desires necessarily increases your freedom. Thus, the aim of equalizing freedom is inherently linked to equalizing material resources (see Section 7.4). And because capitalism leads to inequality of resources, on this view, it necessarily involves unequal freedom.

Liberal advocates of capitalism thus reject this conception of freedom. Writes F. A. Hayek,

> This confusion of liberty as power with liberty in its original meaning inevitably leads to the identification of liberty with wealth; and this makes it possible to exploit all the appeal which the word "liberty" carries in the support of the demand for the redistribution of wealth. Yet, though freedom and wealth are both good things which most of us desire and though we often need both to obtain what we wish, they still remain different. Whether I am my own master and can follow my own choice and whether the possibilities from which I must choose are many or few are two entirely different questions. The courtier living in the lap of luxury but at the beck and call of his prince may be much less free than a poor peasant or artisan, less able to live his own life, and to choose his own opportunities for usefulness.
>
> . . . Liberty does not mean all good things or the absence of all evils. It is true that to be free may mean freedom to starve, to make costly mistakes, or to run mortal risks. In the sense in which we use the term, the penniless vagabond who lives precariously by constant improvisation is indeed freer than the conscripted soldier with all his security and relative comfort. But if liberty may not therefore be preferable to other goods, it is a distinctive good that needs a distinctive name.[6]

Notice that just as Isaiah Berlin appealed to pluralism (Section 3.2) in his defense of negative liberty against liberty as autonomy (Section 4.2),

Hayek too appeals to pluralism. Freedom is just one of the good things in life; material wealth and security are others, and they too are important if we are to achieve our aims and purposes. But Hayek, like Berlin, insists that it is a mistake to include all these good things in the concept of liberty; the pursuit of freedom and other good things can conflict, and one may have to choose, say, freedom over security, or freedom over material well-being. Including all of these good things in the concept of liberty belies a monistic belief that they all are part of the same ideal and we can avoid the necessity of choosing among them.

The Ideal of a Free Person

Although freedom as power is in many ways a much more straight-forward notion of positive liberty than that presented by T. H. Green, it has a serious problem that Green's theory does not. Green's theory helps us make sense of the ideal of a free person. Green can argue that a liberty-enhancing social policy ought to aim at encouraging the development of free, autonomous, people. According to freedom as effective power, however, the general idea of a free person becomes lost. What is a free person? The proponent of negative liberty has an answer: someone who is not being restrained by others. Green has an answer: someone who can act autonomously, and so is not a slave to passions or prejudices. But the proponent of freedom as effective power does not have a clear answer: a person can be free to do this or free to do that, but the ideal of *a free person* appears to evaporate. Since freedom requires resources, and since no one will ever have all the resources to do everything she wants, people will always be free to do some things and not others. The only way to reconcile freedom as power with the idea of a free person is to rely on a social environmentalist theory of human nature (Section 3.3), according to which people's wants are formed by their society. As many socialists have argued, although people's wants in capitalist societies are endless—no matter what we have we always want something more—it does not follow that people living in a socialist society would be "limitless consumers." If, under socialism, people only wanted what they needed, or in some way their wants were limited and modest, then everyone might have the power to do everything they wanted to do, and then everyone could be called a free person.

In the absence of such a radical change in the nature of people's wants, however, the conception of freedom as effective power switches the focus of freedom discourse from the general value of freedom to the value of being able to do this thing (go to university) or do that thing (take a vacation). That is, if we take this second conception of positive freedom as basic, we will no longer be committed to the idea of a free person, but must focus on particular sorts of freedom. Should you be free to travel to the moon? Are we to worry if people are unfree in this sense? Clearly some unfreedoms (that is, lack of powers) are not to be regretted, and some freedoms (that is, powers) are not to be pursued. But if that is so, then we need criteria to distinguish valuable freedoms from silly freedoms. Why are some powers essential and other powers unimportant? Somewhat surprising, developing such criteria is apt to lead us back to freedom as autonomy, or freedom as self-realization (Sections 4.2, 4.3). We can distinguish important from trivial liberties if, accepting an ideal of self-realization or self-development, we can distinguish those liberties (powers) that are critical for achieving self-realization from those that do little to advance it—indeed, perhaps even are impediments to it. Suppose, for example, that great wealth is actually an obstacle to self-development; it has been said that it distracts us and tempts us to pursue self-indulgent, but ultimately not self-satisfying, lives. Equipped with a theory about which freedoms are important, the advocate of freedom as power could now say what types of freedom (abilities) are necessary for a satisfying, free life. But note that at this point freedom as power has collapsed into freedom as self-realization: the free life is a self-realized or autonomous life, not simply a life rich with effective powers.

5.2 Power and Freedom

"Power to" and "Power over"

The notion of positive freedom as power to act has led us into one of the enduring disputes in political theory—the relation of freedom and power. We cannot really understand freedom until we grasp its relation to power. Unfortunately, like other important political concepts, power itself seems essentially contested (see Section 2.1).[7] The discussion in Section 5.1 relied on what might be called the Hobbesian conception of power. According to Thomas Hobbes, "The power of a man . . . is his present means, to obtain some future or apparent good."[8] So understood, power belongs to a person if he has the means to achieve his goals, desires, and so on. One's power is one's ability to do what one wishes. Such *power to* depends on one's natural capacities, information, and resources. All these could be employed by Robinson Crusoe alone on a desert island. What he could not have until another person appeared was *power over* another. If a person possesses "power over" others, he can somehow affect their interests and lives; he can typically make them do things they would not otherwise have done or believe things they would not have otherwise believed.[9]

It would seem that "power to" is the more general idea. A person can have the power to do things for many different reasons, one of which is that he has "power over" others. Having power over others is one way, but only one way, of being able to secure what one desires. Let us say, then, that "power over" is a subset of "power to." A person who has "power over" another necessarily has "power to" affect that person in certain ways, but one can have the power to, say, build one's own house without having power over anyone.

Control Versus Effect Theories of "Power over"

Political theorists have long debated precisely what is involved in one person having power over another. Simplifying a complex debate, we can distinguish two broad families of theories. According to *control theories* of power over, to possess power over others evinces an ability to control them.[10] Alf is thus said to have power over Betty when Alf can control some aspect of Betty's life. Alf has power over Betty's dreams if he can in some way control her dreams; he has power over her desires if he can control which ones she adopts; he has power over her actions if he can control what she does. "Control" is to be distinguished from influencing another through reasoning with her or exchange with her. When I try to convince you to join the American Civil Liberties Union, I do not control you, even if you decide to join up; when I offer the car dealer $20,000, I do not control her, even if she takes up the offer. In neither case do I have power over the other in the sense of control. But if I influence your decisions by brainwashing you or by coercing you, then I do exercise control, and so have power over you. Some, however, have denied this. It has been maintained by Felix Oppenheim that control was exercised by President Eisenhower when he persuaded voters to elect him by promising an end to the Korean war.[11] Although, to be sure, if there really is such a thing as "hidden persuasion" in the form of subliminal advertising, that would indeed be a type of control; but simply persuading voters that you will do what they want you to do hardly seems a way to control them. If, on the other hand, the president withheld crucial information so as to manipulate the people, then we may well see him as exercising control.

If we adopt the control view, it does not seem that Alf has power over Betty just because he can affect her, even greatly affect her, in ways that he cannot control. A bull in a china shop greatly affects the owners of the shop, indeed in ways that go against their interests, but the bull does not exercise power over the owners. This is important, for we see that a person may possess a great amount of "power to" do things that tremendously affect people, yet still not have "power over" them in the sense of control.

Control theories explain the notion of power over in terms of one person being subject to the will of another. They thus place great stress on the way in which power is tied to intentional or conscious purposes. It has been said that "power may be defined as the production of intended effects."[12] Control of another seems to imply that one wishes person A to Φ, and because one has control one is able to make it the case that person A performs action Φ. To be sure, one who has control can accidentally use it—my daughter may accidentally hit the control button on her video game and make it turn off when she does not want it to. In that case, her control of the game led to a result she did not intend or wish. But unless you can generally make the other do what you wish, you do not control her. And unless you *have* control (can guide things to do what you want them to do), you cannot *lose* it and cause an unintended outcome.

Many have disputed that for person A to have power over B with regard to Φ, A must intend that B Φ. According to *effect theories of power over*, the heart of power is the ability to adversely affect the interests of others, usually in a way that benefits the power holder.[13] Thus, according to Steven Lukes's famous account, "A exercises power over B when A affects B in a manner contrary to B's interests."[14] Consider, for example, the following story presented by William Connelly:

> Suppose . . . as a white employer in control of important and scarce job opportunities, I fail through inattention and habit to consider candidates for employment other than lower-class white males. I could do otherwise if I were to attend carefully to the consequences of my actions, but I don't, contributing thereby to the high unemployment of minorities.[15]

To the advocate of the control theory, this looks more like a bull in a china shop than an exercise of control over people. The employer has great power to do things, and his exercise of this "power to" has effects on others, but it is hard to see how in any way it exhibits a control of them. In one way, of course, the owner is clearly different from the bull in the china shop: he is responsible for his actions, and could have done otherwise. For some, this is crucial: if person A is responsible for an obstacle confronting B, some insist that he is exercising power over her.[16] To many, what is also salient in this case is that because the white employer holds a "strategic position with regard to employment chances," he can reasonably be said to "exercise power over them."[17] The core idea is that the employer's actions have a systematic, adverse effect on the interests of the blacks, and that is why he holds power over them. On this effect view of power over, person A has power over person B if person A (systematically) acts in ways that adversely affect the interest of B while advancing his own.

What is not important to effect theories is that the power holder controls people in the sense of making them do what he wants them to do.

Which conception of "power over" a theorist thinks best will, as is the case with any essentially contested concept, turn on the rest of his political theory. With respect to theories of power, an especially important consideration will be the individualist or collectivist commitments of the theory. As we saw in Section 3.4, a methodological collectivist believes that the beliefs, actions, and interests of individuals are to be explained by the social system in which they find themselves. In explaining a person's life and its conditions, then, the collectivist insists on the primary importance of one's place in the social system, not the aims, desires, and intentions of individual agents. Such collectivism, then, inclines strongly to effect theories of "power over." To use Connolly's term, it is the "strategic position" in the overall social and economic system that gives one person power over another. We locate power not in one agent's ability to make another do what he wishes, but in the way the social system systematically disadvantages some interests over others, allowing some people to thrive and others to be dominated. Political theories that combine a collectivist method and a view of society that stresses conflicts of interest thus tend to place effect theories of "power over" close to their core. Not surprising, then, socialist analyses of capitalist society are apt to make the most of this conception of power. For example, according to Harold Laski, one of the twentieth century's foremost socialist political theorists, socialism

> is not a movement the summary of which is simple. There go to its making ideas derived from the most disparate sources. But it is not, I think, inaccurate to say that the essence of its attack [on liberalism] derived from the realization that the liberal idea secured to the middle-class its full share of privilege, while it left the proletariat in chains.[18]

The core of socialism's criticism of liberal capitalist society is that its basic arrangements leave some well off while others are impoverished; in this sense the workers are in "chains," and the owning classes have power over them. Of course, Laski does not mean either that the workers are literally in chains or even that they are consciously controlled by capitalists: he is pointing to their place in the economic system and how it disadvantages them.

In contrast, classical liberals adopt some version of methodological individualism. They understand society in terms of the beliefs, actions, and desires of individuals and the relations between them. Consequently, when analyzing what is involved in one person having power over others, liberal individualists identify relations in which one person is able to, or actually does, control the beliefs, desires, and actions of another individual. Although classical liberals are likely to acknowledge that rules and institutions are usually employed in this power relation, the core case of "power over" is one person intentionally controlling another.[19]

Liberty, Power, and Competition

We began the chapter by examining the conception of positive liberty according to which freedom is equated with "power to." We are now in a position to appreciate one of the worries raised by such conceptions: because one form of "power to" do something is to have "power over" others, if to have freedom is to possess power, one's freedom may be enhanced by having power over others. Exercising power over another, however, inherently limits that person's liberty.[20] If, say, I control you, then your actions respond to my wishes; should you want to do otherwise, you could not, or could only do so at considerable costs. It would not, I think, make much sense to say that I controlled you, but you were perfectly free to act against my wishes—in what sense do I then control you? Recall that for Hayek (Section 4.1), coercion limits your liberty because it makes you "someone's else's tool." That too is the right metaphor for being controlled by another: if you exercise power over me I am to some extent your tool, and so not free.

Now, if one way to have power is to have power over others, and if Alf's having power over Betty implies that Betty's liberty is limited, then according to freedom as power to act, one person's liberty inherently limits another person's. If Alf has power over Betty, he is free, but her freedom is limited. If Alf does not have power over Betty, her freedom shows that his power is limited; but if freedom is power, then Betty's freedom necessarily limits Alf's freedom. Insofar as freedom involves having power over others, freedom thus becomes *an inherently competitive good*. We can distinguish three types of goods. Let us call a good a *common good* if one person's share of it cannot detract from other people's share—it is "not diminished by sharing."[21] Listening to a concert together is such a good; my listening does not diminish the amount of concert open to you to hear. And if I get more of the good—the performer does an encore, say—you also get more of the good. A *partially competitive* good is one that, in some cases, both Alf and Betty can gain more of at the same time, whereas in other cases Alf gains more by diminishing Betty's share. Wealth is such a good. In productive enterprises, the cooperating parties both increase their wealth; plunderers, however, gain through taking the wealth of others. Last, an inherently competitive good is one in which the only way for you to increase your amount is to decrease the amount of someone else. The good of "being best" on a team is such a good; the only way you can get it is to take it away from someone else.

Insofar as freedom is sought through power over others, it is inherently competitive. The only way I can achieve such freedom is by limiting your liberty (that is, power) to do as you please. If, then, we understand freedom as "power over" others, we cannot even contemplate the ideal of a society of free people. We can no more imagine a society in which everyone is free (in the sense of having power) than we can imagine a society in which everyone is the best baseball player. Freedom thus understood can be redistributed—moved from person to person—but its total amount cannot be increased.[22] It is certainly troubling for a conception of freedom that it seems to undermine the very ideal of a free society. If, however, we restrict freedom as power to the notion of "power to," where this does not imply "power over," the pursuit of freedom is not inherently competitive. It is then a good like wealth (indeed, freedom becomes very closely linked to wealth). We can all simultaneously increase our wealth (or freedom), but I also can increase my wealth (or freedom) by taking some of your wealth (freedom qua power to).

Is it possible to understand freedom as a common good—one that is not diminished by sharing? Negative liberty seems to render freedom noncompetitive insofar as my share of freedom does not in itself diminish yours. Alf is negatively free insofar as no one acts in such a way as to render options ineligible for him; Betty is free insofar as no one renders options ineligible for her (Section 4.1). The absence of obstacles to Alf in no way necessitates obstacles for Betty; his "share" of nonintervention does not in itself decrease her share. The problem, as classical liberals have long recognized, is that although there is no inherent conflict between Alf and Betty's negative freedom, as soon as they employ their freedom to do things, they may end up limiting each other's freedom. Should Betty use her freedom to capture Alf, or to block his path when walking down the street, she limits his freedom. As soon as we begin to *use* our negative freedom, it is very hard not to, as it were, bump into each other in ways that limit each other's negative freedom. Thus, liberals have argued, a condition in which each was free to use her freedom in any way she wished—a "state of nature"—would be characterized by conflict and insecurity (Sections 4.3, 8.2). Classical liberals have often insisted that to ensure a generally free society, we must give up the liberty to "bump into each other" in certain ways—say, by attacking each other. This suggests that as a practical matter, even negative freedom is a partially competitive good.

5.3 Freedom, Power, and Property

Liberty and Private Property: Classical Liberal Views

Instrumentalist Defenses of Freedom.   Since at least the seventeenth century, liberals have not only upheld liberty as their core value, they have insisted that private property is necessary for liberty. Liberals, however, have presented two markedly different accounts of this relation. According to what we might call *liberty-protecting cases for property,* private property is justified because it supplies individuals with the power they need to counteract the power of government. Although, as we have just seen, liberals recognize that government is necessary to protect us from each other, they also insist that the power of government is the chief threat to liberty. To exercise power is to limit someone else's freedom; since government is the most powerful single actor in society, it poses the greatest threat to freedom. Consequently, liberals have insisted that only an economic system based on private property disperses power and resources, ensuring that private people have the resources to oppose the state. Property provides individuals with the power to resist government. As Hayek argues, "There can be no freedom of press if the instruments of printing are under government control, no freedom of assembly if the needed rooms are so controlled, no freedom of movement if the means of transport are a government monopoly."[23] Another, similar defense of property insists only those with property have the independence necessary for a free society: because they do not depend on the state or others for their livelihood, they can afford to speak their mind and oppose those who would use their power to dominate society.[24] Liberty-protecting defenses of property, then, see property as involving "power to": if I have property, I have the power to act on my desires, including desires that the government opposes.

None of this constitutes a denial that Alf's property limits Betty's freedom. If *P* is Alf's property, he has a "bundle of rights" regarding it, most important of which are

(1) *Right of Use:* Alf has a right to use *P*, that is,
   (a) It is not wrong for Alf to use *P*, and
   (b) It is wrong for others to interfere with Alf's using *P*.
(2) *Right of Exclusion:* Others (including Betty) may use *P* if and only if Alf consents, that is,
   (a) If Alf consents, it is, other things being equal, not wrong for others (including Betty) to use *P*;
   (b) If Alf does not consent, it is, other things being equal, wrong for others to use *P*.
(3) *Right of Transfer:* Alf may permanently transfer the rights in rules (1) and (2) to specific persons by consent.[25]

The right of exclusion—(2)—clearly limits Betty's liberty: Alf's property right to *P* limits Betty's liberty to use it. Liberal defenses of private property do not deny that Alf's property limits Betty's freedom to use *P*. After all, *all of Alf's rights* limit the freedom of others: Alf's right not to be mugged limits the freedom of others to mug him (see Section 8.1).[26] But, says the classical liberal, that Alf has property does not imply that he exercises "power over" Betty, even if Alf has a great deal of property and Betty has little. Everything depends on precisely how Alf employs his property. If Alf uses his property to hire thugs to intimidate his neighbors and get them to do what he wants, then his property clearly is the basis of his power over them. He uses his property to *control* them by making some options ineligible. Consider a different case: Alf is a rich entrepreneur who offers Betty a low-wage job. Classical liberals would insist that he is not exercising power over her, because he is not controlling her. He is not limiting her options: indeed, as we have seen, since offers expand one's options, many liberals insist that they can never render options ineligible (Section 4.1). This being so, although Betty agrees to obey Alf's instructions, he does not exercise power over her: he has increased her choices. Since she is free to not obey him and to quit her job, she is not controlled by Alf. After all, when you order a hamburger at McDonald's, you do not exercise power over the person behind the counter, even though he does what you want him to do—he gives you a Big Mac. Because it is a free exchange, the classical liberal insists that neither party controls the other—exercises power over the other—and so neither limits the other's freedom.

For classical liberals, then, a private property market order is absolutely necessary for a free society. More than that, in the eyes of classical liberals, the market has the unique virtue of producing (1) an orderly system of social cooperation (2) among people with diverse ends while (3) respecting their freedom. It is easy to see how two of these can be combined; the trick is accommodating all three. It is relatively easy, for example, to produce a system of cooperation that respects freedom if we all happen to value the same thing, for then we will voluntarily cooperate to attain the thing we all desire. And it is relatively easy to respect freedom while allowing for a diversity of ends if we do not care about social cooperation and are content to live in a condition of anarchy (see Section 8.2). And of course, we can produce order even with a diversity of ends if we do not care about freedom: an authoritarian can take charge and command us to cooperate (see Section 10.4). The market order, insists the classical liberal, allows for all three. It requires a diversity of ends or goals; it is only because we want different things that exchange is possible. If everyone wanted the same things—if we all valued everything in the same way—exchange could not occur. People enter market transactions, they trade, in order to obtain those goods and services that will better allow them to pursue their aims. And because our aims differ, we pursue different things. The market thus allows free, that is, noncoerced, cooperative behavior without any agreement on ultimate ends.

The market thus coheres with classical liberalism's pluralism (Section 3.2) and its self-interested view of human nature (Section 3.3). When you go to McDonald's and ask for a Big Mac, a possibility of exchange occurs because you and McDonald's have different values: they would prefer having your money to keeping their burger, and you would prefer having the burger to keeping your money. As Hayek sees it, the great accomplishment of the market is that it allows people pursuing a tremendous diversity of aims to cooperate in such a way that they assist each other in their pursuits without having any intention of doing so. Thus, as Adam Smith (1723–1790) put it, each person "intends only his own gain, and he is in this, as in many other cases, led by an invisible hand to promote an end which was no part of his intention."[27]

According to the liberty-protecting defenses of property, then, (1) your property rights *do* necessarily limit the freedom of others insofar as they exclude others from using your property. (2) Property, unlike freedom, gives one "power to" do what one wants. Property is necessary for a free society because it is essential that private citizens have the power to do things without asking the approval of government. (3) The use of property does *not* inherently involve the exercise of "power over" others. As a resource giving one power to do what one wants, it can be used to acquire power over others, but such power is not the norm in free exchange. Indeed, for the classical liberal the market order is the only way for people to freely coordinate their actions.

Property as Freedom.   Liberals have not only insisted that property is a means to preserving liberty, they have often conceived of it as an embodiment of liberty, or as a type of liberty, or indeed as identical to liberty. This view is popular among many contemporary classical liberals. Jan Narveson, for instance, bluntly asserts, "Liberty is Property."[28] There are, once again, a number of variations on this claim.[29] The main idea, though, is that one's freedom is a "zone" or "space" in which one can act without interference from others. Property defines this zone: a person who has property can do what she wants with it, and others cannot interfere. So, the zone defined by one's property is simply a manifestation of one's freedom. To be free is just to be free to use what is yours—your property.[30]

Although advocates of this view typically see themselves as advocating negative liberty, their argument seems to confuse negative liberty and liberty as power (Sections 4.1, 5.1). A person with property is a person with the resources to translate her desires into reality. If that is a sort of freedom, it is just the sort of positive freedom that classical liberals such as Hayek strongly and explicitly reject; as I argued, it seems much more at home in socialist political theories.

Private Property and Power: Socialist Views

Private Property and the Transfer of "Power to."   Socialists have long insisted that capitalist private property inevitably and crucially involves
power relations between the owners and workers. Following Karl Marx,
socialists have often understood private property as a mechanism that allows capitalists to extract the productive powers of the workers and use
them for the benefit of the capitalist class. Under capitalism, it is argued,
those with private property systematically employ the productive powers of the workers to enrich themselves; consequently, on this view, the
whole point of private property is to transfer "power to" from the producers (workers) to owners. According to C. B. Macpherson,

> Most simply, what is transferred, from the non-owner to the owner of the
> means of labour (i.e., of the land and capital), is the non-owner's ability to
> labour, i.e., his ability to use his own capacities productively, during the time
> contracted for. The owner purchases that ability for a certain time and puts it
> to work. The ability, the labour-*power,* is transferred. The actual work is *per-
> formed* by the non-owner. But in a very real sense the actual work is *owned* by
> the owner of the capital. He, having purchased the other's ability to labour,
> has the rights of ownership in the labour that is actually performed. . . . He
> also owns the product, including the value added to the materials of the
> work. . . .
>   What is transferred, then, is both the ability to work and the ownership of
> work itself.[31]

Thus, whereas the liberal sees private property rights as providing every
property owner with the power to do as she wishes, Marxists such as
Macpherson insist that because capitalism is based on the sale of labor
power by the workers to the owners, capitalism is a systematic redistribu
tion of "power to" from workers to capitalists.

Property and "Power over."   A core theme of socialist writings has been
that private property constitutes the capitalists' "power over" the working class. Some socialists such as R. H. Tawney employed the narrower
notion of "power over" as "control" to make this point:

> For the characteristic of modern industry, and of the financial arrangements
> associated with it, is not only that it increases, by its technological triumphs,
> man's power over nature, but that, in the absence of deliberate restraints im-
> posed by society, it heightens that of some men over others, by organizing
> and concentrating it. It concentrates it because it normally involves the con-
> centration of ownership, and therefore of the rights which ownership con-

fers; because its method is mass-production, and mass-production involves
the control of large armies of workers, who execute, by small groups, who
direct and plan; because it makes all, or nearly all, types of economic activity
interdependent, so that those who control a key service can impose their
terms on the remainder.[32]

Capitalists have power over workers because they can direct the workers
according to their plans. Thus, in the eyes of Tawney, as well as revisionist liberals such as L. T. Hobhouse, protecting the liberty of the workers
required constraining the power of employers. "There is no intrinsic and
inevitable conflict between liberty and compulsion," since coercive restraints in the form of government regulation—concerning, say, working
hours, factory conditions, and wages—are necessary to protect the workers from the power of capitalism.[33]

The contemporary socialist philosopher Kai Nielsen employs an effect
account of power in his criticism of capitalism. In commenting on the
power of the famous capitalist John D. Rockefeller (1839–1937), Nielsen,
in contrast to Tawney, does not make much of the way in which Rockefeller's "capitalist property rights" allowed him to intentionally control
his workers or consumers. Instead, Nielsen stresses how Rockefeller's
decisions produced "unintended" public consequences for the entire society.[34] Capitalism, a socialist might say, constitutes a power structure insofar as the holders of property rights systematically act in ways that advance their interests while adversely affecting the interests of workers
and other non–property-owning classes. This second criticism of the
power inherent in capitalist property relations goes much deeper than
Tawney's. The power of a capitalist such as Rockefeller is not located in
his ability to control and manipulate his workers or government officials,
but his ability to act on his interests in a way that, whether intended or
unintended, has far-reaching effects throughout the economy that work
to the disadvantage of the working class. And because the capitalist's
power runs so much deeper, controlling it requires much more radical action. Insofar as the capitalist's "power over" others consists in his power
to consciously *control* his workers, legislation that protects workers can
check the power of control. But if the power of capitalism resides in the
tremendous effect of owners' decisions on the entire economy, only the
elimination of the capitalist system will free the workers by eliminating
this power over them.

The reader may have noticed that not only do the liberal defense of private property and the socialist criticism clash on the nature of power, they
also deeply disagree on how markets are to be understood. To the classical liberal, markets are realms of freedom and mutual benefit; to the socialist they are arenas of intense competition and conflict. Socialists, for

instance, almost always see profits as deriving from exploitation of the workers: that the capitalist gains means that others lose. And that is why socialists insist that the capitalist system must rest on power, since it takes from some to give to others. In contrast, defenders of liberal capitalism insist that profits are the result of mutually beneficial activity. Because both owners and workers gain from their market relations, there is no need to assume that the entire edifice rests on power rather than free choice.[35]

5.4 Freedom, Power, and the Law

Negative Liberty and the Law: A Basic View

Recall from Section 5.3 that according to a typical classical liberal argument, if each was free to use her negative liberty in any way whatsoever, people would, as I put it, "bump" into each other in ways that would limit each other's freedom. In short, we would often use our freedom to construct obstacles that limit the freedom of others. To prevent us from limiting each other's freedom in this way, we require a system of laws that protect the freedom and property of each (see Section 8.2). Of course, in creating a system of laws, we construct a power over us: the government can control us by threatening us with coercion unless we obey. Thus, to check the power of other people, we create the power of government. But of course, government checks not only the liberty of others, it checks your and my liberty too.

Because government uses its power to construct obstacles to our action, most classical liberals have held that each law, at least insofar as it threatens us with coercion (see Section 4.1)—that is, punishment—is itself a limitation of our liberty. Thus, we accept some coercion by the state, and the limits on liberty it implies, in order to protect ourselves against the coercion of private individuals.[36] Law is thus two-edged: it protects us from coercion by coercion, it protects our liberty by taking some of it away. Law provides *security* for most of our freedom by limiting some of it. People wish their freedom to be secure from attack; to provide that security we institute a power that can block those who would limit our liberty. But the pluralism of classical liberals (Section 3.2) inclines them to insist that although security is a good, it is not the same good as freedom. And as the pluralist tells us is usually the case, to gain the good of security we must give up some of another good—in this case, some of our freedom.[37]

Freedom, Law, and Morality: Kant's Liberal Rationalist View

Immanuel Kant (1724–1804) agreed that rational, moral people would abandon the "wild, lawless" freedom of the state of nature—in which one person can use her freedom to harm others—and agree to live under laws of justice (Section 8.2). Kant, though, refused to see this as involving any loss of freedom, however:

> Any opposition that counters the hindrance of an effect promotes that effect and is consistent with it. Now, everything that is unjust is a hindrance to freedom according to universal laws. Coercion, however, is a hindrance or opposition to freedom. Consequently, if a certain use of freedom is itself a hindrance to freedom according to universal laws (that is, it is unjust), then the use of coercion to counteract it, inasmuch as it is the prevention of a hindrance to freedom, is consistent with freedom according to universal laws; in other words, this use of coercion is just.[38]

Kant's argument seems to be that

(1) If a person employs his freedom in a way that coerces others
(2) And which cannot be justified by universal laws of justice, then
(3) That person's use of his freedom is itself unjust.
(4) The prevention of such a hindrance to freedom is consistent with freedom according to rules of justice, that is, just freedom.
(5) Therefore, acts upholding universal justice are not opposed to (just) freedom.

Although law does indeed restrict "wild" freedom, it is essential for "just" freedom. Thus, argues Kant, when we enter society we give up our wild lawless freedom and accept a rational freedom, under the rules of just laws. Note the rationalist claim (Sections 3.2, 4.3): true freedom must conform to the dictates of reason, which tells us to live according to just laws that protect the freedom of everyone. Properly understood, there is no conflict between law, freedom, and reason.

Freedom as Antipower

Alf's *exercise* of power over Betty inherently limits her freedom. But what of Alf's mere *possession* of power over her? A person can *possess* power without actually using it; to have power is to have the ability to control or affect others, but not everyone who has an ability actually uses that ability. I have the ability to count to 1,000, but have never done so; someone who has thousands of loyal followers may have great power, since *should* she tell her followers to do something, they would. But she may not tell them—that is, she may not exercise that power.

According to most liberal advocates of negative liberty, a person is free if she is not being interfered with by others. Consequently, that others *possess* great power does not in itself limit your freedom. Recently, Philip Pettit has criticized this understanding of freedom. As Pettit sees it, Betty is not free if, although as a matter of fact she is left alone, at any moment Alf could constrain her choices if he wished to. Perhaps she merely is lucky that so far Alf has not noticed her; or perhaps she ingratiates herself with Alf to protect herself from his power. But none of this, says Pettit, makes her free, for she lives under the constant possibility that Alf may decide to limit her liberty. Thus, for Pettit, "the employer who can fire his employees as whim inclines him" possesses power that limits the liberty of his employees, even if he should never choose to use that power.[39]

Pettit argues for an alternative view: freedom as "antipower." If Alf has power over Betty in one way, but she had power over Alf in another, their mutual power might nullify the power of either to interfere. Each can resist the power of the other; each then is truly free, for not only is each not interfered with, but both are secure from having power exercised over them by the other. Unlike classical liberals, Pettit does not believe that the law takes away some of our freedom to better protect other parts; rather, like Kant, Pettit insists that the rule of law in no way detracts from our freedom because it provides citizens with antipower. The law, says Pettit, neutralizes the power possessed by some citizens that, if left unchecked, would limit the freedom of their fellows. Specifically, Pettit argues that the law promotes antipower in three ways:

(1) The criminal law deters individuals with power from interfering with others.
(2) The law regulates the way in which the powerful may employ their resources. Thus, for example, regulation of economic decisions by corporations protects the liberty of employees and shareholders.
(3) Government provision of transportation, education, and other opportunities empowers ordinary citizens, making them less vulnerable to the more powerful members of society.

Pettit insists that his view is distinct from liberal, socialist, and conservative conceptions of freedom. According to this "republican" theory of government, nonarbitrary legislation does not limit the freedom of citizens.[40] Because being subject to *arbitrary* interference is the mark of an unfree life, systems of nonarbitrary law making—systems based on widespread participation by citizens in the creation of general laws that apply to all—do not constitute limits on freedom. Thus, in the republican tradition, freedom is closely bound with popular participation in legislation and the prevention of the arbitrary use of power. In this respect, the republican tradition embraces Kant's rationalism: arbitrary interference is hostile to freedom because it is not based on rules of justice and reason. This idea was central to the French political philosopher Jean-Jacques Rousseau. Rousseau, like Kant and the republican tradition, emphasizes the difference between being subject to the will of specific people and being subject to impersonal laws. His great work, *The Social Contract*, stresses the way in which a system of law secures each citizen against personal dependence on the wills of others. The theme of personal dependence runs very deep in Rousseau's writings. The crucial sort of unfreedom for Rousseau is when you are forced to obey the will of another individual: when another has control over you. For Rousseau, and the republican and to some extent the socialist traditions, such personal dependency is avoided by making each person subject only to the laws he had a part in making. This, says Rousseau, is the only sort of freedom that can be had by humans-in-society (as opposed the wild and lawless freedom of people in a "state of nature")—freedom under the rule of law. Without the rule of general laws, there would only be personal dependency and so slavery (see Section 10.4).

The General Will: Law and Positive Freedom

Perhaps the most radical proposal for reconciling law and freedom has been proposed by those upholding the ideal of the "general will." Although Rousseau is the most important theorist of the general will, the idea was most completely developed by later political philosophers such as Bernard Bosanquet. Abstracting from the specifics of their particular treatments, the basic argument can be broken into four claims:

(1) *Self-imposed restraints do not limit freedom.* According to Bosanquet and others, restraints that you impose on yourself do not limit your freedom. This idea of freedom is a version of freedom as autonomy (Section 4.2). A person is free when she can do what she really wants to do: if she imposes a restraint on herself—if she decides that she does not want to do something—the restraint does not interfere with her freedom. Self-imposed restraints, then, are not a limitation of one's autonomy, as one desires to act on them. So those who really will a law, who wish to have the law, do not have their freedom limited by it: they remain free. In a democracy, Rousseau believed, all citizens deliberate and vote on the laws, and the laws apply to all. In a democracy, then, laws seem to be a form of self-imposed restraints.

(2) *The minority are free if they too can somehow "will" the law.* The problem is the dissenting minority, that is, those who vote against the law. On the face of it, the law seems to genuinely restrict their freedom, since it is not a self-imposed restraint: they voted against it. And if so, it would

seem that the law limits their autonomy. But if there was some way in which the minority could embrace the majority's verdict as their own—if they could come to will the result—then they too would be free.

(3) *Laws that express the general will are willed by everyone.* The minority could will the laws (that they voted against) if the laws were really in the interests of all citizens. That is, we might distinguish two types of law: (a) Some laws favor the majority at the expense of the minority, and so could never be embraced by the minority. (b) Other laws, however, apply to all citizens equally and serve the common interests of all citizens. Even if the minority voted against such laws, as members of the community desiring the common good they actually do will the laws insofar as they promote the general good. Recall again T. H. Green's distinction between a person's "real" and "actual" will (Section 4.2); a person's real will consists of the things he really cares about—his long-term aims, interests, and goals—whereas a person's "actual" will is distorted by impulses and errors. Now, to the extent that the minority will the common good, if the law promotes the common good, then that is what the minority really will, even if they do not know it.

(4) *Since the minority will the laws, they are free even when they are forced to obey them.* If being free is to do what you really want to do, and if the minority really want to act on the general will, then the minority act freely when they act on the general will. True, they voted against the law because they believed that the law did not express the general will; but if the majority are correct that the law articulates the general will, the minority should accept the majority's judgment.

> When a law is proposed in the people's assembly, what is asked of them is not precisely whether they approve of the proposition or reject it, but whether it is in conformity to the general will which is theirs; each by giving his vote gives his opinion on this question, and the counting of votes yields a declaration of the general will. When, therefore, the opinion contrary to mine prevails, this proves only that I have made a mistake, and what I believed to be the general will was not so. If my particular opinion had prevailed against the general will, I should have done something other than what I had willed, and then I should not have been free.[41]

Once the general will has been revealed by the majority, those who continue to oppose it are captives of their particular wills. Recall here Green's analysis of freedom: those who act on their "actual will" rather than their "real will" are unfree. Rousseau agrees. According to Rousseau, compelling someone to submit to the general will "means nothing other than that he shall be forced to be free; for this is the necessary condition which . . . secures him against all personal dependence."[42]

Bosanquet apparently approves of "Rousseau's observation (*Social Contract*, Book IV, chap. ii, n.) that the convicts in the galleys at Genoa had 'liberty' stamped on their chains. The fetters of the bad self are the symbol of freedom."[43] Again, we confront Berlin's worry about positive liberty: forcing a person to act on his "real will" can itself be a way of making him free.

The doctrine of the general will reconciles law and positive freedom by presupposing a collectivist theory of society (Section 3.4). Rousseau himself explicitly embraces such a conception. In *The Social Contract*, he insists that society is more than an "aggregation"—it is an "association" with a real unity and shares a genuine "common good."[44] If individuals are members of an association in which the good of each is bound to the common good, and in which each thus wills the common good as a crucial constituent of her own good, it is possible to claim that each really wills the general will, and so is autonomous when acting on it. Hence Rousseau's insistence that a society is a "people" rather than a collection of individuals. For if all we have is a collection of individuals, it seems dubious indeed that all share a general will, and are free when they follow it.

Conservatism and Legal Liberties

In concluding our analysis of liberty and the law, we should note a more modest proposal, characteristic of much conservative thought. As I stressed in Section 3.2, conservative antirationalism leads to valuing traditions, as embodying the accumulated practical knowledge of a political culture. Rather than seeking to develop an abstract theory of freedom— as do liberals and socialists—conservatives are wont to stress that our understanding of what liberties are fundamental to political life is determined by our political traditions. In his *Reflections on the Revolution in France*, Burke criticized the liberal doctrine of universal natural rights to liberty. Instead, Burke argued that the liberties of the English were an "inheritance derived to us from our forefathers, and to be transmitted to our posterity—as an estate specially belonging to the people of this kingdom, without any reference whatever to any other more general or prior right."[45] Moreover, Burke, drawing on a typical conservative theory of human nature, stressed the dangers of human passions for political society (Section 3.3). Burke maintained,

> Society requires not only that the passions of individuals should be subjected, but that even in the mass and body, as well as in the individuals, the inclinations of men should frequently be thwarted, their will controlled, and their passions brought into subjection. This can only be done by a *power out*

of themselves, and not, in the exercise of its function, subject to that will and to those passions which it is its office to bridle and subdue. In this sense the restraints on men, as well as their liberties, are to be reckoned among their rights. But as the liberties and the restrictions vary with times and circumstances and admit to infinite modifications, they cannot be settled upon any abstract rule; and nothing is so foolish as to discuss them upon that principle.[46]

Thus, for Burke, the law—"a power out of themselves"—is needed to identify specific liberties of, and put restrictions on, too-passionate people. No general law or principle can be laid out in advance, specifying precisely what these will be; they are an inheritance of a people's political and legal traditions.

Burke's account is resolutely antirationalist, in many ways far more so than even Berlin's defense of negative liberty (Section 4.3). No philosophical theory of liberty in general is sound. Specific liberties, such as freedom of the press and freedom of association are the outcomes of a complex legal tradition; what liberties are important, and what such liberties imply, is not a matter for a philosophical theory of liberty, but a historical and legal study of a complex political community. For Burke and conservatives who follow him, although there are no "human rights" or "rights of man," there are rights more precious and important: "the rights of Englishmen . . . as a patrimony derived from their forefathers."[47] Indeed, the conservative is sure to criticize the liberal endorsement of freedom in general as destructive of social traditions, and ultimately to freedom itself. Although some freedoms are central to our traditions, others are not; and liberalism's constant attack on limits to freedom—its "liberationist" proposals—destroys social customs and paves the way for authoritarian leaders.

> Where the liberal sees a probable increase in freedom and creativeness the result of these liberations, the conservative is more likely to see, or at least fear, insecurity and alienation.
>
> The chief accusation made against liberalism by conservatives is . . . that liberalism is a kind of Judas goat for totalitarianism. By its incessant liberationist work on the traditional authorities and roles in society, liberalism, it is argued, weakens the social structure, encourages the multiplication of "mass-types" of human beings and thus beckons in its way to waiting totalitarian masters. "By destroying the social habits of the people," wrote Elliot, "by dissolving their natural collective consciousness into individual constituents. . . . Liberalism can prepare the way for that which is its own negation."[48]

It is interesting to observe here the reply of liberal theorists. "Liberty," says Hayek, "is one. Liberties appear only when liberty is lacking; they are special privileges and exemptions that groups and individuals may acquire while the rest are more or less unfree."[49]

Conservatism displays a cleavage about the relative importance of economic freedoms. Burke himself harshly criticized the French revolutionaries for praising moneymaking—success in the marketplace—rather than landed property. Landed property, as he saw it, represented society's traditions, whereas the marketplace undermined them. John Gray, a contemporary conservative, continues this tradition; he has been increasingly critical of "market capitalism" and the way that it undermines cultural and natural values.[50] Although these latter-day Burkeans are not opponents of private property and the market, they stress the way that it can undermine traditional institutions, and so are willing to limit economic liberties to protect cultural traditions. In contrast, what are sometimes called "new right" conservatives—most notably, Margaret Thatcher, the former prime minister of the United Kingdom—put great stress on the importance of economic liberty, as necessary to promote the traditional virtues of self-reliance, prudence, hard work, and care for one's family (see Section 9.3). This difference, then, stems from competing interpretations of the relation of economic liberty to traditional liberties and values—does it undermine them, protect them, or form a part of them?

5.5 Summary

This chapter considered the relation of freedom to power. I began in Section 5.1 by examining a conception of positive liberty that identifies freedom with the power to act on one's desires. Manifestly, this view of freedom greatly expands the task of a "freedom-valuing state": to protect and promote the freedom of citizens requires supplying them with the resources necessary to achieve their aims. Section 5.2 examined in more detail the notion of power and its relation to freedom; we distinguished "power over" and "power to." Whereas power to can be seen as enhancing freedom, it seems that one person's power over another inherently limits the freedom of the person over whom he exercises that power. Like freedom, power, especially "power over," is a contested concept; we examined the debate between a liberal-individualist analysis emphasizing control and a socialist conception stressing systematic adverse effects on the interests of some while benefiting others. The debate between liberals and socialists carried over into Section 5.3, which examined differing views of the relation of property and freedom. Drawing together liberal analyses of power and freedom, we saw how liberals argue that property is necessary to protect freedom while insisting it does not necessarily involve power over others, whereas socialists insist that it inherently involves liberty-limiting power. In Section 5.4, the relation of liberty and law was examined. Starting with the basic classical liberal claim that all law, qua coercive restraint, limits liberty, we went on to examine several proposals that seek to show how, properly understood, general justified legal restraints do not limit civil freedom. Finally, we briefly examined Burke's conservative, antirationalist view, which abjures a general analysis of freedom, locating the important liberties of a people in their historical-legal tradition.

Notes

1. T. H. Green, "On the Different Senses of 'Freedom' As Applied to the Will and the Moral Progress of Man," in Paul Harris and John Morrow, eds., *Green's Lectures on the Principles of Political Obligation* (Cambridge: Cambridge University Press, 1986), p. 235.

2. R. H. Tawney, *Equality* (New York: Harcourt, Brace, 1931), p. 221.

3. John Rawls, *A Theory of Justice* (Cambridge, MA: Harvard University Press, 1971), p. 204.

4. See, for example, Kai Nielsen, *Equality and Liberty: A Defense of Radical Egalitarianism* (Totowa, NJ: Rowman and Allanheld, 1985), p. 84.

5. Richard Norman, *Free and Equal: A Philosophical Examination of Political Values* (Oxford: Oxford University Press, 1987), p. 44.

6. F. A. Hayek, *The Constitution of Liberty* (London: Routledge, 1960), pp. 17–18.

7. See Steven Lukes, *Power: A Radical View* (London: Macmillan, 1974).

8. Thomas Hobbes, *Leviathan*, Michael Oakeshott, ed., (Oxford: Blackwell, 1948), p. 56 (Book 1, chap. 10).

9. See S. I. Benn, "Power," in Paul Edwards, ed., *The Encyclopedia of Philosophy* (New York: Macmillan and the Free Press, 1965).

10. See here Felix Oppenheim, *Dimensions of Freedom* (New York: St. Martin's, Press, 1961).

11. Ibid., pp. 82–83.

12. Bertrand Russell, *Power* (London: Unwin Books, 1960), p. 25.

13. See Christian Bay, *The Structure of Freedom* (New York: Atheneum, 1965), p. 257; William E. Connolly, *The Terms of Political Discourse*, 2nd ed. (Princeton: Princeton University Press, 1983), chap. 3.

14. Lukes, *Power: A Radical View*, p. 34.

15. Connolly, *The Terms of Political Discourse*, p. 106.

16. See Kristján Kristjánsson, *Social Freedom: The Responsibility View* (Cambridge: Cambridge University Press, 1996), pp. 150ff.

17. Connolly, *The Terms of Political Discourse*, p. 106.

18. Harold J. Laski, *The Rise of European Liberalism* (London: George Allen and Unwin, 1936), p. 239.

19. Again, we need to stress that political theories are complex, and can exemplify different sorts of connections. See Kristjánsson, *Social Freedom*, chap. 6.

20. See ibid.

21. See Bernard Bosanquet, *The Philosophical Theory of the State*, in Gerald F. Gaus and William Sweet, eds., *The Philosophical Theory of the State and Related Essays* (Indianapolis, IN: St. Augustine Press, 2000), p. 46.

22. This claim is disputed by C. B. Macpherson, *Democratic Theory: Essays in Retrieval* (Oxford: Clarendon Press, 1973), pp. 40ff.

23. F. A. Hayek, "Liberalism," in his *New Studies in Philosophy, Politics, Economics and the History of Ideas* (London: Routledge and Kegan Paul, 1978), p. 149.

24. See Alan Ryan, *Property* (Milton Keynes, UK: Open University Press, 1987).

25. I am following here Frank Snare, "The Concept of Property," *American Philosophical Quarterly*, vol. 9 (April 1972), pp. 200–206. I have significantly altered some of these conditions. See also Lawrence C. Becker, *Property Rights* (London: Routledge and Kegan Paul, 1977), pp. 18–19.

26. This claim is argued for in Gerald F. Gaus and Loren E. Lomasky, "Are Property Rights Problematic?" *The Monist*, vol. 73 (October, 1990), pp. 483–503.

27. Adam Smith, *An Inquiry into the Nature and Causes of the Wealth of Nations*, R. H. Campbell and A. S. Skinner, eds. (Indianapolis, IN: Liberty Fund, 1981), p. 456.

28. Jan Narveson, *The Libertarian Idea* (Philadelphia: Temple University Press, 1988), p. 66.

29. I have considered these in detail in "Property, Rights and Freedom," *Social Philosophy & Policy*, vol. 11 (Summer 1994), pp. 209–240.

30. Narveson, *The Libertarian Idea*, p. 66.

31. Macpherson, *Democratic Theory*, pp. 64–65. For Marx's views on the sale of labor power, see *Capital*, in Robert C. Tucker, ed., *The Marx-Engels Reader*, 2nd ed. (New York: W. W. Norton, 1978), pp. 351ff. See Section 9.1 below.

32. Tawney, *Equality*, p. 214.

33. L. T. Hobhouse, *Liberalism* (New York: Oxford University Press, 1964 [1911]), p. 78.

34. Nielsen, *Equality and Liberty*, pp. 234–235.

35. For an examination of profit as an essentially contested concept, see James W. Child, "Profit: The Concept and Its Moral Features," *Social Philosophy & Policy*, vol. 15 (Summer 1998), pp. 243–282.

36. See Hayek, *The Constitution of Liberty*, p. 21.

37. See Bertrand de Jouvenel, *On Power* (Boston: Beacon Press, 1962), chap.17.

38. Immanuel Kant, *The Metaphysical Elements of Justice*, John Ladd, trans. (Indianapolis, IN: Bobbs-Merrill, 1965), p. 36.

39. Philip Pettit, "Freedom As Antipower," *Ethics*, vol. 106 (April 1996), p. 581.

40. See Pettit's *Republicanism: A Theory of Freedom and Government* (Oxford: Clarendon Press, 1997).

41. Jean-Jacques Rousseau, *The Social Contract*, Maurice Cranston, trans. (London: Penguin Books, 1968 [1762]), Book 4, chap. 2.

42. Ibid., Book 1, chap. 7.

43. Bosanquet, *The Philosophical Theory of the State*, p. 150.

44. Rousseau, *The Social Contract*, Book 1, chap. 5.

45. Edmund Burke, *Reflections on the Revolution in France* (Harmondsworth, UK: Penguin, 1968), p. 119.

46. Ibid., p. 151.

47. Ibid., p. 118.

48. Robert Nisbet, *Conservatism* (Milton Keynes, UK: Open University Press, 1986), p. 50.

49. Hayek, *The Constitution of Liberty,* p. 19.

50. See, for example, John Gray, *Beyond the New Right: Markets, Government and Common Environment* (London: Routledge, 1993).

6

EQUALITY

6.1 Equality and the Grounds for Equal Treatment

In contrast to liberty, equality seems a simple idea. We all know, for example, what is meant by saying, "Alf and Betty are of equal height" or "Charlie's and Doris's weights are equal." In these contexts, there is a scale of measurement, and both people have the same score on the scale. Let us call this the *tied score conception of equality*. Things are equal when they are tied: they have the same score. Other standard uses of equality, however, are less precise. If I say, for example, that I like chocolate and coffee ice cream equally well, I am probably not saying anything so precise as "on my scoring system for ice cream, chocolate and coffee flavors have the same score." To be sure, if one did have a scoring system for ice cream, then indeed the tied score conception would be appropriate. We typically do not have scoring systems, yet we often employ the idea of equality. In the ice cream case, I am probably saying that I do not prefer chocolate to coffee and I do not prefer coffee to chocolate.[1] In this sense, "*A* and *B* are equal" means "neither is to be preferred to the other." Let us call this *the nonpreferential conception of equality*. This is a broader conception than the tied score notion: one reason for not preferring *A* to *B* or *B* to *A* is that they have a tied score, but we might have less numerical reasons as well.

As a political ideal, equality has most often expressed something akin to the nonpreferential conception. Throughout the history of political thought, advocates of equality have been opponents of political and economic systems in which one person or group of people is given preference over others. Thus, as the English socialist R. H. Tawney observed, the egalitarian program of the eighteenth century opposed legal privileges that gave a select group of citizens legal rights withheld from others.[2] In legal matters, insisted these early egalitarians, one class of citizens (for example, aristocrats) is not to be preferred to another (for example, commoners). Later egalitarians extended their opposition to inequality, attacking the economic privileges that accompanied property ownership as well as the informal social privileges (for example, those stemming from having attended private schools, being a member of the "right" ethnic group, having a high-status occupation, and so on). As a political ideal, then, equality has usually implied a criticism of preferential treatment—of preferring one person or class to another. Of course, as we shall see, other understandings of equality, such as the tied score conception, have also been advanced; we would do well to begin, though, by focusing on the nonpreferential conception.

We can immediately appreciate the core problem of equality: equality does not always seem a good thing, and inequality is not always to be avoided. In many contexts, it is totally unobjectionable to prefer one person to another. Many people, for instance, believe that it is right and proper—indeed, demanded by justice—to give preference (in the distribution of money) to the hardworking over the lazy, (in the distribution of help) to our neighbors over distant strangers, (in the distribution of punishment) to the guilty over the innocent, (in the distribution of love) to our family over strangers, and (in the distribution of assistance) to the needy over the well-off (see Section 9.3). Aristotle famously observed that justice demands treating those who are equals in an equal way *and* treating those who are unequal—say in merit—in an unequal way.[3] As Aristotle noted, it "is the origin of quarrels and complaints—when either equals have and are awarded unequal shares, or unequals equal shares."[4] To be sure, some ultraradical egalitarians have wished to abolish all ways in which one person is to be preferred to another. According to the followers of the radical egalitarian François-Noël Babeuf (1760–1797), "any price" should be paid to achieve "true equality"; so deeply did Babeuf hate any privilege or preference between people that in the interests of maintaining equality, he was willing to restrain those who would work extra hard to prevent them from having a claim to additional rewards.[5] For Babeuf and his followers, equality was essentially *sameness:* the more we are alike, the more equal we are. Few, however, are willing to go so far down the egalitarian road. Devotion to the political ideal of equality is almost always an insistence that in *some* important ways people should be treated as equals—in some important matters one person should not be preferred to another although, of course, in other ways preference and distinction are entirely acceptable.

A case for equality, then, must (1) specify the ways in which people are to be treated equally, and (2) provide the grounds, or justifying reasons, for equal treatment in that way. In what ways should we be treated equally, and why should we be treated equally? Why is it so important to treat people equally—that is, not to prefer some to others? The main task of this chapter is to get clearer about the grounds for equality and the types of equal treatment that political theorists have thought important.

In Sections 6.2 and 6.3, I consider different grounds for equal treatment; in Section 6.4, I examine proposals about the ways in which it is important not to treat some people better than others.

6.2 Why Equality? External Arguments for the Importance of Equality

Utilitarian Egalitarianism

Our first concern is why many political theorists have insisted that people must be treated equally. What I shall call *external arguments for equality* maintain that equal treatment is desirable because it advances some other good thing or important goal. The best-known example of an external argument for equality is utilitarian. As we saw earlier (Section 1.4), the utilitarian tradition in social and political philosophy has insisted that the one, supreme, proper goal of political institutions is to promote the greatest happiness of the greatest number. According to Jeremy Bentham, the "father" of modern utilitarianism, an action is "conformable to the principle of utility, or for shortness' sake, to utility (meaning with respect to the community at large) when the tendency it has to augment the happiness of the community is greater than it has to diminish it."[6] The utilitarian seeks to maximize the overall *net happiness* for society as a whole. Suppose that one is a Benthamite utilitarian, seeking to maximize pleasure and minimize pain. To do this, one must be able to compare the pleasures and pains of different people. That is, suppose that the Benthamite utilitarian is trying to decide whether policy X or Y is required by morality in a three-person society composed of Alf, Betty, and Charlie; his question is, roughly, whether X or Y will lead to the greater surplus of pleasure over pain. So for each policy, he needs to calculate the following: (Alf's pleasure) + (Betty's pleasure) + (Charlie's pleasure) − (Alf's pain) − (Betty's pain) − (Charlie's pain) = overall net pleasure or happiness. The Benthamite's aim is to maximize net pleasure or happiness.

Now, many utilitarians have argued that if a society is distributing a good such as money, food, or housing it will usually maximize net happiness to distribute the good *equally*. This argument rests on the assumption of *marginal decreasing utility* of these goods, an example of which is illustrated in Figure 6.1. In this case, Betty presently has $100 and Alf presently has $600. One hundred additional dollars are to be distributed. If our only goal is to generate the most possible "utility" (or happiness), how should we divide up the money? As Figure 6.1 shows, if we give the additional $100 to Alf, it will move his overall utility level from Alf_1 to Alf_2; if we give it to Betty it will move her utility from $Betty_1$ to $Betty_2$. We can see that giving Betty the $100 yields a much greater gain in utility

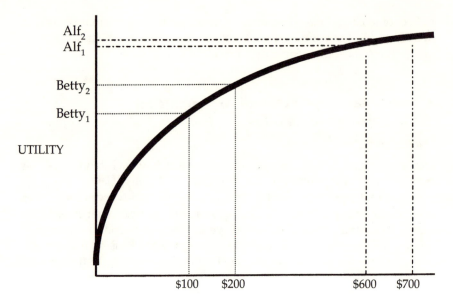

FIGURE 6.1   Decreasing Marginal Utility

than giving it to Alf. This is because of the slope of the *utility function:* the more one already has, the less extra happiness an additional unit of the good gives you. More formally, we can say that the $n+1$ unit of any good always yields less utility than did the nth unit. It is important to stress that more of the good always yields some additional utility: in Figure 6.1 Alf does gain some utility by moving from Alf_1 to Alf_2, but, on this as- sumption, *utility increases at a diminishing rate.*

Now, argues the egalitarian utilitarian, given the decreasing marginal utility of goods such as money, because it always yields more utility to distribute a good to those lower on the utility function than to those fur- ther up on it (in our case, to Betty rather than Alf), the distributions of goods that will maximize utility will always be that which promotes equality: we should keep on giving to those who have less (since, as it were, they get more utility per dollar than do those who are richer), until everyone is at exactly the same point on the utility function. Once every- one is at the same point, we will distribute money equally, because, once again, that would maximize overall utility. Note that this argument does not depend on the intrinsic desirability of the value of equality. The value being promoted is not itself egalitarian: it is the moral collectivist aim of maximization of utility in society (see Section 3.4). It just so happens that given the assumption of decreasing marginal utility, the best way to pro- mote utility is to promote equality.

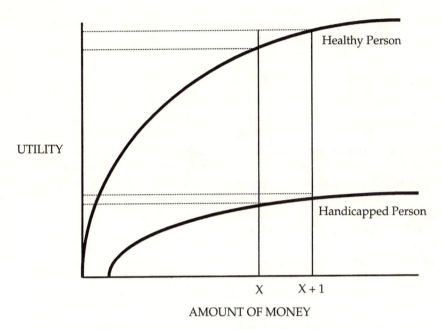

FIGURE 6.2   Different Utility Functions: Healthy and Handicapped

Just because the utilitarian case for equality does not depend on the intrinsic desirability of equality, if we vary the assumptions a bit, or add additional considerations, the utilitarian can become a strong defender of
*in*equality. Crucial to the utilitarian egalitarian argument is that everyone's utility function—the rate at which they get utility from a good—is
the same. But consider Figure 6.2, which depicts the utility functions of a
healthy and a handicapped person.[7] Notice that at any level of income,
the handicapped person receives less utility than does the healthy person.
Given her handicap, it takes much more money to raise her to the same
level of utility; in fact, it is often impossible for her to reach the same level
of utility as the healthy person. Add to this that it often takes a lot of
money to raise the handicapped person's utility even a little bit: she
needs expensive help to even get small increases of utility. This is depicted by the flatness of the handicapped person's utility function. Even
at the move from amount $X to $X+1, the healthy person gets more marginal utility than does the handicapped person. Thus, if Figure 6.2 accurately describes the utility (happiness and so on) that different people receive from different amounts of money, the utilitarian will advocate an
unequal distribution, *giving money to the healthy person rather than the handicapped person.* The utilitarian case for equality is thus highly sensitive to

the assumptions made about the rate at which people turn money and goods into happiness (or utility).

Impartiality and Formal Equality

Some political theorists have held that we should endorse equality because it expresses a truly impartial or objective view of our relations with others. Each of us is tempted to think that his or her own life is special. After all, your life is special *to you:* you directly experience your own life, and the trials and triumphs of your own life are, to you, of immense importance. But, argues the "impartialist egalitarian," that your own life is in some way more important to you does not show that it is, or should be, especially important to others. More than that, from the "objective point of view" we can see that each person's life is, in itself, no more or less important than anyone else's. From the objective point of view, Alf's life is no more important than Betty's, and Betty's is no more important than Alf's. As was proclaimed in the famous debate at Putney in 1647–1649, "The poorest he that is in England has a life to live as the greatest."[8]

From the impartial viewpoint, the life of neither the poorest nor the greatest is to be preferred. But, argues Thomas Nagel,

> if everyone matters just as much as everyone else, it is appalling that the most effective social systems we have been able to devise permit so many people to be born into conditions of harsh deprivation which crush their prospects for leading a decent life, while many others are well provided for from birth, come to control substantial resources, and are free to enjoy advantages vastly beyond the conditions of mere decency.[9]

As Nagel sees it, if we take an impartial perspective and so come to value equality, we cannot condone the vastly unequal distribution of goods and life chances that results from our economic institutions. Thus, continues Nagel, "impartiality generates a greater interest in benefiting the worse off than in benefiting the better off—a kind of priority to the former over the latter."[10] For Nagel, then, a commitment to impartiality and equality leads us to favor those with less over those with more.

On reflection, it is doubtful that a commitment to the abstract ideal of impartiality so quickly leads to social policies that favor less well off over better-off citizens. For although an objective attitude may well indicate that governments should not be partial toward some citizens or classes (for example, government policies should not favor the rich just because they are rich), it is manifest that governments *should* be partial in some ways: in many contexts they should favor the innocent over the guilty and perhaps the hardworking over the lazy. To be *objectionably partial*—

partial in a way that manifests a lack of objectivity—is to favor some over others without good reasons. It appears that rather than leading directly to egalitarian social policies, a devotion to impartiality justifies a principle of "formal equality," which asserts "the presumption in favor of equality."

> *Formal Equality:* Any discriminatory act—any action that provides differential advantages or burdens—stands in need of justification; any unjustified discriminatory act is wrong.

Formal equality asserts a blanket moral presumption in favor of equality. If, say, someone wishes to be partial to Alf over Charlie, she must show that she has good reasons for this partiality. If she has good reasons, then she is still acting from the objective point of view. She is not favoring Alf just because he is Alf (that would be objectionably partial), but for good reasons. Formal equality "requires that if two people are being treated, or are treated, differently, there should be some relevant difference between them."[11] As Stanley Benn and R. S. Peters put it, "None shall be held to have a claim to better treatment than another, in advance of good grounds being produced."[12] They continue,

> Understood in this way, the principle of equality does not prescribe positively that all humans be treated alike; it is a presumption against treating them differently, in any respect, until grounds for distinction have been shewn [sic]. It does not assume, therefore, a quality which all men have to the same degree, which is the ground of the presumption, for to say that there is a presumption means that no grounds need be shewn. The onus of justification rests on whoever would make distinctions.
> ... Presume equality until there is a reason to presume otherwise.[13]

As Benn claimed in a later essay, "Discrimination in treatment between persons requires moral justification: it is not enough simply to prefer one to another since that involves regarding another person from the point of view of one's own satisfaction; respect for a person involves a right to be considered from his own standpoint."[14]

In itself, formal equality does not justify egalitarian social policies of the sort Nagel has in mind (that favor the poor over the better off in the distribution of resources, advantages, and opportunities). Formal equality simply requires that any differential treatment be justified. But it takes on a much more strongly egalitarian character when it is combined with a second principle, asserting the moral arbitrariness of natural endowments, such as a person's innate skills and abilities. It has been argued—by revisionist liberals and socialists—that inequalities that stem from the "natural lottery" of birth, in which people get natural and social advantages that they do not deserve, are unjust: "All inequalities of birth constitute undeserved discriminations." [15] Because these inequalities cannot be justified, argue some egalitarians, an impartial government must "redress" them by giving additional resources to those who have lost out in the lottery of birth: "Without such special justification all persons, whether equal or unequal, ought to have equal shares."[16] The crucial claim here is that these advantages are undeserved, and so unjustified. Taken together, then, (1) the principle of formal equality and (2) the claim that advantages and liabilities based on natural gifts and social advantages cannot be justified lead to (3) the sort of egalitarian-redistributionist policies that Nagel advocates.

Whether this argument is persuasive largely turns on whether we believe that advantages flowing from one's natural gifts and social position are morally arbitrary and so cannot be justified. Some, such as the leading revisionist liberal, John Rawls, are adamant that one does not deserve one's talents—they are the result of a natural lottery, in which some people are winners (they have extensive talents that are in demand) and others lose (they have few special talents, or few talents in high demand). Thus, from Rawls's perspective, whether one is talented or not is irrelevant to an impartial evaluation of principles of justice. According to Rawls, the best principles of justice would represent "an agreement to regard the distribution of natural talents as a common asset and to share in the benefits of this distribution whatever it turns out to be. Those who have been favored by nature, whoever they are, may gain from their good fortune only on terms that improve the situation of those who have lost out."[17] Indeed, it would seem that for Rawls even the extent to which one makes an effort and tries to succeed is largely a matter of luck, being dependent on one's being born into a "happy family and social circumstances."[18] This is a matter of deep dispute. Although, to be sure, one does not deserve one's talents, it does not follow that one does not deserve the fruits of those talents. Indeed, a widely shared belief about distributive justice is that a producer of a good has a special claim over what she has produced—the fruits of her labor. And it is widely believed that those who work hard deserve greater rewards than those who do not. We shall return to this dispute about justice and desert in Sections 8.2 and 8.3.

Incommensurability and Equality

We have thus far considered two types of arguments supporting the importance of equality, and in particular equal distributions of the good things in life: the utilitarian argument that such distributions maximize overall happiness, and the argument from impartiality. Many have been persuaded by a different case for equality, which maintains that people should be treated equally just because each person is a unique individual and cannot be compared to, or ranked above or below, others.

If I *can* say whether *A* is better than *B* or vice versa, then they *are* commensurable: I can compare and rank them. And in most cases we can, at least roughly, make such comparisons. When I go to the malt shop, I rank a chocolate malt above a strawberry malt and so I choose the chocolate over the strawberry. Indeed, whenever one makes a reasoned choice—for example, every time you buy something at the store, or decide to turn down one date and accept another—you are making an implicit ranking, and so are comparing two different options or valuable things. We make such comparisons with more or less effort, but we make them constantly. Sometimes, though, we cannot compare two things. To say that two things, *A* and *B*, are *incommensurable* is to say that they cannot be ranked in terms of "better than" and "worse than." In the novel *Sophie's Choice*, the Nazis offer a Polish mother a choice: she can choose which of her children will live and which will die.[19] Sophie is unable to make the choice; she cannot compare the importance of the lives of her children—they are literally incommensurable.

Some think that all individuals are incommensurable: each individual is unique and cannot be ranked as, overall, above or below others. Of course, proponents of the view readily admit, we can rank people for specific purposes: teachers rank students in terms of academic merit, students rank teachers in terms of their teaching performance or popularity, Olympic officials rank athletes according to their performances, and so on. But although "it is of the essence of merit . . . to be a grading concept . . . there is no way of grading individuals as such. We can grade them with respect to their qualities, hence only by abstracting from their individuality."[20] We can rank people in terms of their possession of certain features (for example, academic talents, teaching ability, popularity, speed), but any such ranking abstracts from their full individuality and uniqueness, focusing on some specific attributes. What we cannot do, on this view, is rank *individuals as such*, for each individual is a unique combination of traits, abilities, and so on. This is often what is meant by the claim that each individual is of "infinite" worth: we cannot rank individuals on some overall scale, because each individual is unique. And as we saw in Section 6.1, according to the nonpreferential conception of equality this is precisely what is meant by equality: *A* is not preferred to *B*, and *B* is not preferred to *A*.

Although the argument from incommensurability shows why claims to rank individuals can be rejected, it is not entirely clear how it shows that people should be treated equally. After all, if *A* and *B* cannot be compared, then we cannot say that they are equal. The claim to equality is itself a comparison. In mathematics, if *A* is not greater than *B*, and if *B* is not greater than *A*, it follows that *A* and *B* are equal. But according to the incommensurability argument, we cannot say "*A* is not greater than *B*" or "*B* is not greater than *A*," because we cannot make any sensible comparison of *A* and *B*. If so, then we also cannot say that *A* and *B* are equal. If the value of Sophie's children was incommensurable, her problem was not that she valued them equally, but that she was totally unable to make any comparisons at all. She was unable to choose because there was no way to compare their value. This points to a basic worry about the very idea of nonpreferential conception of equality: to claim that neither person should be preferred to the other does not necessarily show that they are equals. It may show simply we are unable to make any comparisons at all.

The nonpreferential notion is only egalitarian on the supposition that if we are not to prefer one person to another, we should treat them equally: if $A \not> B$, and $B \not> A$, then $A = B$. It is here that an egalitarian may well resort to the presumption in favor of equality that we examined above. If a presumption in favor of treating people as equals is our "default" or "baseline" assumption, then if *A* is not better than *B*, and if *B* is not better than *A*, we will have a good reason to treat *A* and *B* equally. If, then, we accept the presumption in favor of equality, the argument from incommensurability does generate a case for treating people equally.

6.3 Why Equality? Arguments from Fundamental Human Equality

External Grounds Versus Arguments from Fundamental Human Equality

Thus far, we have been examining arguments that endorse equal treatment because such treatment is called for by some other value or consideration. Thus, for the utilitarian egalitarian, to maximize overall *utility* we ought to distribute goods equally; for the impartialist, to treat people impartially and objectively we must treat them equally. The proponent of incommensurability maintains that given our inability to compare the value of individuals, the rational thing to do is to prefer no one, and so treat people equally. "External" (or mixed) arguments for equality are thus of the form: *given value or principle X, where X is not itself about the importance of equality, we should treat people equally.*

Let us contrast such external cases for equal treatment to what I shall call arguments from *fundamental human equality*, which have the form: *people should be treated equally because they are in some important or funda-*

mental respect equal. Equals, Aristotle said, should be treated equally. If in some important respect people really are equal, then Aristotle's dictum indicates that we should treat them equally in some relevant way. A number of arguments in favor of equal treatment thus have been defenses of the ways in which humans are basically equal. Of course, to show that people should be treated equally, it is not enough to show that in *some* way we are equal: that almost everyone has an equal number of fingers does not help much in showing that everyone should be treated equally. An argument from fundamental human equality must establish three claims: (1) that in some respect, *R*, humans are equal: (2) that *R* is important; and (3) that *R* is relevant to the case for equal treatment.

Shared Human Nature: The Theological Foundations

Perhaps the most important egalitarian argument has called attention to our shared human nature, or our shared nature as human beings: all of us are humans, and equally so. As J. R. Lucas has pointed out, however, this seems to rely on fallacious reasoning.[21]

All humans are human;
∴ All humans are equally human;
∴ All humans are equal.

But, Lucas points out, this cannot be a valid argument; an argument of exactly the same form is

All numbers are numbers;
∴ All numbers are equally numbers;
∴ All numbers are equal.

Nevertheless, it seems wrong to simply dismiss arguments for equal treatment grounded on the idea that humans are basically equal. The American *Declaration of Independence* declares it to be self-evident that "all men are created equal." This famous claim from the *Declaration* points to an important tie between egalitarianism and Christian doctrine. If we are all God's children, and if he loves all his children equally, then we are equal in our most important trait—being loved by God. Any inequalities between people almost vanish when compared to this crucial equality of human beings. Since God loves the poorest as much as the richest of his children, the welfare of each is equally important; since the poor are in greater need, the Christian-egalitarian response is to devote special attention to their welfare and problems. In the words of the *Virginia Declaration of Rights,* it is "the mutual duty of all to practise [sic] Christian forbearance, love, and charity toward each other."[22] Egalitarian thought has been much more deeply influenced by Christian ideals than has thinking about liberty. This influence continues right up to the present day: the liberation theology of the Catholic Church and "social justice" movements in Protestant denominations place great stress on the "brotherhood" of all humans, and so their basic claim to be treated as equals. Indeed, the socialism of R. H. Tawney—who was a guiding intellectual force in the Labour Party of the United Kingdom—was premised on this Christian ideal of equality.[23]

Fundamental Equality and Ordinary Language

An argument from fundamental equality, then, maintains that because we really are equal, we should be treated as equals. As we have just seen, one way to defend fundamental human equality is to rely on theological claims about God's equal love for each of us; most egalitarians, though, insist on a purely secular defense of fundamental equality. The problem with such defenses, as Bernard Williams, a contemporary philosopher, has observed, is that "to say that all men are equal in all those characteristics in respect of which it makes sense to say that all men are equal or unequal, is a patent falsehood; and even if some more restricted selection is made of these characteristics, the statement does not look much better."[24] Confronted with the obvious ways in which we are unequal, many egalitarians resort to what might be called the weak argument for fundamental equality. "On this interpretation," says Williams, "we should not seek some special characteristics in respect of which all men are equal, but merely remind ourselves that we are all men."[25] Williams believes that this reminder is more powerful than one might think:

> That all men are human is, if a tautology, a useful one, serving as a reminder that those who belong anatomically to the species *homo sapiens* and can speak a language, use tools, live in societies, can interbreed despite racial differences, etc. are also alike in certain respects more likely to be forgotten. These respects are notably the capacity to feel pain, both from immediate physical causes and from various situations represented in perception and thought; and the capacity to feel affection for others.[26]

Is this acknowledgment of our similarity really important? Suppose some cruel dictator acknowledges this fact of human similarity, but insists that this tells her nothing about what she should *do*. How can a mere fact about the ways in which people are similar tell us how we ought to treat them? How can *facts* about human beings lead me to *value* equality? Williams, following Wittgenstein (Section 1.3), maintains that facts and values are not two distinct realms, but are intermixed in our language and the form of life in which our language is embodied. To be a speaker of a language is to be committed to certain forms of discourse; in particular, to use a language, Williams, believes, is to accept severe constraints on what can count as a reason for doing something. Consider, for example, someone who denies racial equality, insisting that black people's welfare simply does not matter.

> Few can be found who explain their practice [of discrimination] merely by saying "But they're black; and it is my principle to treat black men differently than others." If any reasons are given at all, they will be reasons that seek to conflate the fact of blackness with certain other characteristics which are at least candidates for relevance to the question of how a man should be treated: such as insensitivity, brute stupidity, ineducable irresponsibility, etc.[27]

Williams, of course, realizes that such charges are false rationalizations; his point is that a defender of unequal treatment sees the need to give some relevant reasons for discrimination, and our language does not allow the mere fact of skin color as a relevant reason for, say, denying medical care or education to a person. A defender of discrimination must try to advance some relevant reason for his actions. And, Williams argues, what constitutes a relevant reason for doing something is drastically constrained by our language.

Williams believes that this insight shows that the recognition of our common humanity gives us strong reasons to treat people equally. Consider, for instance, the distribution of medical care in the light of our common humanity. What constitutes a relevant reason for distributing medical care? To Williams, the answer is clear: medical care should go to those who are in ill health. "Leaving aside preventative medicine," he argues, "the proper ground of distribution of medical care is ill-health: this is a necessary truth."[28] His point is that our understanding of medical care and health, embedded in our form of life, greatly constrains what reasons can be relevant in distributing medical care. Given that we are all human, and so display basic human needs, we have reason to ensure that those who need medical care receive it. Of course, this argument does not directly show that medical needs should be equally satisfied, but it does suggest that those who are equally needy have an equally strong claim to medical care.

On this view, our basic human equality derives from our basic similarity: we have a common nature, which gives rise to common needs. Basic human equality is, at bottom, the basic sameness of people: we share the same nature, which gives rise to common needs. To treat people equally is to recognize that in their essential characteristic they are the same and so there is no reason to prefer one to the other. Note here the way in which equality as *sameness* is said to give rise to equality as *nonpreferential* treatment: because we are basically the same, no one should be preferred to others (see Section 6.1). It is important to stress that although the basic ground for our equality is our similarity, the treatment that is argued for is not that everyone be treated exactly the same, but that needs be met in a nonpreferential way. That we share a common human nature that gives rise to common needs does not imply that at every moment each person has the same needs: at any given time some may require medical care, others education, and so on. What is crucial is that these common needs be equally satisfied. As Tawny pointed out, "Equality of provision is not identity of provision. It is to be achieved, not by treating different needs in the same way, but by devoting equal care to ensuring that they are met in the different ways most appropriate to them."[29]

Williams, then, believes that our language provides a secular basis for showing that our shared humanity gives us reason to help the needy. The difficulty with Williams's argument is revealed if we recall the analysis of conceptual disputes in Chapter 2. Our language is remarkably open-textured and allows people to sensibly employ terms in opposing ways. It was Gallie's insight that the sensible use of language is consistent with great differences about the best interpretation of our political concepts. The same lesson applies to notions like "medical care." It is simply wrong to say that an advocate of the free market who claims that "Alf should get good medical care because he can pay for it" is misusing language. One might disagree with him and try to provide an argument that, when distributing medical care, needs are more important than ability to pay. The issue, though, cannot be settled by proclaiming that since "it is a matter of logic that particular sorts of needs constitute a reason for receiving particular sorts of goods,"[30] the advocate of the free market is simply misusing language.

Two Views of Human Essence: Marx and Kant

The strength of Williams's proposal is that he does not make any controversial claims about the way in which we are equal (for example, that we are all equally loved by God). Many secular proponents of fundamental equality, however, have been prepared to identify some core, shared human characteristic that defines the "human essence." Karl Marx, for example, argued for the basic equality of humans insofar as all humans share a common human nature (Section 3.3) or essence, which generates similar needs. According to Marx, humans need to "objectify" themselves.[31] To objectify oneself is to turn one's thoughts and plans into something objective by changing the world. In short, it is transforming the world in such a way as to reflect one's aims and intentions. That, as Marx sees it, is what makes the works of humans so special; they are ways in which humans have changed the world to conform with their aims. When humans act on the world, their action is conscious: they are seeking to shape the world in accordance with their conscious purposes. In more familiar language, we might say that we are planners and doers; our labor is the way in which our plans are expressed in doing. Animals are doers, but not, Marx thinks, conscious planners. Thus, our essence—our distinctively human feature—shows that we have basically the same needs: to create and produce. Because, Marx insisted, capitalist society stifles this creative impulse for almost everyone, it dehumanizes us (see Section 9.1).

Followers of Immanuel Kant, in contrast, maintain that our fundamental human characteristic is our ability to act morally. For Kant, it will be recalled, freedom never conflicts with justice (Section 5.4): to act freely is to act in accordance with rules of justice. To Kant, our dignity and worth stem from our ability to restrain our impulses and act autonomously (Section 4.2) on principles of justice. This ability to restrain our impulses and instead do the right thing is our *moral personality*: it is the feature that enables us to live morally and to respect the moral rights of others. If we did not possess such a moral personality, there would be no point in having rights or rules or justice, for no one would pay attention to them when they clashed with her passions or impulses. Only because we have the ability to put aside our impulses and act according to reason, Kant argues, does morality make any difference to us. Thus, for Kant, our fundamental human equality is our shared rational nature (Section 3.2). Our equal rationality, in particular our equal capacity for moral personality, is our fundamental human equality.[32] And it is this equality of moral personality that gives us an entitlement to equal justice.[33]

The problem is that we do not seem to have an equal moral personality, if this means an equal capacity to restrain our impulses and desires and to instead act on rules of justice. Some people seem to have precious little capacity to do so—they have an extremely hard time resisting temptation—whereas other people are able to resist almost any temptation. Some people are always getting into trouble, whereas others hardly ever break moral rules or act unjustly. In what sense, then, can it be claimed that we are equally rational or have an equal capacity for moral personality? This is actually a general problem for most claims about fundamental equality. No matter what characteristic we identify as a common, fundamental human characteristic, it will almost surely be open to some variation among humans. People possess different degrees of rationality, different capacities and desires to "objectify" themselves, different needs, and so on. We do not all have "tied scores" on rationality, moral personality, or capacity for objectification. If we are never all really equal, can arguments from fundamental equality ever succeed?

An interesting response to this problem is to change continuous concepts into *threshold* concepts.[34] For example, consider a continuous concept such as "age"—we have a continuous scale (years old), and score each person on the scale. We find, of course, that many people beat out others—they have higher ages. To the extent equality requires a tied score (Section 6.1), most people are unequal on this continuous concept. Threshold concepts hold out the possibility for a huge number of ties, however. Consider, for example, the concept "old enough to drive." Someone who is fourteen years old is ranked below (that is, "too young") someone who is twenty (who is "old enough"). But those who are twenty, thirty, forty, fifty, and sixty are *equal*: they get the same score— "old enough." Thus, even though twenty-, thirty-, forty-, fifty- and sixty-year-old people are unequal in ages, they are equal in satisfying the criterion of being old enough to drive. The thirty-year-old person does not better satisfy the criterion than does the twenty-year-old. We can apply this same idea to a fundamental equality claim. Although we do not all possess equal moral personality (in the sense of an equal ability to control our impulses and act on reason), we may all be equally capable of minimal moral personality: we are able to usually follow the basic rules of morality. Perhaps a few do not even meet this minimum criterion, but such people really might be special cases who are not on par with the rest of us (for example, small children and psychopaths). The great majority of functioning adults are indeed equal insofar as they meet the minimum conditions for moral personality and thus have a "tied score" on that threshold trait.

Equal Freedom

The Virginia Declaration of Rights of 1776—which in many ways was the model for the *Declaration of Independence*—proclaims in its first article, "That all men are by nature equally free and independent."[35] In *The Second Treatise on Civil Government*, one of the most important works in liberal political theory, John Locke (1632–1704), makes a very similar claim about the condition "all men are naturally in." It is a condition not only of liberty (Section 4.3) but

> also of equality, wherein all the power and jurisdiction is reciprocal, no one having more than another; there being nothing more evident, than that creatures of the same species and rank, promiscuously born to all the same advantages of nature, and the use of the same faculties, should also be equal

one amongst another without subordination or subjection, unless the lord and master of them all should, by any manifest declaration of his will, set one above another, and confer on him, by an evident and clear appointment, an undoubted right to dominion and sovereignty.[36]

For Locke—and the entire liberal tradition in political theory—the fundamental human equality is the absence of any natural ranking of individuals into those who command and those who obey. We are not born under any natural authority (except, Locke would add, God's). Thus, given the nonpreferential conception of equality, since no one is to be ranked above or below any one else in terms of authority, we are naturally equal. Thus, by nature, people have equal freedom. This fundamental equality, argues Locke, shows that justified political authority cannot be derived from the natural status of some as rulers over others, but must be based on the consent of all citizens. We will turn to the relation of equality and authority in Chapter 10; for present purposes what is crucial is that, in liberal political theory, the fundamental equality is an *equality of freedom*.

Two Worries about Arguments from Fundamental Equality

Thus far, I have been assuming that arguments from fundamental equality are the key egalitarian arguments. But Joseph Raz, a contemporary political philosopher, gives us reason to wonder whether arguments from fundamental equality are really egalitarian arguments at all![37] Following Raz, let us consider a version of what I have called the argument from fundamental equality (FE):

FE: All who are equally *F* are equally entitled to *G*.

Thus, as many egalitarians have argued, those who are equally needy are equally entitled to have their needs met. Now, it seems that we can rephrase FE along the lines of

FE*: If *G*s are being distributed solely on the basis of feature *F*, then those who are equally *F* are equally entitled to *G*s.

Thus, again, if we are distributing health care simply on the basis of need, then those who have equal needs have equal claim to health care. On reflection, however, FE* is not an egalitarian principle at all—it is a principle of nonarbitrary distribution. If we are really distributing *G*s simply on the criterion of possession of *F*, and if two people are equally *F*, to say that one person has a stronger claim to *G* must imply one of two things.

(1) It may show that possession of F was not really the sole grounds for distributing G. For example, suppose a teacher says that a 90 on the final exam is the complete grounds for awarding an A in the course, and that two students receive 90 on the final, but only one gets an A. If the two students receive different final grades for the course, it may be that, after all, the teacher is using two criteria rather than one. Perhaps, in addition to performance on the final exam, the teacher is taking into account class participation, call it factor E. In that case, all those who are equally F and equally E should receive equal grades. (2) Alternatively, the teacher may assign the grades arbitrarily: he randomly assigns grades regardless of one's score on the final exam. In this case, we would not expect those with equal Fs to receive equal Gs.

But if the teacher is not being arbitrary, and if the teacher has specified all the criteria for giving grades, then those who score the same on the criteria have equal claims to an A, and will both receive an A. This will not be because the teacher is an egalitarian: it is because the teacher is distributing the good on the basis of the stated criterion. This seems to mean that the fundamental egalitarian argument does not really depend on any commitment to the value of equality, but simply to nonarbitrary, rational distribution of the goods at stake.

It may well be argued, however, that FE is not the best statement of the argument from fundamental equality. More in the spirit of egalitarianism seems to be

TrueFE: All those who are equally F are to receive equal shares of G.

TrueFE is distinct from FE. Whereas as FE generates *equal claims to G*, True FE endorses *claims to equal amounts of G*. We can reinterpret TrueFE as

TrueFE*: If Gs are being distributed solely on the basis of feature F, then those who are equally F are entitled to equal amounts of G.

In most cases, the same general point holds for TrueFE as for FE. In our case of the teacher, TrueFE tells the teacher to give equal grades to those who have equal F-scores. As Aristotle put it, the teacher is treating equally (giving equal Gs to) those who are equals (have equals Fs), and treating unequally (giving different Gs to) those who are unequal (have different Fs). TrueFE is, though, a true egalitarian principle—it is more than a mere statement of nonarbitrary distribution of G. Consider, for instance, a case in which we have nine indivisible units of G and five people to distribute them to, all of whom are equally F. If we are to give those who are equally F equal Gs, and we cannot give fractions of Gs, then TrueFE requires us to give each person one *G*. This leaves four *G*s wasted, but there is no way to equally distribute them, so TrueFE requires that they must be left undistributed. This is important: although one way to promote equality is to give more to those with less, another way is simply to take away from those with more until everyone has the same amount. Indeed, often it is impossible to raise everyone to the highest standard, and the only way to satisfy TrueFE is to lower some people. For example, if all who have equal health care needs are to have equal health care, and if we cannot afford some very expensive treatment for everyone (say, dialysis machines), then it satisfies TrueFE if no one receives the health care.

Raz, then, concludes that principles such as FE are reasonable principles, but are not really egalitarian. On the other hand, TrueFE, which seems most truly egalitarian, may be very wasteful and that appears unreasonable.

6.4 Equality of What?

Thus far, our main focus has been on arguments in favor of equality. In Section 6.2, we examined attempts to ground the case for equal treatment on utility, impartiality, and incommensurability; Section 6.3 focused on arguments that we should be treated equally because we are, in some fundamental respect, really equal. Throughout, we have considered various ways people can be treated equally—goods can be distributed equally, needs can be fulfilled equally, people can have equal liberty. Not only do political theorists offer very different reasons why we should treat people equally, they deeply disagree on the ways in which people should be treated equally. The aim of this section is to briefly review the different ways in which it has been said people should, or should not, be treated equally.

Equal Welfare

It is plausible to suppose that if we want to truly treat everyone as equals, we should seek to make everyone's life go equally well.[38] After all, is not the real point of giving people goods, such as money or education, to make their lives go better? Consider an "equal" distribution of a good such as music compact disks (CDs): everyone in society gets a certain number of CDs every year. Some of these people, though, are tone deaf, or entirely deaf, and have no use for CDs. It hardly seems that we are treating equals equally if we give CDs to everyone, including the deaf. If we wish to treat the deaf equally, it seems that we should give them something that they want just as much as a music lover wants a CD.

More generally, if some people have pressing needs—say, they are handicapped and require additional assistance to lead a normal life—it may seem that giving them the same income as a healthy person is not really to treat them equally. If they are to lead a life that is equally satisfying, they will require additional funds (see Figure 6.2 above).

Following a standard view in economics and political theory, let us define a person's welfare as the satisfaction of her wants or "preferences." Suppose each person ranks her preferences—her desires or wants—from those things that she wants most to what she wants the least. We can then say that a person's welfare (or utility) level is a function of the number of her preferences that are satisfied and how highly these preferences are ranked.[39] So, someone who gets her top preference satisfied has a higher level of welfare than someone who gets only her forty-fifth preference satisfied. If we adopt the view that to treat people equally is to ensure that they have an equality of welfare, we will equally satisfy everyone's preferences.

Equality of welfare, however, is open to at least two objections.[40] (1) Although most people's preferences concern how their own lives go—preferences for nicer houses, cars, good health, and so on—all of us some of the time, and some of us most of the time, have preferences about how other people's lives go. Indeed, we often encourage this: we teach our children not to think only of themselves, but to want to help others. We can say, then, that people entertain "external" preferences—preferences about other people getting their preferences satisfied. Alf, for instance, might have a preference that Betty gets what she wants—this would be an external preference. External preferences raise problems for the egalitarian. For one thing, they may be nasty: if one of my preferences is to see you fail to get what you want, the pursuit of equal satisfaction of welfare must admit that the very thing that satisfies your preference stifles my preference. You getting what you want makes my life worse. So, perhaps you ought not to get it. But even "nice" external preferences cause problems for the egalitarian. If Alf has a preference that Betty gets what she wants, Betty's preferences will in a sense be "double-counted": giving it to her will satisfy her preference and Alf's too, thus making two people's lives better off. Perhaps this is not a decisive problem, since Alf is getting something he wants: the satisfaction of Betty's preference. It will, however, be likely to have the consequence that selfish people will receive more goods in an egalitarian system. All the selfish person's preferences will be about her receiving goods; but the unselfish (altruistic) people will have split preferences—some of their preferences will be about their receiving goods, and some will be about other people, including presumably selfish people, receiving goods. If so, then the equal satisfaction of preferences will lead to additional goods for selfish people, some to satisfy the preferences of the selfish people and some to satisfy the external preferences of the altruistic people.

A more serious objection to equality of welfare is that we choose many of our preferences, and some people choose very expensive ones. Some people want a life of luxury filled with extremely expensive things; others are more modest. Now, the equal satisfaction of preferences would lead to giving more goods to those who have expensive tastes, since it takes so much more to satisfy the preferences of such people. We thus are faced with the possibility of an "egalitarian state" that supports some in a life of luxury. The case of the person with expensive tastes, it should be noted, is very similar to the handicapped person we considered above (see Figure 6.2). The handicapped person needs more goods to give her the same level of preference satisfaction as that obtained by the healthy person; the person with expensive tastes is in a similar position. If we think there is an important difference between the cases, it is because we think that the person with luxurious tastes is responsible for having expensive tastes whereas the handicapped person did not choose her expensive preferences. It seems, then, that a plausible defense of equal welfare must develop an account of "freely chosen expensive tastes" and "nonvoluntary expensive preferences." Although in some cases this distinction will seem clear, it will raise intractable problems in a host of others. Compare, for example, someone who, for as long as she can remember, has had an overwhelming desire to be a political leader, and a person who has suffered paralysis in a car accident. Can we say that the first person somehow is responsible for her costly preferences whereas the second person did not voluntarily choose his now-expensive preferences? But the paralyzed person chose to drive in cars, and so run the risk of injury, whereas our would-be leader cannot recall ever making any choice to desperately want to lead others. What does equality of welfare instruct us to do?

Equal Satisfaction of Needs

One way to avoid these problems is to adopt a needs-based conception of welfare. Instead of understanding a person's welfare in terms of what she wants and whether she gets it, we may characterize a person's welfare in terms of the satisfaction of her basic needs. The notion of a "need" points to standard conditions or goods that are required by everyone.[41] Thus, for example, one political philosopher had advanced the following list of "course-of-life needs":

(1) The need to have life-supporting relation to the environment
(2) The need for food and water

(3) The need to excrete
(4) The need for exercise
(5) The need for periodic rest, including sleep
(6) The need (beyond what is covered by the preceding needs) for whatever is indispensable for preserving the body intact in important respects
(7) The need for companionship
(8) The need for education
(9) The need for social acceptance and recognition
(10) The need for sexual activity
(11) The need to be free from harassment, including not being continually frightened
(12) The need for recognition[42]

Such needs do not depend on preferences: on a needs-based account of welfare, these are the things that people need, regardless of what they want. Equal treatment, then, would entail the equal satisfaction of these basic needs.[43] Thus, said Marx, the ultimate achievement of a communist society would be to distribute "to each according to his needs" (see Sections 3.3, 9.1).

To the extent needs-based accounts indicate that a person's overall welfare does not depend on her own view of what she wants, they are controversial. Suppose, for example, that a person has no interest in companionship, wishing to live (as did Wittgenstein for a period) as a hermit. It seems contentious indeed to say that we are furthering her welfare by providing her with companionship (need 7 above), something for which she has no desire. Needs-based accounts of welfare are typically linked to theories of human nature, such as Marx's, that depict humans as having an essence that we must fulfill if we are to lead satisfied lives (Sections 3.3, 6.3). Such a theory gives a basis for deeming some things (such as companionship) a true need, but others (such as doing philosophy) a mere desire. One of the attractions—as well, ultimately, as one of the drawbacks—of the preference-based account of welfare is that it makes each individual authoritative in deciding what her welfare is; needs-based accounts make authoritative a theory of human nature, or a rationalist insight into the true proper life for humans (Sections 3.2, 3.3).

Equal Resources

The problems with equal welfare interpretations of equal treatment have led many egalitarians to defend an equal resource view.[44] To treat people equally is to give them equal resources. Having received their equal share of the resources, it is up to each person whether he or she will use them wisely to help construct a satisfying life or waste them in the pursuit of empty pleasures. Thus, a person who cultivates expensive tastes will have to use her equal share of the resources to satisfy them; given how expensive they are, she will probably not be able to satisfy many of them, and so her welfare level will be lower than someone with more modest tastes.

Equal resource theories must identify what is a resource. It seems clear that money is a resource, but what about eyes? If a resource is something that is instrumental to achieving your purposes, then having eyes is a crucial resource. There would thus seem a case for an equal distribution of eyes, perhaps justifying taking an eye from some to transplant into the blind. Some resource theorists have been ambivalent whether body parts and personal traits are to be viewed as resources. Although John Rawls, for example, is explicit that body parts are not to be distributed, he also believes that a just society treats everyone's natural talents as a "collective asset" that should work to the advantage of the poor.[45] Although Rawls seems somewhat attracted to such an expansive view of resources, he ultimately advocates a list of "primary goods," which are all-purpose resources that everyone must have to pursue their aims in life. Thus, says Rawls, we require liberty, income, opportunities, and the social basis of self-respect, whatever our plan of life is; the distribution of resources, for Rawls, is the distribution of these goods.

We may well query, however, whether an equal share of such goods constitutes an adequate interpretation of equal treatment. Some people may not be able to use their goods or may require a great deal of additional goods for an adequate life. Amartya Sen draws our attention to the handicapped person, who would not receive any additional goods under a simple equal resource view: she would get her share, and only her share, even though she can do comparatively little with it. Sen suggests that such a view suffers from a "goods fetish"[46]—its only concern is goods, but goods are only a means, not an end. The end or goal is that people's lives go well. In response to problems raised by the handicapped and the ill, equal resource views have developed complex insurance schemes, which try to accommodate extra assistance for some in an equal resource distribution.[47]

Basic Capability Equality and Needs

Sen's own proposal is to focus on equal capabilities, rather than either welfare or resources:

> It is arguable that what is missing in all this . . . is some notion of "basic capabilities": a person being able to do certain basic things. The ability to

move about is relevant here, but one can consider others, e.g. the ability to meet one's nutritional requirements, the wherewithal to be clothed and sheltered, the power to participate in social life of the community. . . . [Rawls's idea of] primary goods suffers from the fetish handicap in being concerned with goods . . . rather than what these good things *do* to human beings. Utility [i.e., preference satisfaction welfarism], on the other hand, *is* concerned with what these things do to human beings, but uses a metric that focusses not on the person's capabilities but on his mental reaction. There is still something missing in the combined list of primary goods and utilities.[48]

Once again citing the case of the handicapped person, Sen concludes that what is required by the egalitarian is an "interpretation of needs in the form of capabilities."[49] Note here that Sen himself sees his account as a version of needs theory. Rather than conceiving of needs as more-or-less passive resource requirements, Sen understands them as active powers or abilities—capabilities or "functionings" that one must possess to lead an adequate life. Although we cannot go into the details of Sen's account here, it should be manifest that insofar as his account is needs based, it has the general rationalist trait of such accounts of presupposing a notion of an adequately or properly functioning person.

Equal Civil Status

All of the modes of equal treatment thus far examined have employed an extremely wide conception of "treatment." Having one's life go well, having resources, having needs satisfied, or possessing capabilities are all seen as ways that people can be treated. To understand "treatment" in this way presupposes that almost all of one's life constitutes a "treatment" of you by your society or government. Thus, if your life has not gone as well as other people's, some seem tempted to say that you thus have not been treated as well; if you have less resources than others, you thus have been treated unequally. Understanding treatment in this way would seem more at home in collectivist accounts of individuals-in-society (Section 3.4), which understand most attributes of the individual in terms of collective or social facts. It thus should come as no surprise that the political theorists discussed thus far in Section 6.4 embrace either socialism or revisionist liberalism.

A more modest understanding of "treatment"—and one that is more consistent with classical liberalism's individualist analysis of individuals-in-society (Sections 2.1, 3.4)—focuses on cases in which some individuals (officials of the state) are explicitly meting out treatments such as punishments, rewards, and positions to others (citizens). According to the notion of civic equality, when treating people in these ways public officials are not to simply prefer some group of citizens to others, but must employ general, public criteria for any difference in treatment. If all have equal status as citizens, no group of citizens, just because of their group membership, will be preferred to others, nor will any group be ranked lower than others. Hence they will be treated equally in the sense of the nonpreferential conception.

One aspect of this equality of civil status is *equality before the law*. In meting out legal punishment, government officials are to be concerned only with a person's legal rights, not extralegal considerations such as class, race, sex, or ethnic background. Of course, different people have different legal rights—the law creates different classes of people, such as landlords and tenants, doctors and patients, public officials and private persons. [50] The ideal of equality before the law is that when being treated by the law, one's treatment is determined solely by one's legal status (as determined by one's rights and duties), not by one's nonlegal social status. In itself, equality before the law is consistent with giving some groups legal privileges; thus aristocrats may have legal rights denied to commoners. A stronger conception of civic equality, and one that has been at the heart of the liberal tradition, is *equal basic rights of all citizens*, and a general opposition to legal distinctions based on class, sex, or race. An ideal of equal citizenship is expressed by the Fourteenth and Fifteenth Amendments to the U.S. Constitution:

AMENDMENT XIV. . . . No state shall make or enforce any law which shall abridge the privileges or immunities of citizens of the United States; nor shall any State deprive any person of life, liberty, or property, without due process of law; nor deny to any person within its jurisdiction the equal protection of the laws.

AMENDMENT XV. . . . The right of citizens of the United States to vote shall not be denied or abridged by the United States or by any State on account of race, color, or previous condition of servitude.

The Fifteenth Amendment outright prohibits legal distinctions based on race in matters of voting. The Fourteenth Amendment holds that no citizen is to be denied "equal protection of the law." In interpreting this clause, the Supreme Court has developed a doctrine of "suspicious classifications," which include race and national origin, and at times has been interpreted to include status as an alien and as poor, and might plausibly be extended to include homosexuals and women. In evaluating whether the Fourteenth Amendment has been violated, the Supreme Court looks especially hard at any laws that employ any of the "suspicious classifications." If a law invokes such a classification, it must be shown that (1) the law serves a legitimate public goal of considerable importance, and (2) using the classification fits the public goal perfectly—it is precisely the classification that is required if the goal is to be achieved.[51] Thus, for example, race might be used as a classification in a desegregation law, since it would be necessary to achieve the goal of the law, but in most cases the court would prohibit use of the classification as a denial of equal citizenship. Some, however, have opposed any laws that allot different treatment to citizens on the basis of such "suspicious categories," arguing that all such laws undermine equal citizenship.

Political and Social Equality

Advocates of democracy—and the Fifteenth Amendment—have argued that equal citizenship endorses *political equality*, according to which each citizen has an equal say in elections. The ideal of one person, one vote, is an expression of political equality: each citizen is the political equal of any other insofar as the vote of each counts equally. Other interpretations have been much more expansive; to one socialist, political equality "is the demand to be equally involved in the authorization of a total way of life, and it is the fundamental demand of democracy."[52] In Chapter 9, in our examination of social justice, we will return to the socialist notion of political equality.

Some egalitarians have insisted that the ultimate expression of the value of equality is *social equality*, in which all citizens have the same social status and perhaps the same power. Social equality is usually taken to require both economic equality (say, in the form of equality of resources) and political equality, but it goes beyond those. It has sometimes been called "social democracy"—a way of life characterized by the absence of social and occupational hierarchies. Thus, to advocates of social equality, it is necessary to reform the "division of labor itself . . . the way that people sort themselves out (or are sorted out) to accomplish their goals of production and distribution."[53] People must not be sorted out according to occupational status hierarchies or into groups of owners and workers, bosses and bossed. Carried to its extreme, the pursuit of social equality can lead to regulations concerning dress and consumption, for both of these are ways in which some people display their higher status over others. Thus, in Maoist China uniform styles of dress were mandated; on a smaller scale, social egalitarians often favor school uniforms. Social equality thus seems to lead to equality as sameness (Section 6.1).

On reflection, however, it seems impossible to really eliminate social hierarchies: although in Maoist China leaders and the led dressed alike, no one was in doubt about who the leaders were, or their prerogatives. Indeed, it seems impossible to educate without creating a hierarchy of educational attainments, impossible to engage in sports without creating athletic hierarchies (standings), impossible to have art without producing artistic inequalities. Almost every field of endeavor creates ranking of those who are better or worse, more or less praiseworthy, and so on. In response to this inevitability of social rankings, Michael Walzer, a contemporary egalitarian, has advocated "complex equality."[54] By this, Walzer means that in a socially egalitarian society, the rankings from one field of endeavor will not translate into an overall social hierarchy. Being better at sports will give one high status in sports, but will not translate into better medical care, higher wealth, and overall high status; being a scholar will give one high academic status, but, again, not more political status or better medical care. For Walzer, rather than eliminating social hierarchies, equal treatment requires that they be contained. As he is a socialist, his deepest worry is about economic equalities; although he allows that they are necessary for production, he wishes to contain their influence, so that high economic status does not automatically bring high political status, the best education, and the best medical care. Like Williams (Section 6.3), Walzer believes that we share socially agreed upon understandings of what the distributive criteria should be for different parts of social life—academic fame should go to great scholars, and medical care should go to the sick. Walzer's proposal thus raises a very similar problem to that we considered in relation to Williams's analysis of human equality: the diversity of our language and culture leads to sensible disagreements about the nature of the practices of medicine or education, and so disagreements about just what are the correct criteria for distributing their goods.

Equality of Opportunity

An important aspect of civic equality concerns competition for public positions: in competing for public offices, citizens are not to be discriminated against on the grounds of race, national origin, or sex. Understood in this way, *equality of opportunity* requires nonpreferential treatment in competition for government positions. The development of modern civil services is an expression of this ideal, in which appointments are made on the basis of criteria relevant to the performance of the position. The ideal has been expanded in more recent times to include the treatment of citizens by nongovernmental organizations such as business corporations and private universities. One ground for this extension is an expanded view of what constitutes a public organization. Rather than restricting the ideal of equal citizenship to public qua governmental organizations, there has been a movement in legislation to include "private" organizations that are open to the public or serve the public. Hence, according to the United Kingdom Race Relations Act of 1968, it is "unlawful for any person concerned with the provision to the public . . . of any goods, facilities or services to discriminate" on the grounds of color, race, ethnic or national origin.[55]

The ideal of equality of opportunity as open competition, barring preferential treatment except on grounds relevant to the performance of the task in question, is distinct from a more encompassing ideal of equality of opportunity, sometimes called "equality of fair opportunity."[56] The core of this latter idea is that social factors such as class, race, and sex should not affect one's chances to obtain desired positions in society. Those equally endowed should have equal chances of success. It is important to note that not even equality of fair opportunity seeks to guarantee equal success: to have an opportunity is to have some obstacles to success—such as being a women or being poor—eliminated, not to be guaranteed success, if only because the positions being competed for are scarce.[57] Whereas the original ideal saw each competition for each position as a different competition that should be conducted fairly, equality of fair opportunity extends this idea of a fair competition to life prospects as a whole. Is it fair, ask the proponents of equality of fair opportunity, that the competent poor child stands less of a chance of eventually getting favored positions in our society than does the equally competent rich child? Is that treating equals equally? Note that if we embrace this conception of equality of fair opportunity, we are again taking an encompassing and abstract view of "treatment"—*society is treating* people unequally because some are born in positions that do not allow them to effectively compete with others who are no more competent than they.

6.5 Summary

In this chapter, I have explored two groups of questions. (1) Why is equality to be valued or pursued? (2) In what ways are people to be treated equally? In answering the first question, I distinguished "external arguments" for equality, which endorse equality because it promotes or expresses some other value, and arguments from fundamental equality, which hold that we ought to treat people equally because in some deep sense we really are equal. Section 6.2 considered three external arguments for equality: that based on promoting overall utility, that based on impartiality, and that based on incommensurability. Section 6.3 examined arguments maintaining that we are fundamentally equal because we are all human, because we share a common human essence, and because we are equally naturally free. Section 6.3 closed by considering some concerns about arguments from fundamental equality, most importantly whether they really are egalitarian at all. Section 6.4 turned to modes of equal treatment. People can be treated equally in an almost limitless variety of ways; only a sample of the main proposals were discussed. Examined were arguments in favor of (1) equal welfare, (2) equal satisfaction of needs, (3) equal resources, (4) equal capabilities, (5) equal civic status, (6) political and social equality, and (7) equality of opportunity.

Notes

1. See here J. R. Lucas, *The Principles of Politics* (Oxford: Clarendon Press, 1966), pp. 243ff.

2. R. H. Tawney, *Equality* (New York: Harcourt, Brace, 1931), pp. 110–111.

3. Aristotle, *The Politics*, in Richard. McKeon, ed., *The Basic Works of Aristotle* (New York: Random House, 1941), Book 3 [1280a–1281a].

4. Aristotle, *Nicomachean Ethics*, W. D. Ross, trans. (Oxford: Oxford University Press), Book 5, 3 [1131a6–1132a2].

5. François-Noël Babeuf and Slyvain Marechal, "The Manifesto of Equality," in Louis P. Pojman and Robert Westmorland, eds., *Equality* (Oxford: Oxford University Press, 1987), pp. 49–52.

6. Jeremy Bentham, *Introduction to the Principles of Morals and Legislation*, in Alan Ryan, ed., *Utilitarianism and Other Essays* (Harmondsworth, UK: Penguin, 1987), chap. 1.

7. This is an alteration of a case given by Amartya Sen, "Equality of What?" in Sterling McMurrin, ed., *Liberty, Equality and the Law* (Cambridge: Cambridge University Press, 1987), pp. 145ff. See Section 6.4.

8. Quoted in Bernard Crick, *Socialism* (Milton Keynes, UK: Open University Press, 1987), p. 8.

9. Thomas Nagel, *Equality and Partiality* (New York: Oxford University Press, 1991), p. 64.

10. Ibid., p. 66.

11. J. R. Lucas, "Against Equality," in Hugo A. Bedau, ed., *Justice and Equality* (Englewood Cliffs, NJ: Prentice-Hall, 1971), p. 139.

12. S. I. Benn and R. S. Peters, *Social Principles and the Democratic State* (London: George Allen and Unwin, 1959), p. 110.

13. Ibid., p. 111.

14. Stanley I. Benn, "Human Rights—for Whom and for What?" in Eugene Kamenka and Alice Erh-Soon Tay, eds., *Human Rights* (New York: St. Martin's Press, 1978), p. 67.

15. Herbert Spiegelberg, "A Defense of Human Equality," *Philosophical Review*, vol. 53 (March 1944), p. 114.

16. Ibid.

17. See Rawls, *A Theory of Justice* (Cambridge, MA: Harvard University Press, 1971), p. 101.

18. Ibid., p. 74.

19. William Styron, *Sophie's Choice* (New York: Vintage Books, 1992).

20. See Gregory Vlastos, "Justice and Equality," in R. B. Brandt, ed., *Social Justice* (Englewood Cliffs, NJ: Prentice-Hall, 1962).

21. Lucas, *The Principles of Politics*, p. 251.

22. Online at http://www.constitution.org/bcp/virg_dor.htm.

23. See Tawney, *Equality*. See Also Sanford A. Lakoff, "Christianity and Equality" in J. Roland Pennock and John W. Chapman, eds., *NOMOS IX: Equality* (New York: Atherton, 1967), pp. 115–133. For an argument that the idea of equal human worth is essentially religious, see Louis P. Pojman, "On Equal Human Worth: A Critique of Contemporary Egalitarianism," in Pojman and Westmorland, eds., *Equality*, pp. 282–299.

24. Bernard Williams, "The Idea of Equality," in his *Problems of the Self* (Cambridge: Cambridge University Press, 1973), p. 230.

25. Ibid.

26. Ibid., p. 232.

27. Ibid., p. 233.

28. Ibid.

29. Tawney, *Equality*, p. xx. See also David Braybrooke, *Meeting Needs* (Princeton: Princeton University Press, 1987), pp. 144–145.

30. Braybrooke, *Meeting Needs*, pp. 241–242.

31. See here John Plamenatz, *Karl Marx's Philosophy of Man* (Oxford: Oxford University Press, 1975), p. 115. See also Jon Elster, *An Introduction to Karl Marx* (Cambridge: Cambridge University Press, 1986), pp. 44ff.

32. See Amy Gutmann, *Liberal Equality* (Princeton: Princeton University Press, 1980), pp. 27–41.

33. Rawls, *A Theory of Justice*, p. 505.

34. See here Alan Gewirth, *Reason and Morality* (Chicago: University of Chicago Press, 1978), pp. 121–122.

35. Online at http://www.constitution.org/bcp/virg_dor.htm.

36. John Locke, *Second Treatise of Government*, in Peter Laslett, ed., *Two Treatises of Government* (Cambridge: Cambridge University Press, 1960), sect. 4.

37. The following discussion is drawn from Joseph Raz, *The Morality of Freedom* (Oxford: Clarendon Press, 1986), chap. 9.

38. This view is endorsed by Kai Nielsen, *Equality and Liberty* (Totowa, NJ: Rowman and Allenheld, 1985), for example, p. 7.

39. This is a very basic view, which requires modification. I consider the idea of preference satisfaction in more depth in my *Social Philosophy* (Armonk, NY: M. E. Sharpe, 1999), pp. 50–58.

40. Much of what I say here is drawn from Ronald Dworkin, "What Is Equality? Part 1: Equality of Welfare," *Philosophy & Public Affairs*, vol. 10 (Summer 1981), pp. 185–246; and Eric Rakowski, *Equal Justice* (Oxford: Clarendon Press, 1991), pp. 23ff. I leave aside here serious objections to the very idea of comparing the degree to which different people have had their preferences satisfied; I discuss these problems in *Social Philosophy*, chap. 4.

41. For a somewhat different view, see James Griffin's notion of well-being as based on certain "prudential values" that are held to be valuable by everyone. *Well-being: Its meaning, Measurement and Moral Importance* (Oxford: Oxford University Press, 1986).

42. Braybrooke, *Meeting Needs*, p. 36.

43. For complications, see ibid., pp. 138ff.

44. See Ronald Dworkin, "What Is Equality? Part 2: Equality of Resources," *Philosophy & Public Affairs*, vol. 10 (Fall 1981), pp. 283–345; Eric Rakowski, *Equal Justice*.

45. Rawls, *A Theory of Justice*, p. 101.

46. Sen, "Equality of What?" p. 160.

47. See Dworkin, "What Is Equality? Part 2: Equality of Resources."

48. Sen, "Equality of What?" p. 160.

49. Ibid. See also Amartya Sen, *Inequality Reexamined* (Cambridge: Harvard University Press, 1992).

50. See Benn and Peters, *Social Principles and the Democratic State*, pp. 122–123.

51. For an excellent analysis, see John Hart Ely, *Democracy and Distrust* (Cambridge: Harvard University Press, 1980), pp. 145ff.

52. Philip Green, *Retrieving Democracy: In Search of Civic Equality* (London: Methuen, 1985), p. 5.

53. Ibid., p. 9.

54. Michael Walzer, *Spheres of Justice* (New York: Basic Books, 1983).

55. For a discussion of this act, see S. I. Benn and G. F. Gaus, "The Liberal Conception of the Public and Private," in S. I. Benn and G. F. Gaus, eds., *Public and Private in Social Life* (New York: St. Martin's, 1983), pp. 36–38.

56. See Rawls, *A Theory of Justice*, pp. 65ff.

57. See Peter Westin, "The Concept of Equal Opportunity," *Ethics*, vol. 95 (July 1985), pp. 837–850.

7

EQUALITY AND LIBERTY
IN POLITICAL THEORIES

7.1 Do Liberty and Equality Conflict?

In *The Social Contract*, Jean-Jacques Rousseau tells us,

> If we enquire wherein lies precisely the greatest good of all, which ought to
> be the goal of every system of law, we shall find that it comes to two main
> objects, *freedom* and *equality*: freedom, because any individual dependence
> means that much strength taken from the body of the state, and equality, be-
> cause freedom cannot exist without it.[1]

For Rousseau, not only are liberty and equality the two chief components
of the common good, but equality supports liberty—there is no clash between the pursuit of liberty and equality. In contrast, J. Roland Pennock,
a leading theorist of democracy, insisted that liberty and equality are, at
best, in "tension" with each other; we need to somehow accommodate
both, even though they tend to pull us in opposite directions.[2] More
radically, many have believed that "liberty and equality are in essence
contradictory."[3]

From the analyses of Chapters 4 to 6, one reason for these radically different views about the relation of liberty and equality should be obvious.
Both "liberty" and "equality" can mean many different things; depending on what view is taken of liberty, what grounds for equal treatment
are endorsed, and what type of equal treatment is advocated, a multitude
of different relations between liberty and equality can result. A theorist
who adopts a negative conception of liberty and sees equality as "social
equality" will have a different view of the relation of liberty and equality
from a political theorist who adopts a positive conception of liberty and
understands equality in terms of "equality before the law." This, though,
is only part of the story. This long-standing debate in political theory can-

not be reduced to a bunch of confused people thinking that they are having an argument about whether freedom and equality conflict, when actually they are not having any argument at all, since they are using the words "freedom" and "equality" in very different ways. Recall again Gallie's notion of essentially contested concept (Section 2.1); each side is not simply employing particular understandings of freedom and equality, but maintaining that their interpretations of the concepts are the best interpretations and so their view of the relation between freedom and equality is the most enlightening. To understand the debate between liberals, socialists, and conservatives about the relation between freedom and equality, we need to grasp not only the different conceptions of freedom and equality they employ, but why they employ these conceptions and why they claim that these are the preferred conceptions.

7.2 Classical Liberalism: Liberty and Basic Equality

Social Contract Theory: An Example of Classical Liberal Egalitarianism

Although, as we shall see, classical liberals are apt to insist on the many ways in which liberty and equality clash, it is clearly wrong to understand classical liberalism as devoted simply to liberty with no concern whatsoever for any sort of equality.[4] Most important, liberals have typically asserted the fundamental equality of each person insofar as each person has natural liberty. As John Locke said, humans are naturally in a "State of perfect Freedom to order their actions . . . as they think fit . . . without asking leave, or depending on the Will of any other Man"[5] (Section 4.3). Thus, Locke argued, because each person is by nature equally free, and not under the authority of any person, political authority can only be justified by the consent of each free and equal person (see Sections 6.3, 10.3).

> Men being, as has been said, by nature, all free, equal, and independent, no one can be put out of this estate, and subjected to the political power of another, without his own consent. The only way whereby any one divests himself of his natural liberty, and puts on the bonds of civil society, is by agreeing with other men to join and unite into a community for their comfortable, safe, and peaceable living one amongst another, in a secure enjoyment of their properties, and a greater security against any, that are not of it.[6]

Now, given that legitimate political authority must be based on the consent of all equally free persons, it follows that only if the authority is impartial (Section 6.2) will everyone agree to it. Any political system that favored some citizens over others would be rejected by those who are disfavored: only an impartial political authority, upholding a system of equal rights, could possibly be accepted by all equally free people. Thus, fundamental to social contract theory is that our status as equally free justifies a political order that is egalitarian insofar as it treats all citizens impartially: no citizen is to be privileged in relation to any other.

In classical liberal theory, this fundamental equality requires a regime that guarantees the equal citizenship (Section 6.4) of each person. Classical liberal equal citizenship has three core elements: (1) It requires that all citizens possess equal rights to negative liberty and equal rights to acquire property and have their property protected. We have already seen how their individualist and pluralist commitments lead classical liberals to favor negative liberty (Section 4.1); importantly, we have also seen how fundamental to classical liberalism is the claim that liberty is only secure when accompanied by private property (Section 5.3). Classical liberals thus posit a world of essentially self-interested individuals, whose main concern is leading their own lives, while disagreeing fundamentally on what is good or what makes life worth living (Sections 3.3, 4.3). Thus, all are concerned to protect their own "Lives, Liberties and Estates."[7] (2) To enforce these rights, individuals require a system of settled law, specifying the extent of their rights, and impartial judges, to fairly decide disputes, with the power to enforce their verdicts (see Sections 5.4, 10.3). Equal citizenship thus requires equality before the law: the impartial resolution of disputes is the defining feature of the classical liberal state, and this can only be achieved if government officials treat individuals strictly according to their legal rights, treating equally those with equal legal rights. This idea of equality before the law applies not only to criminal matters, but to all the administrative functions of the state. What has been called the *Rechtsstaat* is the "legal state," in which administrative as well as criminal functions express equality under the law.[8] (3) Last, the full application of the rule of law to the state requires that its offices be filled on terms that are impartial and do not treat some groups of citizens as privileged over others. Thus, equality of opportunity, applied to public positions, is a development of the ideal of the rule of law.

Mill, Individuality, Utilitarianism, and Classical Liberalism

As I have stressed throughout this book, political theories are complex and diverse. There is more than one form of classical liberalism and more than one classical liberal argument for civic equality. The most important alternative to the social contract argument is advanced by the classical liberal utilitarians. Although many contemporary utilitarians adopt some form of revisionist liberalism, the early utilitarians (and many economists today) employ utilitarian reasoning to endorse classical liberal equal citizenship.

John Stuart Mill provided a utilitarian case for equal liberty rights (Section 4.3). It will be recalled that according to Mill, each person seeks to develop her own capacities; each thus requires freedom to make her own choices about what sort of life best suits her. Thus, says Mill, the proper role of coercive legal rules "is to enforce upon everyone the conduct necessary to give all other persons their fair chance: conduct which chiefly consists in not doing them harm, and not impeding them in anything which without harming others does good to themselves."[9] As we saw earlier (Section 3.1), Mill argues that a society that enforces only these minimum requirements will spur the development of human nature (Sections 3.3, 4.3): once human nature is prevented from growing in "noxious" directions by respecting the basic liberty rights of others, it will "expand itself in useful ones."[10] Thus, given human nature, granting people liberty rights produces overall happiness and development. Assuming that this establishes a case for liberty, does it lead to *equal* liberty? Why not give more liberty to those more capable of development and less liberty to those who, in any case, are not really capable of much? Mill certainly does not believe that everyone is capable of equal development: some people excel at many things and some find it very difficult to do much of anything. Why should liberty be distributed equally? Mill relies here on another developmental argument based on his theory of human nature. In chapter 3 of *On Liberty*, he explicitly considers what to do about those whose development might seem held back by insisting on an equal liberty for all. Mill answers,

> As much compression as is necessary to prevent the stronger specimens of human nature from encroaching on the rights of others, cannot be dispensed with; but for this there is ample compensation even in the point of view of human development. The means of development which the individual loses by being prevented from gratifying his inclinations to the injury of others, are chiefly at the expense of the development of other people. And even to himself there is a full equivalent in the better development of the social part of his nature, rendered possible by the restraint upon the selfish part. To be held to rigid rules of justice for the sake of others, develops the feelings and capacities which have the good of others for their object.[11]

Mill thus advances two arguments for restraining the "stronger specimens of human nature." First, controlling them aids the development of the "weaker specimens" whose lives they would encroach on. But second, and I think more interestingly, Mill thinks that the "stronger specimens" so restrained receive a "full equivalent": whatever opportunities for individual development are closed off to them, the development of their social nature is enhanced by a system that secures equal rights for everyone.

The argument based on the development of human nature is, I think, the core of *On Liberty*, and, indeed, of John Stuart Mill's whole political philosophy. And Mill manifestly thinks it is a utilitarian argument: those who develop their capacities lead rich, fulfilled, and satisfying lives, whereas those who fail to develop their natures are lethargic and un-happy. But about midway through chapter 3, Mill pauses and reflects,

> Having said that Individuality is the same thing with development, and that it is only the cultivation of individuality which produces, or can produce, well-developed human beings, I might here close the argument: for what more or better can be said of any condition of human affairs, than that it brings human beings themselves nearer to the best they can be? Or what worse can be said of any obstruction to good, than that it prevents this?[12]

Nevertheless, Mill thinks that the argument based on human nature might not be enough. Those who most need convincing, Mill says, are not those who cherish the ideal of development, but those who do not much care about the ideal. So, after giving all these inspiring arguments about the development of human nature and making each person the best being she can be, Mill turns to a more mundane issue: what good are developed people to those who are unconcerned with development?

Mill's answer focuses on the idea of *progress*. Progress in societies, he maintains, depends on allowing freedom so that people of genius can grow. Mill paints a picture of the exceptional individual versus the collec-tive mass. The mass of society, according to Mill, is a "collective medioc-rity": it is composed of people who tend to *conform* and are not interested in new ideas. Mill insists, however, that even this collective mass benefits from allowing people of genius to develop in an atmosphere of freedom. The few who do think and invent are "the salt of the earth: without them, human life would become a stagnant pool."[13] As Mill sees it, "The initia-tion of all wise or noble things, comes and must come from individuals, generally at first from some one individual."[14] Mill, writing in 1859, pointed to China as an example of a civilization that had managed to root out individuality. And in China, he thought, progress had halted. The un-dermining of individuality had thus resulted in the development of a stagnant society. The upshot of Mill's account, then, is that for a society to advance—to increase material abundance and the comforts of life, as well as intellectual improvements—at the very least the elite needs freedom.

The question, however, is whether Mill's argument establishes the need for specialized freedom applying only to the elite or freedom for the society as a whole. According to Mill, it is the latter. He says, "Genius can only breathe freely in an *atmosphere* of freedom."[15] Only a general freedom—a society in which there is a wide-ranging freedom for citizens to act as they choose—will genius prosper. So, although this case for liberty stresses the role of the exceptional individual in spurring progress, Mill advocates equal liberty for all. Only such a general freedom, he thinks, will lead to progress; and even those who are not interested in liberty or development will benefit from material progress.

Liberty Versus Equality: The Dangers of Social Equality

Implicit in Mill's argument for equal liberty is a concern that social equality is a danger to individuality. Mill was greatly influenced by Alexis de Tocqueville's *Democracy in America*. Tocqueville (1805–1859) was convinced that countries such as France were developing toward greater political and social equality; he saw the United States as the country that had gone furthest down this egalitarian road. He traveled to America in 1831 to study this new regime of social equality. His findings were ambivalent; he reported, "I am full of apprehensions and of hopes. I perceive mighty dangers which it is possible to ward off, mighty evils which may be avoided or alleviated."[16] Tocqueville believed that the progress of political and social equality led to a society of "a countless multitude of beings, shaped in each other's likeness, amid whom nothing rises and nothing falls."[17] He observed an America with tremendous pressures to conform—for each to be like his or her neighbor. The spirit of social equality favored sameness (Section 6.4); no one wished to stand out as exceptional, defying the democratic mass:

> As the conditions of men become equal among a people, individuals seem of less and society of greater importance; or rather every citizen, being assimilated in the rest, is lost in a crowd, and nothing stands conspicuous but the great and imposing image of the people at large. This naturally gives the man of democratic periods a lofty opinion of the privileges of society and a very humble notion of the rights of individuals; they are ready to admit that the interests of the former are everything and those of the latter nothing.[18]

This becomes a fundamental theme in classical liberal thought: social equality is understood as allied to a moral collectivism, which counts the good of the collective as "everything" and that of the individual as "nothing."[19] Equality thus understood is in conflict with Millian individuality and his case for negative liberty.

This is not to say, however, that either Tocqueville or Mill opposed the movement toward greater equality. As Tocqueville put it, "A state of equality is perhaps less elevated, but it is more just. . . . [However] No man on the earth can as yet affirm, absolutely and generally, that the new state of the world is better than its [inegalitarian] former one."[20] For Mill, the spirit of equality and democracy can, under some conditions, protect freedom, whereas under others it can destroy it: "Equality may be equal freedom or equal servitude."[21] If equality is understood as equal liberty for each to live his own life as he pleases, and equal citizenship, classical liberals see no danger in it. But following Tocqueville's analysis, if the spirit of equality leads to elevation of "the people" over the individual, and to conformity over individuality, then liberty and equality are in inherent conflict. Tocqueville concluded *Democracy in America* by observing, "The nations of our time cannot prevent the conditions of men from becoming equal, but it depends upon themselves whether the principle of equality is to lead them to servitude or freedom, to knowledge or barbarism, to prosperity or wretchedness."[22]

Liberty Versus Economic Equality

Equality is in conflict with liberty and individuality insofar as it takes the form of social equality, which is both morally collectivist (Section 3.4) and conformist. Classical liberals also insist that the pursuit of economic equality is at odds with individual liberty. Or as it is sometimes put, people's liberty upsets the pattern of income and wealth that economic equality strives after. This position has been upheld by a contemporary classical liberal, Robert Nozick. To make his point, Nozick tells the following story about Wilt Chamberlain, a star basketball player who is in great demand. Living is a fully egalitarian society, Wilt decides on a way to improve his salary: He will only agree to play if a box is put outside the arena with "For Wilt, 25¢" written on it and each spectator pays the extra twenty-five cents. If one million people go to home games, Wilt ends up with $250,000 more than he was allotted in the egalitarian distribution. Now, it would appear that to sustain the equal distribution the government must interfere with free transactions between Wilt and his fans: the government must stop the fans from giving him the additional quarter of a million dollars. So, Nozick argues, any attempt to ensure economic equality will require interfering with the liberty of citizens to do as they wish, and this makes the pursuit of economic egalitarianism objectionable.[23]

Some object that that an egalitarian taxation system does not interfere with people's liberty, it simply taxes them—it alters the relation between their gross and net incomes. But, say these critics, that hardly constitutes a limitation of freedom. No one is forcing you to act against your will. Nozick has a strong (and controversial) reply: he maintains that such taxation is essentially the same thing as forced labor—that is, slavery. He reasons that since a person must work extra to pay the egalitarian tax, some proportion of her working day is devoted to paying the tax, that is, working so that others will benefit. But to be forced to work to benefit others is precisely what is meant by forced labor. One concern about Nozick's argument is that it appears to prove too much: it would seem to show that all taxation is forced labor. But all classical liberals endorse some governmental activities, so all endorse some form of taxation; but if taxation is forced labor, all classical liberals endorse forced labor, hardly an inviting conclusion. Nozick's main point, however, can be less controversially put. Insofar as economic egalitarianism requires coercive transfers of funds from some to others, egalitarianism intrinsically limits liberty. To be sure, this does not show that it is unjustified, for all laws limit liberty. It does, though, indicate that the pursuit of economic equality inevitably clashes with negative liberty, which is the crucial point of Nozick's tale about Wilt Chamberlain. Moreover, because classical liberals have insisted that property rights have a fundamental role in protecting individual liberty (Section 5.4), coercive impositions that redistribute property are especially hostile to a system of negative liberty.

This classical liberal argument against any sort of economic equality depends on two claims:

(1) Economic equality requires a certain pattern of property holdings; and

(2) The natural result of negative liberty is to upset such a pattern.

Claim (2) is crucial. As F. A. Hayek, argues, "From the fact that people are very different it follows that if we treat them equally [that is, primarily by ensuring that all have equal liberty], the result must be inequality in their actual position."[24] Ludwig von Mises, another great classical liberal of the twentieth century, is even more adamant:

Nothing . . . is as ill-founded as the assertion of the alleged equality of all members of the human race. Men are altogether unequal. Even between brothers there exists the most marked differences in physical and mental attributes. Nature never repeats itself in its creations: it produces nothing by the dozen, nor are its products standardized. Each man who leaves her workshop bears the imprint of the individual, the unique never-to-recur. Men are not equal.[25]

Thus, if we seek to ensure equal results—an equal distribution of resources or welfare, for example—we can only do so by interfering with equal liberty: some people must be restrained, or granted additional favors denied to others, if we are to obtain equal results. So, the natural differences in human nature, coupled with equal liberty, according to the

classical liberal, translate into inequalities in property holdings; to equalize property holdings requires that some people's liberty be restricted. Of
course, as socialists have noted, this presupposes a liberal theory of human nature (Section 3.3): it supposes that in the light of the human differences, people will wish to pursue their own aims and accumulate resources rather than seek to aid each other and maintain an egalitarian
distribution.[26] If people were thoroughly cooperative, the pursuit of
equality need not conflict with individual liberty.

7.3 Revisionist Liberalisms

Liberal Egalitarianism: Liberty Reduced to Equality

We have seen that classical liberalism has a significant egalitarian element. Only a system of laws that is impartial, and thus enshrines equal
liberty and equal civic status, would be agreed to by equally free persons.
A number of contemporary liberal philosophers have sought to make
equality and impartiality the very heart of liberalism. According to
Ronald Dworkin, for example, "a certain conception of equality," which
he calls "the liberal conception of equality . . . is the nerve of liberalism."[27] Dworkin argues that at the heart of liberalism is a commitment to
treat all individuals equally—with equal concern and respect. For
Dworkin, this equality derives from pluralism (Section 3.2) and the fundamental requirement of being impartial between competing conceptions of the good life (Section 6.2):

> Equality supposes that political decisions must be, so far as possible, inde-
> pendent of any particular conception of the good life, or whatever gives
> value to life. Since the citizens differ in their conceptions, the government
> does not treat them as equals if it prefers one conception to another, either
> because the officials believe that one is intrinsically superior, or because one
> is held by the more numerous or powerful group.[28]

Thus far, most classical liberals would concur. But for Dworkin and his
followers, this generates a case not simply for equal civic status, but for
equality of resources and opportunities. As Dworkin sees it, for the political system to distribute resources on any other basis would be to "assume either that the fate of some people should be of greater concern
than that of others, or that the ambitions and talents of some are more
worthy, and so should be supported more generously on that account."[29]
    What is of particular interest in Dworkin's proposal, however, is not
simply that he bases an argument for equal resources and opportunities
on impartiality, but that he also grounds individual liberty rights on im-

partiality. Dworkin is critical of a hybrid view of liberalism, which conceives of liberalism as devoted to both liberty and equality as independent values. On the hybrid view, liberals care deeply for liberty, but give equality an important, though limited, role. Dworkin suggests that those who adopt this hybrid conception are apt to contrast liberalism to conservatism and socialism, arguing that conservatism gives greater weight to liberty and less to equality than does liberalism, whereas socialism gives equality a more dominant role than does liberalism. Dworkin, however, understands liberalism in a monistic way: its core value is equality, not liberty. Indeed, he believes that the very idea of a general right to liberty is confused. There is, he insists, no general "commodity" liberty that we always value. On the traditional classical liberal view (Sections 4.3, 5.4), liberty is itself always a good thing; of course, we may give up some of it to secure other goods such as security from attack, but, in itself, it is always better to have liberty than lose it. Dworkin disagrees. The liberty to drive on the left side of the street is of no value at all in the United States, he maintains, and no sane person thinks she loses something by giving it up. In place of the general concept of liberty, then, Dworkin follows the traditional conservative route of identifying a list of basic liberties (Section 5.4). What is important is not liberty, but certain civil liberties.[30]

What makes Dworkin's version of liberalism so radical is that he not only dismisses the general concept of liberty but maintains that the important civil liberties are grounded in equality. According to his egalitarian liberalism, liberties such as freedom of speech and association are ways to achieve equal concern and respect. The equal distribution of liberties is an instance of the general case for an equal distribution of resources and opportunities. The special status attributed to these basic liberties in liberal thought does not derive from the unique importance of freedom, but from our commitment to equal concern and respect and the need to protect people from the external preferences of others (Section 6.4). External preferences, it will be recalled, are a person's preferences that other people act in the way he wants; if you are a Catholic, you might have an external preference that everyone be Catholic. To make me conform to your external preferences, presumably, would not be to treat me with equal concern and respect; freedom of religion ensures me protection from your external preferences.

Egalitarian liberalism, then, avoids conflicts between liberty and equality by putting equality on center stage and entirely banishing liberty in general. It must be wondered whether liberalism is rendered more plausible by, first, almost entirely removing its traditional core and, second, depicting it as expressing simply one value—and a value that has traditionally had a complex and difficult place in liberal theory.[31] In any event, it seems clear that egalitarian liberalism is a narrow understanding of liberalism: liberalism is depicted as a theory about how a distributor of good things should distribute them. It takes the perspective of a distributor of treatments for a society as a whole—for example, the distribution of resources, rights, or opportunities—and provides an impartial criterion for all these distributions: distribute them in a way that accords with equal concern and respect. The theory, then, assumes that liberalism is essentially a theory to guide an organization that distributes benefits. Interestingly, the theory does not adequately explain why an individual demands that the distributor-government respect her choices about how she is to live her life. To the egalitarian liberal, the individual's demand for respect stems from her right to be treated as an equal to others: her objection to nonrespectful state interference is that it fails to treat her equally with others. But it is at best dubious that the individual's real complaint here is that she is not being treated as an equal; much more plausible, I think, is the simpler idea that she just wishes to live her life as she sees fit—she seeks to be free to pursue a vision of the good life without undue interference by others. Liberalism certainly presupposes that individuals are free and equal; it is much more doubtful that it claims we are equal, and so must in some ways be treated as free.

Hobhouse's Revisionist Liberalism: Self-Determination, the Common Good, and Equality

Thus far, we have seen that classical liberals endorse a basic requirement of equal treatment—equal civic status—while stressing the ways in which social and economic equality conflict with liberty and individuality. Dworkin's egalitarian liberalism seeks to overcome the clash between liberty and equality by grounding liberalism, including its basic liberty rights, purely on equality. The "new liberal" theory of L. T. Hobhouse offers a different way to reconcile liberty and equality within the liberal tradition. Unlike Dworkin, Hobhouse never denies that liberty is the heart of liberalism. Following T. H. Green (Section 4.2), though, Hobhouse advocates a positive account of freedom: a free person is "self-determined"—we might say autonomous—in that her self constitutes a "harmonious whole."[32] Hobhouse believes, however, that such internal "moral" freedom needs to be supplemented by social freedom—the freedom of "man in society." Now, social freedom, as liberals generally recognize, requires constraints; if people are to be self-determined in society, there must be limits on what others may do to them and what they may do to others. In a state of nature or anarchy, people can constantly interfere with my self-determination by coercing and restraining me (Sections 4.3, 8.2). Thus, argues Hobhouse, social freedom presupposes a system of

social restraints. Unlike classical liberals, who see law as a system of restraints that takes away some of our liberty so as to better protect the rest,
Hobhouse sees no clash between law and freedom (Section 5.4):

> If Liberty involves restraint, it may be asked whether its pursuit is not illu-
> sory. What is gained from the point of view of liberty by substituting one
> system of restraints [that is, law] for another [that is, restraint by other indi-
> viduals]? Can we find a system of restraints which is consistent with liberty,
> while others are inconsistent?[33]

Hobhouse's answer is that the "the liberty of each . . . must, on the principle of the common good, be limited by the rights of all."[34] Basic to Hobhouse's argument is a strongly monistic view (Section 3.2) that the good
of the individual and the common good of society necessarily are harmonious. Following Green, Hobhouse believes that the good for individuals
is to develop their personalities, but that such development is only possible in a society of developed individuals (see Section 3.3). For both Hobhouse and Green, there is no ultimate conflict between one person's development and the development of others: all persons can only realize
what is best in themselves by participating in a social life with other developed personalities. A free person follows his rational will, and a rational person wills the common good. A free person "comes to realize that
his true good not in some course dictated by self-will but in a modification of that course which opens to him a life compatible with and contributing to the life of society."[35]

The common good, Hobhouse maintains, requires equal rights for all,
so that everyone may develop his or her personality. Equal rights, then, in
no way detract from the individual's good or his true (positive) liberty;
indeed, equal rights are *required* by true liberty. On Hobhouse's view,
equal rights to contribute to the common good, including not only the
traditional liberal liberties but "equal satisfaction of equal needs"[36] (Section 6.4), are implied by liberty. It is fairly obvious how the plausibility of
this reconciliation of liberty and equality depends on accepting a rationalistic and monistic view of liberty and a collectivist view of society. Liberty
is rationalistic (Section 4.3) insofar as true freedom requires a self-determined will that pursues its true good; the theory is monistic (Section 3.2)
insofar as the true good for one person necessarily involves and supports
the true good for other people. In contrast to Berlin's pluralism (Sections
3.2, 4.3), there is no tragic conflict of competing conceptions of the good
life in Hobhouse's theory. Last, as Hobhouse himself was apt to point out,
the theory is collectivistic (Section 3.4): it supposes that the good for one
person is intimately bound up with the common good of his society.

Pluralism, Liberty, and Equality

There is a much simpler route from classical liberalism to a revisionist liberalism that seeks to advance economic equality. A pluralist liberal might insist that although negative liberty is a crucial social value in a world in which people must choose what values to pursue (Section 4.3), a pluralist political theory need not always choose liberty over equality. Indeed, Isaiah Berlin, the most prominent exponent of pluralism and negative liberty, is very clear about this:

> I do not wish to say that individual freedom is, even in the most liberal societies, the sole, or even the dominant, criterion of social action. We compel children to be educated, and we forbid public executions. These are certainly curbs to freedom. We justify them on the ground that ignorance, or a barbarian upbringing, or cruel pleasures and excitements are worse for us than the amount of restraint needed to repress them. . . .
>
> The extent of a man's, or a people's, liberty to choose to live as they desire must be weighed against the claims of many other values, of which equality, or justice, or happiness, or security, or public order are perhaps the most obvious examples.[37]

That liberty and equality clash—that we cannot have all of both, and so we must weigh them and choose between them—does not itself imply that we must always choose liberty. Because classical liberals are devoted to individuals and their ends, and see most forms of equality as a threat to individuality, they typically oppose equality. But pluralism itself does not lead to this strong ranking of liberty over equality. Some revisionist liberals view the modern welfare state as a balancing of the demands of liberty and equality: civil liberties such as freedom of speech, association, the press, and religion take precedence over equality, but once those liberties have been secured, the pursuit of economic equality is justified.[38] Thus, at the heart of much revisionist liberal thinking is the claim that economic liberties to buy, to sell, and to advertise are less important than civil liberties and more easily overridden for the sake of economic and social equality.

7.4 A Socialist Reconciliation Proposal

As I pointed out in Section 3.1, almost all socialist theories agree in claiming that, properly understood, liberty and equality do not conflict (in this respect, Hobhouse's revisionist liberalism concurs). A very nice example of a socialist case for the harmony of liberty and equality is presented by

Richard Norman in his book *Free and Equal,* in which he explicitly challenges the claim that liberty and equality are at odds.

Norman on Effective Choice and Liberty

Let us begin by briefly considering Norman's views on liberty, which combine a view of liberty as a self-chosen life (Section 4.2) with freedom as power (Section 5.1). According to Norman, "You are free in so far as you are in a position to make choices":

> In maintaining that freedom consists in being able to make choices, we must add that the degree of freedom is determined not by the sheer number of choices available, but by the range of meaningful choice. And here the phrase "range of meaningful choice" must refer both to the areas of people's lives in which they can make choices and the options from which they can choose. [39]

Norman argues that in addition to noninterference, effective choice requires (1) political, (2) material, and (3) cultural conditions. The *political conditions* concern one's ability to participate in collective decision-making. "It seems plausible," he writes, "to suppose that institutional arrangements which give me some degree of political power will, to that extent, increase my capacity to make choices about the affairs of the society in which I live, and therefore about my own life. In other words, an increase in democracy would seem to be an increase in freedom."[40] As we have already seen (Section 5.1), it is clear how *material conditions* increase one's effective choice.

> If I inherit a fortune or win the pools or, less spectacularly, get a new job which will provide me with a larger income, new opportunities become available to me which were previously inaccessible: I can travel to different places, engage in different activities or pastimes—new worlds, geographically new or culturally new, are opened up for me. The connection with freedom lies not in the greater material comforts or enjoyments, but in the increase of possibilities—the greater scope for choice.[41]

Norman's third condition for freedom concerns education and other *cultural opportunities.* As we saw in Section 4.3, for the advocate of positive freedom education is liberating: it adds to freedom by expanding the options available. Education also adds to freedom because it seeks to make people into better choosers, promoting the critical capacities necessary for an autonomous life.

Cooperation and Equality

Fundamental to almost all socialist theories is a cooperative view of un-corrupted human nature and the ideal society. Competitive individual-ism, socialists typically argue, is a pathological psychological state pro-duced by capitalist productive relations, which give some power over others (Section 5.3). Humans are, by nature, social creatures, more in-clined to cooperation than conflict. "To enter into co-operative relations with others," writes Norman, is "to commit oneself to the point of view of a shared project, it is to replace the question, 'What will benefit me?' with the question 'What will benefit us?'"[42] If people adopt this collec-tivist view of our nature and our projects, two things follow:

> First, this will affect the way they make decisions. It will be a joint decision, not one imposed by some of them on others. Everyone will be able to have their say. If possible, they will try to agree on a decision acceptable to them all. If they cannot reach an agreement, they will at any rate make sure that everyone's view is taken into account. . . .
>
> [The second thing that follows from a commitment to co-operation is that the] set of arrangements which is adopted by the group must be one which can be justified to each of its members. If a co-operative group is one in which each person has an equal say, then each of them can make an equal claim on the group; those claims, therefore, can properly be satisfied only by a state of affairs in which all benefit equally overall.[43]

The cooperative society, then, will require, first, *political equality*. Norman is clear that political equality requires more than just equal voting rights: "It requires a shift of the balance of power between electors and elected. It requires that political representatives should be more answerable to those whom they represent, so that genuine power lies with the latter."[44] Norman also thinks equal power requires economic democracy (Section 9.2), according to which the principles of majority rule should be applied to the management of the firm, such that the workers, through represen-tatives, manage the firm for themselves. Norman thus believes that this cooperative social life is incompatible with capitalism, in which the own-ers manage the firm and instruct the workers what to do. It requires a so-cial ownership of industry that allows the workers to democratically manage their own firms.

Norman also endorses *resource equality* in the cooperative society. He does not mean by this that everyone is to have precisely the same goods, or that those with special needs are not to be accorded more. Rather, he argues that "everyone should benefit equally overall from their participa-tion in a co-operative community."[45] There should be "free communal

The Conditions for Effective Choice	The Conditions for Cooperative Equality
1. Political Power	1. Equal Political Power
2. Material Resources for Development	2. Equal Material Benefits from Cooperation
3. Cultural Resources	3. Equal Cultural Resources

FIGURE 7.1   Conditions for Effective Choice and Cooperative Equality

provision of goods to satisfy basic needs, and, beyond that, the distribution of wealth in such a way that everyone benefits equally overall
from the work of the community on the condition that, if they are able to,
they participate in such work."[46] Norman thus appears to allow that
those who have special burdens or who work at hard jobs require extra
compensation. He sees this as reflecting a more basic equality. They receive extra rewards to cancel out the extra work they did: in the end
everyone should receive something like equal overall benefits.

Last, Norman maintains that the cooperative socialist society will provide *equal cultural opportunities*. Educational equality, he says, is especially important in producing an egalitarian society. What is particularly
important is the equal opportunity of each child to develop his or her capacities. Norman, of course, does not accept the liberal ideal of equal opportunity as the equal opportunity to compete for the best jobs and so
climb to the top of society (he calls this the "ladder" notion of equality of
opportunity). Instead, he argues that each person, regardless of his or her
capacities, should have the opportunity to develop them.

The Convergence of the Demands for Liberty and Equality

It now should be clear why Norman thinks his notion of positive liberty
is not in conflict with the demands of equality. As Figure 7.1 shows, the
conditions for cooperative equality are simply the equalization of the
conditions for freedom as effective choice!

It is worth emphasizing again in what way Norman's theory is monistic. Like T. H. Green—whom he explicitly follows—Norman believes that
there is a true goal for each of us: to develop into good choosers with developed capacities. He thus adopts a positive notion of freedom: to be a
free person is to be such a developed chooser. Norman's cooperative society gives everyone the things he or she needs to become such a chooser:
because we all have the same general goal, we all need these resources if
we are to do what we desire. Moreover, Norman's effort to show that no
conflict exists between freedom and equality is itself monistic: it manifests a conviction that, properly understood, the values worth having

must go together. We cannot be faced with choice between two desirable values, having to sacrifice some of one to achieve more of the other.

7.5 The Conservative Critique of Equality

According to Robert Nisbet,

> There is no principle more basic in the conservative philosophy than that of the inherent and absolute incompatibility between liberty and equality. Such incompatibility springs from the contrary objectives of the two values. The abiding purpose of liberty is its protection of individual and family property—a word used in its widest sense to include the immaterial as well as the material in life. The inherent objective of equality, on the other hand, is that of some kind of redistribution or leveling of the unequally shared material and immaterial values of a community. Moreover, individual strengths of mind and body being different from birth, all efforts to compensate through law and government for this diversity of strength can only cripple the liberties of those involved; especially the liberties of the strongest and the most brilliant. This is, in brief, the view which conservative philosophers have unfailingly taken, from Burke on, on the relation between liberty and equality.[47]

We can trace the conservative hostility to equality to its theory of human nature, its antirationalism, and its theory of society.

Human Nature and Inequality

"Men are by nature unequal. It is vain, therefore, to treat them as if they were equal."[48] More than even the classical liberal, the conservative is struck by the basic and ineradicable inequalities between people. It is not society, but nature, that makes people unequal, and it makes them unequal in every possible dimension of life. They are unequally moral; unequally patriotic; unequal in physically abilities; unequally fit for leadership; unequally intellectually talented; unequally good at being fathers, or mothers, or teachers; and so on. Hobhouse (Section 6.3) once insisted that despite the many ways in which people were different, their common human nature "lies far deeper than all the differences between them."[49] No so for a conservative. What is common is largely overshadowed by our differences.

In light of this, calls for equality are apt to be seen not only as vain but as motivated by pride and envy. Those who are too proud to admit that others are their betters are constantly insisting on the equality of everyone. "All men are equal," the conservative suspects, is motivated by a boastful conviction that "no one is better than me"—and it is almost certainly false. Alternatively, equality may be motivated by envy and spite; seeing others more successful, seeing their high status and their wealth, those without it want it; and if they cannot have it, they will insist that no one has it. Recall that equality can be satisfied by denying goods to some, as well as providing them to everyone (Section 6.3). Thus, Nisbet worries that calls for equality are attacks on the brilliant and talented, for it is often they who have what others want. In this regard, the conservative might point out that in Australia, a distinctly egalitarian country, when a public figure or business person is disgraced or suffers a social or economic fall, people often contentedly remark on the desirability of cutting "tall poppies"—those who have stood out and grown too high require cutting down to size.[50]

Antirationalism and Social Complexity

Because people are so different and unequal, and because societies develop over long periods of time and are thus not planned, all human societies are characterized by numerous institutions and associations that displease egalitarians. The economy is divided into those who have wealth and those who do not. The institution of the family produces economic inequality, because the children of good parents as a rule are more successful than the children of parental failures; within the family, parents have authority over children, and to the exasperation of egalitarians, the family continues to divide tasks on sexual lines. The Catholic Church is officially sexist, universities are intellectually elitist, athletic clubs disfavor the physically handicapped, and so on. As a conservative sees it, these institutions, some of which are voluntary and some not, have functions in society, although no one can give a complete account of any complex institution and its functions. Given the complexity of human society, no single person or group of people can fully understand its workings. What we call a "society" is the complex system of these institutions: take away business corporations, the family, universities, schools, churches, and the rest, and there would be nothing left of American society.

The conservative charges that because each of these institutions is in some way a source of inequality, egalitarian socialists dream of reforming each and every one of them according to an egalitarian plan. But, says the conservative, this rationalist project is doomed to failure, since societies are far too complex to be guided by any rational plan or theory. Furthermore, to produce social and economic equality requires a plan backed by a political authority with tremendous power (see further Section 10.4). Of such collectivism, Michael Oakeshott observes,

The opposition of collectivism to freedom appears first in the collective rejection of the whole notion of the diffusion of power and of a society organized by a means of a multitude of genuinely voluntary associations. . . .
The organization to be imposed upon society springs from the minds of
those who compose the government. It is a comprehensive organization.
. . . And great power is required for the over-all control of this organization.
. . . Having discouraged all other means of social and industrial regulation, a
collectivist government must enforce its imposed order or allow society to
relapse into chaos. . . . All this is, clearly, an impediment to freedom; but
there is more to follow. In addition to the rule of law, and often in place of it,
collectivism depends for its working upon a lavish use of discretionary authority. The organization it imposes on society is without any inner momen-
tum: it must keep going by promiscuous, day-to-day interventions—controls of prices, licenses to buy and sell, the perpetual readjustment of rations,
and the distribution of privileges and exemptions—by the exercise, in short,
of the kind of power most subject to misuse and corruption.

Collectivism is indifferent to all elements of our freedom and the enemy
of some.[51]

It is important to remember that that the first great conservative work,
Burke's *Reflections on the Revolution in France*, was a criticism of the first
great egalitarian revolution, the French Revolution of 1789. The revolutionaries were willing to sweep away those parts of French political culture that did not correspond to their abstract ideas in order to bring about
thoroughgoing civic and social equality. Burke warned that such a rationalist project could only end in disaster.

Egalitarian Collectivism, Conservative Organicism, and Liberal Individualism

Conservatives, then, join liberals such as Mill (Section 7.2) in heeding
Tocqueville's warning that social egalitarianism is apt to lead to a moral
perspective that counts the good of the collective as "everything" and
that of the individual as "nothing." Millian liberals and conservatives
have different objections to such a collectivism, however. Millian liberals,
as we saw, see it as a threat to individuality and free choice. Of course, it
is not the only such threat: Mill was equally critical of custom, which led
to the servitude of women and often discouraged individuality. Conservatives, in contrast, are defenders of custom: it reflects practical wisdom
that has been slowly accumulated over generations and provides a much
better guide to action than a rationalist defense of liberty such as that offered by Mill. Many conservatives object to egalitarian collectivism, not
because it favors society over the individual, but because it is based on a

confused understanding of society. Egalitarian collectivism, charges a certain sort of conservative, sees society as a machine that can be designed to work just the way we want it to, and indeed a very simple machine, composed of almost identical, equal parts. Indeed, the conservative is apt to suggest that there is an odd sort of individualism at the core of socialist egalitarianism, since it sees the collective as composed of a mass of thoroughly equal individual units. Important to the conservative tradition has been the idea that society is better understood as an organism or a complex animal. An organism such as a mammal is composed of a variety of different parts with different and unequal functions. Most are necessary, but some are not. And some have controlling functions, whereas others, although important, must obey if they are to fulfill their functions (Section 10.1). Moreover, no one really can explain exactly how such an organism works; we certainly cannot alter it to conform to our plans about what ideal animals should look like. If society is to be understood in this sort of "organic" way, a true collectivism will recognize the importance of custom, the institutions of a society, and will be wary of anyone's claim to be able to plan and drastically reform the nature of the organism.

Conservatism and Liberal Egalitarianism

In sum, the typical conservative case against social and economic equality is that (1) people are naturally unequal in a variety of ways, (2) societies develop institutions and practices that reflect this deep inequality, and so these practices themselves are inegalitarian, (3) the project of establishing social and economic equality must therefore involve a radical restructuring of society and so (4) must give great power to government. But (5) because equality can only be achieved by rooting out social practices and negating natural tendencies, this power constantly will be used to interfere with traditional liberties; (6) because no such plan can possibly cope with the full complexity of society, it will inevitably fail, though the efforts to save it may lead to long periods of repression. Classical liberals such as Hayek and von Mises would agree with essentially all of this. Classical liberals and conservatives, then, join in rejecting egalitarian projects. What do conservatives tend to say about liberal egalitarianism?

Conservatives, like liberals and socialists, have differing views about the proper extent of equality. As a reasonable generalization, however, we can say that conservatives favor a more limited interpretation of civic equality than liberals and are more skeptical of equality of opportunity and political equality. Conservatives in the Anglo-American tradition have overwhelmingly endorsed equality before the law, which has been fundamental to British law for centuries.[52] Oakeshott, in particular, has been insistent that only a society founded on the rule of law can secure freedom and avoid collectivism. That said, though, conservatives have been much more reluctant to embrace the idea of civic equality, understood as including not simply equality before the law, but equality of legal rights between classes, sexes, and so on. John Stuart Mill, for example, was a strong proponent of equal legal rights for women, and he was quite prepared to undermine customary notions of the family and marriage to achieve such civic equality. Writing in 1869, Mill proclaimed that "the principle which regulates the existing social relations between sexes—the legal subordination of one sex to another—is wrong in itself, and is now one of the chief impediments to human improvement; and that it ought to be replaced by a principle of perfect equality, admitting no power or privilege on the one side, nor disability on the other."[53] Conservatives, not surprisingly, have long upheld the importance of differentiated roles, including differentiated sexual roles, and conceive of liberal efforts to equalize rights as destructive to social stability. So too have conservatives been critical of equal opportunity; although advocating fairness and efficiency in selection processes, the idea that opportunities can be equalized among citizens of diverse backgrounds is dismissed as another rationalist delusion.[54]

More generally, conservatives have expressed reservations about the egalitarian and rationalist tendencies of all legislation. As Elie Halévy (1870–1937) noted, all laws are egalitarian and individualist because they tend to treat each person as a distinct, abstract, legal individual on par with all the rest. In his discussion of Bentham's liberalism, Halévy points out that general legislation is also inherently rationalist. As will be recalled from Section. 3.2,

> The rationalist is inclined to neglect the particular in order to confine himself to the consideration of the general. The existence of "general facts" provides him with a convenient means of distinguishing, in a roundabout way, the necessary from the accidental. Granted the existence of individuals, he finds it convenient to admit, first of all, that individuals can be considered . . . equal.[55]

This is not to say that conservatives are opposed to legislation, but it does indicate a cautious attitude about quickly resorting to legislation to respond to the difficulties of social life, for it cannot take account of the particularity and context that often are crucial to an adequate response (see Section 5.4).

7.6 Summary

My main aim in this book is to show how and why the main enduring political theories have interpreted political concepts differently. Following on the consideration of the concept of equality in Chapter 6, this chapter examined, first, why classical liberals, revisionist liberals, socialists, and conservatives endorse different types of equal treatment; and, second, how their differing interpretations of the concepts of liberty and equality lead them to competing positions on one of the central questions of political theory: do liberty and equality conflict?

Section 7.2 argued that classical liberals, starting from their assumption of equal freedom and the need for impartial political authority, endorse equality before the law and civic equality. They are firm critics of social and economic equality, however, which they see as threats to the core concept of negative liberty. In general, classical liberals insist that the protection of negative liberty is incompatible with the pursuit of most forms of equality. Sections 7.3 and 7.4 considered attempts to reconcile liberty and equality. Section 7.3 analyzed revisionist liberal proposals. I first examined Dworkin's argument that liberalism is based on equality and basic liberties are derived from an ideal of equal treatment, a view of liberalism about which I expressed some skepticism. Closer to the revisionist liberalism of T. H. Green is Hobhouse's claim that true, positive liberty requires a self-determined will directed to the common good, and because the common good requires an equality of rights, true liberty is necessarily consistent with, in fact requires, an equality of rights, including rights to have needs satisfied. In Section 7.4, I considered a positive liberty argument more typical of socialism than revisionist liberalism—Norman's analysis that equates freedom with the conditions for effective choice. If to be free is to have material, political, and cultural resources necessary for effective choice, and if a cooperative society requires equality of material, political, and cultural resources, equal liberty simply *is* an egalitarian distribution of resources. Finally, Section 7.5 examined conservative critiques of both socialist and liberal notions of equality.

Notes

1. Jean-Jacques Rousseau, *The Social Contract,* Maurice Cranston, trans. (London: Penguin Books, 1968 [1762]), Book 2, chap. 11. Emphasis in original.

2. J. Roland Pennock, *Democratic Political Theory* (Princeton: Princeton University Press, 1979), p. 16.

3. Erik von Kuehnelt-Leddihn, *Liberty or Equality: The Challenge of Our Time* (London: Hollis and Carter, 1952).

4. See Will Kymlicka, *Contemporary Political Philosophy: An Introduction* (Oxford: Oxford University Press, 1990), p. 5.

5. John Locke, *Second Treatise of Government,* in Peter Laslett, ed., *Two Treatises of Government* (Cambridge: Cambridge University Press, 1960), sect. 4.

6. Ibid., sect. 95.

7. Ibid., sect. 124.

8. For a survey of developments in understanding the *Rechtsstaat* in relation to classical liberal ideals, see F. A. Hayek, *The Constitution of Liberty* (London: Routledge and Kegan Paul, 1960), chap. 13.

9. John Stuart Mill, *Auguste Comte and Positivism*, in J. M. Robson, ed., *The Collected Works of John Stuart Mill* (Toronto: University of Toronto Press, 1963), vol. 10, p. 339.

10. Ibid.

11. John Stuart Mill, *On Liberty*, in John Gray, ed., *On Liberty and Other Essays* (New York: Oxford University Press, 1991), chap. 3, para. 9.

12. Ibid., chap. 3, para. 10.

13. Ibid., chap. 3, para. 11.

14. Ibid., chap. 3, para. 13.

15. Ibid., chap. 3, para. 11. Emphasis in original.

16. Alexis de Tocqueville, *Democracy in America*. Henry Reeve, trans. (New York: Alfred A. Knopf, 1946), vol. 2, p. 334.

17. Ibid., p. 332

18. Ibid., p. 290.

19. See, for example, Pennock, *Democratic Political Theory*, chaps. 2 and 3.

20. Tocqueville, *Democracy in America*, vol. 2, p. 333.

21. John Stuart Mill, "Democracy in America," in his *Dissertations and Discussions* (New York: Haskell House, 1973), vol. 2, p. 8.

22. Tocqueville, *Democracy in America*, vol. 2, p. 334.

23. Robert Nozick, *Anarchy, State and Utopia* (New York: Basic Books, 1974), p. 161. For a sustained socialist criticism, see G. A. Cohen, *Self-Ownership, Freedom and Equality* (Cambridge: Cambridge University Press, 1995), chap. 1.

24. Hayek, *The Constitution of Liberty*, p. 87.

25. Ludwig von Mises, *Liberalism in the Classical Tradition* (San Francisco: Cobden Press, 1985), p. 26.

26. See Cohen, *Self-Ownership, Freedom and Equality*, p. 29.

27. Ronald Dworkin, "Liberalism," in Stuart Hampshire, ed., *Public and Private Morality* (Cambridge: Cambridge University Press, 1978), p. 115.

28. Ibid., p. 127.

29. Ibid., p. 129.

30. See Ronald Dworkin, *Taking Rights Seriously* (Cambridge, MA: Harvard University Press, 1978), chap. 12.

31. See further, Michael Freeden, *Ideologies and Political Theory: A Conceptual Approach* (Oxford: Oxford University Press, 1996), p. 241.

32. L. T. Hobhouse, *The Elements of Social Justice* (London: George Allen and Unwin, 1922), pp. 55–57.

33. Ibid., p. 59.

34. Ibid., p. 62.

35. Ibid., p. 70.

36. Ibid., p. 111.

37. Isaiah Berlin, "Two Concepts of Liberty," in his *Four Essays on Liberty* (Oxford: Oxford University Press, 1969), pp. 169–170.

38. See, for example, John Rawls, *A Theory of Justice* (Cambridge, MA: Harvard University Press, 1971), p. 106. James P. Sterba characterizes "welfare liberalism"

as a "blend of liberty and equality" in his *Justice: Alternative Political Perspectives*, 2nd ed. (Belmont, CA: Wadsworth, 1992), p. 4.

39. Richard Norman, *Free and Equal: A Philosophical Examination of Political Values* (Oxford: Oxford University Press, 1987), pp. 34, 38.

40. Ibid., p. 41.

41. Ibid., p. 44.

42. Ibid., p. 78.

43. Ibid., p. 70.

44. Ibid., p. 108.

45. Ibid., p. 113.

46. Ibid., p. 119.

47. Robert Nisbet, *Conservatism* (Milton Keynes, UK: Open University Press, 1986), p. 47.

48. James Anthony Froude (1818–1894), "Party Politics," in his *Short Studies on Great Subjects* , 4 vols., (London: Longmans, Green, 1905–1906).

49. Hobhouse, *The Elements of Social Justice*, p. 95.

50. "*Tall poppy:* very important person; influential person; person with status— often held in contempt by others, who try to bring about this person's downfall or ruin." Lenie Johansen, *The Dinkum Dictionary* (Ringwood, Victoria: Claremont Books, 1997), p. 414.

51. Michael Oakeshott, *Rationalism in Politics and Other Essays,* expanded ed. (Indianapolis, IN: Liberty Press, 1991), p. 401.

52. On the French and German traditions, see Noël O'Sullivan, *Conservatism* (London: J. M. Dent, 1976), chaps. 3 and 4.

53. John Stuart Mill, *The Subjection of Women,* in Alice S. Rossie, ed., *Essays on Sex Equality* (Chicago: University of Chicago Press, 1970), p. 125.

54. See, for example, Lincoln Allison, *Right Principles: A Conservative Philosophy of Politics* (Oxford: Blackwell, 1984), pp. 80–84.

55. Elie Halévy, *The Growth of Philosophical Radicalism*, Mary Morris, trans. (London: Farber and Farber, 1928), p. 52. See also Nisbet, *Conservatism*, p. 53.

8

JUSTICE AND LIBERALISM

8.1 The Elements of Justice

Mill's Five Aspects of Justice

In this chapter, we return to the question with which we began the book—
"What is justice?" Unlike Plato, however, we know that we should not be
assuming there is a definition or a core feature that is shared by all notions
of justice and that only characterizes justice (see Section 1.1). This is an important lesson, for the search for the "common attribute" has dominated
investigation of justice. In 1861—over two thousand years after Plato
wrote—John Stuart Mill was still searching for "the distinguishing character of justice." As was typical with Mill, however, he was more cautious
than most, acknowledging that it was a question to be investigated, rather
than a certain assumption, whether "all modes of conduct" designated as
just or unjust share the same quality. To answer this question, Mill begins
in a sensible way: he tries to get a rough feel for the conceptual terrain of
our uses of justice—our main uses of "just" and "unjust." Only once we
understand the main features of the concept of justice, can we try to
arrange them on a conceptual map (Section 2.3).

Mill identifies five "modes of action and arrangements of human affairs, which are classed, by universal or widely spread opinion, as just or
as unjust."[1] (1) "In the first place," says Mill, "it is mostly considered unjust to deprive any one of his personal liberty, his property, or any other
thing which belongs to him by law. Here, therefore, is one instance of the
application of the terms just and unjust in a perfectly definite sense,
namely, that it is just to respect, unjust to violate, the legal rights of any
one." The concept of justice, then, has especially close ties to the law, and
in particular the laws of the country one is in. It would, for example, be
unjust to punish an American for not voting in a U.S. presidential election, because she has a right to abstain; but it would not seem unjust to
punish an Australian for failing to vote in an Australian parliamentary
election, since he does have a duty to vote. The same can be said for a

variety of laws; if there is a law giving one a right, then, as a rule, it would be unjust to deny one that right.

Mill, however, immediately recognizes that (2) "the legal rights of which he is deprived, may be rights which ought not to have belonged to him; in other words, the law which confers on him these rights, may be a bad law. When it is so, or when (which is the same thing for our purpose) it is supposed to be so, opinions will differ as to the justice or injustice of infringing it." According to the Fugitive Slave Law of 1850, slaves' owners had a right to have their fugitive slaves returned to them. Private slave catchers were employed to assist them in securing their legal rights. In one case, slave catchers seized a black man who had worked for nineteen years as a tailor in Poughkeepsie, New York, and returned him to his owner in South Carolina. In 1850, residents of Boston set up a "vigilance committee" to identify and harass these "man-stealers." They put one hunted black couple, the Crafts, on a ship to England. President Fillmore threatened to send in federal troops to uphold the law (and property rights).[2] Did the vigilance committee act unjustly? Many insist that a law that assigns an immoral claim cannot yield a genuine right, and so violating such a rule is no injustice at all. Indeed, the injustice was suffered by the Crafts, who were hunted down in violation of their moral rights. As Mill observed, when

> a law is thought to be unjust, it seems always to be regarded as being so in the same way in which a breach of law is unjust, namely, by infringing somebody's right; which, as it cannot in this case be a legal right, receives a different appellation, and is called a moral right. We may say, therefore, that a second case of injustice consists in taking or withholding from any person that to which he has a moral right.

Features (1) and (2) point to one of the most perplexing aspects of our thinking about justice. Although in some ways our notions of what is just and unjust are closely tied to our legal and judicial system—often it is called "the justice system"—in other ways justice clearly transcends that system and can be used as a way to criticize our current laws and the ways they are applied. It is tempting to simply say that these are just two different notions of justice—what might be called *legal* justice and *ideal* justice. That, however, would fail to appreciate the intimate relations between the two; as we saw in the case of the Fugitive Slave Law, if legal justice departs in a radical way from ideal justice, it seems to lose claim to being justice at all. Our thinking about justice seems torn between the actual and the ideal.[3]

(3) "Thirdly," observes Mill, "it is universally considered just that each person should obtain that (whether good or evil) which he deserves; and

unjust that he should obtain a good, or be made to undergo an evil, which he does not deserve. This is, perhaps, the clearest and most emphatic form in which the idea of justice is conceived by the general mind." One can deserve both good and evil; criminal justice is sometimes understood as giving criminals their "just deserts," that is, punishment. Of course, people can also deserve rewards. Indeed, to one prominent political theorist, "Desert . . . says 'Thank you.'"[4] Claims about what a person deserves are usually of the form: "Person P deserves some treatment T now because of some act Φ that she performed in the past." That is, in most cases of desert one deserves some sort of treatment now because of something that one has already done. A student might be said to deserve a good grade because she worked so hard; or a worker might be said to deserve more pay because he has produced so much. These two examples point to the two most common grounds for desert claims: effort and production.[5] In the case of the student, the ground of the desert claim (what act she has performed that makes her deserving) was that she put in so much effort; in the case of the worker, the desert claim was grounded on how much he produced.

(4) "Fourthly," as Mill says, "it is confessedly unjust to break faith with any one: to violate an engagement, either express or implied, or disappoint expectations raised by our conduct, at least if we have raised those expectations knowingly and voluntarily." Breaking promises and contracts is quintessentially unjust behavior. Of course, as Mill says, few think that it is always unjust to lie or to break a contract: there can be overriding considerations. For example, suppose that a professional killer is looking for his victim and calls you on the phone to ask you whether you know where the victim is. You do, but you tell him that you do not. It then occurs to him that you might have caller ID, and so know who he is; he asks you to promise him not to call the police and give them his name and number. You reason that he will be more likely to flee if you tell him that you will call the police, so you promise him that you will not. As soon as he hangs up, you call the police and give them his name and number. Few think that you have acted unjustly in breaking your promise. Immanuel Kant, though, disagreed. In a similar case (though not involving caller ID), Kant insisted that you were obligated to tell the truth to the killer. "To be truthful (honest) in all your deliberations . . . is a sacred duty and absolutely commanding decree of reason, limited by no expediency."[6]

(5) "Fifthly," Mill maintains, "it is, by universal admission, inconsistent with justice to be partial; to show favour or preference to one person over another, in matters to which favour and preference do not properly apply." Recall that according to Aristotle, justice is treating equals equally and unequals unequally (Section 6.1). This often-cited definition captures

a great deal of what we mean by justice. To act justly is certainly to act impartially; it is to treat relevantly similar cases equally and to distinguish between those who have unequal merits or claims (Section 6.2). Thus, a judge who sentences black defendants to death but gives whites a lighter sentence for the same crime is unjust, as is a teacher who gives higher grades to attractive students just because they are attractive. But although the ideal of impartial treatment captures much of justice, it leaves much unaccounted for. As Mill recognized, and as I stressed in Section 6.1, we do not always have to be impartial:

> Favour and preference are not always censurable, and indeed the cases in which they are condemned are rather the exception than the rule. A person would be more likely to be blamed than applauded for giving his family or friends no superiority in good offices over strangers, when he could do so without violating any other duty; and no one thinks it unjust to seek one person in preference to another as a friend, connection, or companion. Impartiality where rights are concerned is of course obligatory, but this is involved in the more general obligation of giving to every one his right. A tribunal, for example, must be impartial, because it is bound to award, without regard to any other consideration, a disputed object to the one of two parties who has the right to it.

So, although one should certainly give each person what she has a right to—and so should treat equally those with equal rights—in much of life you *should be partial* to your friends and family.

As Aristotle's famous dictum suggests, and as Mill acknowledges, "allied to the idea of impartiality is that of equality; which often enters as a component part both into the conception of justice and into the practice of it, and, in the eyes of many persons, constitutes its essence." Mill himself seems skeptical; as he saw it, people think that equality is fundamental to justice except when they think inequality is called for! Nevertheless, it is clear that to some extent, the concepts of justice and equality overlap.

What Is a Right? Hohfeld's Classic Analysis

Justice concerns our rights and our duties. There is, however, almost as much diversity in theories of rights as there is about justice in general. The most famous analysis of legal rights was advanced by Wesley Hohfeld (1879–1918). To Hohfeld, the concept of "a right" involves several different ideas, each of which is related to the others. Figure 8.1 sketches part of Hohfeld's analysis: single lines with an arrow at each end represent what Hohfeld called "opposites" or contradictories (legal

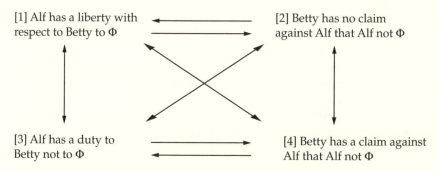

[1] Alf has a liberty with respect to Betty to Φ

[2] Betty has no claim against Alf that Alf not Φ

[3] Alf has a duty to Betty not to Φ

[4] Betty has a claim against Alf that Alf not Φ

FIGURE 8.1   Hohfeld's Analysis of Liberties and Claims

statuses that are inconsistent), whereas lines with single arrows represent "correlatives" (statuses that imply or entail each other).[7]

For Hohfeld, then, Alf has ([1] in Figure 8.1) a *liberty* to engage in act Φ if and only if (2) Betty has no claim against Alf that Alf not Φ. It also follows from Figure 8.1 that if (2) Betty has no claim that Alf refrain from Φ-ing, then (3) he has no duty to Betty to not Φ. For Hohfeld, when we talk about a person having a right to do something, we sometimes mean that he is *at liberty* to do so; he has no duty to refrain. But merely to have a liberty to do something does not imply that you have a claim that others not interfere. The classic example is the liberty of two pedestrians to pick up a dollar bill lying on the sidewalk. Neither has a duty to refrain from picking it up, but neither has a claim on the other to stand aside and let her pick it up. Such "naked liberties" often characterize competitions; people have the liberty to win, but no one has a claim to win. In contrast, Betty has a (4) *claim right* that Alf not Φ if and only if (3) Alf has a duty not to Φ, and so he is not (1) at liberty to Φ. In contrast to liberties, claim rights imply duties on the part of others not to interfere; we might call them rights in the strict sense. Unlike liberties, claim rights limit the freedom of others. If you and I both have a liberty to Φ, neither of us has a duty to refrain from Φ-ing; our liberties represent an absence of duties, and therefore an absence of restrictions on our freedom. To have a claim right, however, is to be able to *demand* that others respect your claim: they have a duty to respect it, and so are not at liberty to ignore it. Your claims, then, concern what is owed to you, and so what people are not free to decline giving you. (Recall here Polemarchus's conception of justice as giving each man his due; Section 1.1.)

Claim rights can be either *negative* or *positive*. If Betty has a claim that Alf refrain from doing something (say, breaking into her house), she has a

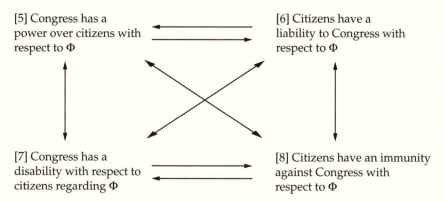

[5] Congress has a power over citizens with respect to Φ

[6] Citizens have a liability to Congress with respect to Φ

[7] Congress has a disability with respect to citizens regarding Φ

[8] Citizens have an immunity against Congress with respect to Φ

FIGURE 8.2   Hohfeld's Analysis of Powers and Immunities

negative claim right. Alf has a duty *not* to perform the action "breaking into Betty's house." A negative claim right corresponds to a duty on someone else's part not to perform an action; it implies that he or she is not at liberty to perform the action. In contrast, if Betty has a positive claim right against Alf (for example, to help when she is in need), Alf has a duty to perform an action. He is thus not at liberty to abstain from performing the required action.

Hohfeld also distinguished between two other legal statuses that are sometimes called "rights."[8] Someone has a *power* if he or she can alter other people's liberties, claim rights, and duties. For example, that Congress has the right to make laws means that ([5] in Figure 8.2) Congress has the legal *power* to alter the liberties, duties, and claim rights of American citizens. It can create new duties, rights, and liberties or abolish old ones. If Congress has the power to make such changes, citizens have (6) a *liability*—their claim rights, liberties, and duties are subject to alteration by Congress. The opposite of a power is (8) an *immunity*. If citizens have an immunity over some area, then Congress does not have the power to alter some liberties, rights, or duties; Hohfeld would describe this as (7) a *disability* on the part of Congress to alter these liberties, claim rights, or duties. An example of a right qua immunity is the U.S. Constitution's First Amendment right of freedom of religion. The First Amendment actually ensures citizens an immunity (8): it bars Congress from enacting laws establishing a religion, thus providing citizens with an immunity from legislation. According to Hohfeld, this immunity held by citizens corresponds to (7) a disability (a lack of power) on the part of Congress to pass such laws; that is, the crux of the right to freedom of religion as specified by the First Amendment is an inability or lack of a power on the part of Congress to pass laws establishing a religion. Alternatively, to say that

Congress has the right to make laws regulating interstate commerce is to say that it has the *power* to enact laws that alter the legal rights and duties of citizens.

Organizing the Elements of Justice

In different ways, Mill and Hohfeld point out some of the main features of our concept of justice. Mill identifies some of the main uses of the notion of justice. Most uses of justice involve the idea of honoring a person's rights, be they legal rights, moral rights, rights to what she deserves, or what you have been promised. The term "right" itself, though, is used in different ways: as Hohfeld shows, when we say that a person has a right to Φ, we might mean (1) she is at liberty to Φ—she has no duty not to Φ— (2) she has a claim on others not to interfere with her Φ-ing or she has a claim on others to assist her in Φ-ing; (3) she has immunity relating to Φ, that is, no one has the power to alter her liberty/claim right to Φ; or (4) she has a power regarding Φ that involves the legal ability to alter the liberty and duties of others.

To sketch out the main aspects of our notion of justice and rights, however, is only the beginning. We need to organize the aspects into a coherent conception, explaining why various parts are important and how they relate to each other. A *theory of justice* seeks to organize, justify, and explain the various aspects of our concept of justice. In many ways, the history of political theory has been about competing theories of justice; we certainly cannot even begin to analyze them all here. In the remainder of this chapter, I will briefly survey some of the main theories proposed by classical and revisionist liberals; in the next chapter I examine socialist and conservative approaches to justice. Throughout, I emphasize how each type of political theory advances a theory of justice that coheres with its understandings of liberty and equality, as well as its positions on the three enduring issues in political theory that we identified in Chapter 3.

8.2 Classical Liberalism: Rules for Equally Free People

The Hobbesian State of Nature

Classical liberalism, it will be recalled, is based on the presupposition that we are equally free (Sections 6.3, 7.2), with freedom being understood as negative liberty. Thomas Hobbes presented a classic, though controversial, depiction of life among equally free people without rules of justice. Hobbes depicts a "state of nature," a condition of anarchy, in which each person is free to do whatever advances her interests. According to Hobbes, individuals in the state of nature have a right to do anything. Note that by "right" Hobbes must mean something very much like Hohfeld's "liberty" (Section 8.1); to say we have a right to do anything is simply to say that we have no duties to not do things. We have no claims on each other in the state of nature ([2] in Figure 8.1), hence we have unlimited liberties ([1] in Figure 8.1). Not only is this a condition of absolute freedom, but it is also one of equality. No one is under the authority of anyone else; more than that, each person is equal insofar as each is vulnerable to attack by others. Or as Hobbes more colorfully puts it, we are equal because anyone can kill anyone else. Hobbes acknowledged that it may be "thought, there was never such a time, nor condition of war, as this"; indeed Hobbes himself believed that "it was never generally so, over all the world," though he did think that some non-European peoples lived in such a state. More important, Hobbes tells us that analyzing life in this state of nature allows us to understand "what manner of life there *would be*" if equally free people lived in anarchy.[9] Hobbes argues that in such a condition equal liberty would lead us into conflict. Each person is as hopeful as the next of obtaining her goals, because no one considers herself the inferior of others. Consequently, if two people both want something, neither is apt to give way, and so they are apt to become enemies. Hobbes's description of life in such a condition is famous:

> In such a condition, there is no place for industry; because the fruit thereof is uncertain: and consequently no culture of the earth; no navigation, nor use of the commodities that may be imported by sea; no commodious building; no instruments of moving, and removing, such things as require much force; no knowledge of the face of the earth; no account of time; no arts; no letters; no society; and which is worst of all, continual fear, and the danger of violent death; and the life of man, solitary, poor, nasty, brutish and short.[10]

Hobbes is especially clear that in such a condition there would be no notion of justice or injustice: "The notions of right and wrong, justice and injustice, have there no place. Where there is no common power, there is no law; where no law, no injustice. Force, and fraud, are in war the two cardinal virtues."[11]

Hobbes's solution to the anarchy of the state of nature is a social contract (Sections 4.3, 7.2). The problem underlying the state of nature is the absence of a distinction between "mine and thine"—there are no claim rights that limit your liberty to use something. Without such claim rights, people might seek to use anything that I possess, including my body. By instituting a system of claim rights, we can create things that are "mine"—things that I have a claim right to use, and so you are not at liberty to use them—and things that are "thine"—which you have a claim right to use, and which I am not at liberty to use. Justice is thus about the creation of property in the very broadest sense: the distinction between what I have a claim right to and what you have a claim right to.

Hobbes believes that equally free people in the state of nature would renounce their unlimited liberties and agree to obey a "sovereign," a government with unlimited powers to determine the rights of its subjects. The crux of Hobbes's social contract is that subjects claim no immunities against the government; to claim that the government was disabled from making some laws would lead to endless disputes about these limits and that, Hobbes thought, would drive us right back into the state of nature. Hobbes's sovereign can do no injustice: he has sole authority to establish laws and determine the rules of property and in so doing set the limits to the liberty of his subjects.[12] Now, obviously, there is nothing at all liberal about this social contract; indeed, it is a remarkably authoritarian contract, insofar as free and equal people create a government with the unlimited right to legislate—it has no disabilities ([7] in Figure 8.2). But it is easy to misunderstand Hobbes here. He does not advocate a political system that denies freedom in the sense of denying subjects claim rights to act; indeed, Hobbes thinks that only the sort of sovereign he advocates can institute an effective system of claim rights. Hobbes's proposed government is authoritarian, then, in the sense that subjects have no immunities against their sovereign; the sovereign has the right (qua power, Figure 8.2) to legislate anything it wishes. In sum, Hobbes argues that we must give up our rights qua unlimited Hohfeldian liberties to act and give the government rights qua unlimited Hohfeldian powers if we are to have an effective system of claim rights.

Because of this, the Hobbesian conception comes close to identifying justice with the requirements of the existing legal system (see Mill's first point, Section 8.1). The sovereign determines what is just. But not even Hobbes manages to simply identify justice with a society's body of laws. Hobbes acknowledges that no one can be bound to give up her life; thus even if the sovereign were to command you to kill yourself or to let him kill you, you are at liberty to disobey (and thus do not have a duty to obey). Even Hobbes—who seeks to equate justice to whatever system of laws the sovereign creates—recognizes some notion of "ideal justice" that is independent of the law (see Mill's point [2], Section 8.1).

Neo-Hobbesian Theory: Justice as Rules for Mutual Benefit

Contemporary philosophers inspired by Hobbes have made great advances in formally modeling the problems in Hobbes's state of nature, as well as what sorts of agreements rational agents would make to extract themselves from it. The point of departure for formal Hobbesian analyses is the now-famous "prisoner's dilemma." In this dilemma, two suspects,

Alf and Betty, have been arrested by the police. The police have enough evidence to convict them both on a relatively minor charge—say, they were caught shoplifting a bag to carry their loot in. If convicted of this charge—and the police can obtain a conviction—each will get a year in prison. The police, however, suspect that they acted together to pull off a really big bank job; unfortunately, the police have no evidence of this, but they hope to get confessions. So this is what they do. Interviewing each separately, they make the following offer to Alf (the same offer is also made to Betty).

> "Alf, turn state's evidence against Betty, and we'll let you go free; we'll demand the maximum penalty for Betty, so she'll get ten years. Of course, if Betty confesses too, we're not going to let you both off: you'll each get seven years. But if you keep quiet and she confesses, we'll let her go free, and you'll be the one to get ten years. We'll be honest with you: if neither of you confess to the bank job, we won't have enough evidence to prosecute. Then we'll proceed with the shoplifting charge, and you'll each get one year."

Their choices can be schematically displayed as in Figure 8.3.

Alf reasons: if Betty confesses, and I keep quiet, I get ten years; if Betty confesses and I confess too, I get seven years. So I know one thing: if Betty confesses, I had better confess too. What if Betty keeps quiet? Alf reasons: If Betty keeps quiet and I keep quiet too, I get a year; if Betty keeps quiet and I confess, I go free. So if Betty keeps quiet, I do best by confessing. But now Alf has shown that confessing is the *dominant strategy:* no matter what Betty does, he does best if he confesses. And Betty will reason in a parallel way; she will conclude that no matter what Alf does, she does best by confessing. So they will both confess, and get seven years.

In some sense, they seem to have outsmarted themselves: by each doing what is individually the best, they both end up with their third option: seven years in jail. There is a clear sense in which it would have been better for both of them to keep quiet, receiving only one year in jail. Yet, they

		BETTY	
		Keep Quiet	*Confess*
ALF	*Keep Quiet*	1 year each	Alf gets 10 years, Betty goes free
	Confess	Alf goes free, Betty gets 10 years	They both get 7 years

FIGURE 8.3   The Prisoner's Dilemma

will not do that, for being rational individuals they will see that if the other keeps quiet, they will do best by confessing. They will thus "defect" or "cheat" on the cooperative policy of keeping quiet. Both Alf and Betty would benefit if, somehow, the option of confessing were not eligible—if it could be excluded from the set of actions they were at liberty to perform. If they could both be convinced that confessing was not a real option for them, they would end up cooperating and both benefit. The lesson is clear: like the parties in Hobbes's state of nature, each would gain from a system of restraint that mandated certain actions (for example, "Do not confess!"). Instituting such a system is therefore mutually beneficial.

Contemporary followers of Hobbes maintain that the prisoner's dilemma models a wide range of social interactions under conditions of unconstrained liberty: those who are equally free are often unable to achieve the fruits of social cooperation. Hence, to better advance their interests rational agents would give up some of their liberty and embrace rules of justice. Without rules of justice, we are caught in prisoner's dilemmas, in which each person's attempt to achieve his or her ends leads to a unproductive conflict. Thus, contemporary classical liberals such as David Gauthier and James Buchanan[13] maintain that rational agents would agree to rules of justice that protect liberty and property rights. These liberals, then, reject Hobbes's claim that free and rational people would create a government with the unlimited right to legislate and determine the content of justice. To live together in peace and to gain the benefits of cooperative social life, insist these recent followers of Hobbes, we require negative claim rights protecting our liberty (claims against others that they do not interfere with our actions) and claim rights to acquire and enjoy property.

The classical liberal analyses of human nature as self-interested (Section 3.3) negative liberty (Section 4.1), the relation of liberty and property (Section 5.4), and the fundamental importance of our status as equally free (Sections 6.3, 7.2) thus set the stage for the Hobbesian-inspired classical liberal theory of justice. To live together in peace, respecting each other's status as equally free people, we require negative claim rights protecting our liberty (claims against others that they do not interfere with our actions) and claim rights to have our property protected. We must add to these two basic aspects of justice a third—claims over our bodies and protection from harm, for unless we are protected from being harmed by others, we cannot be secure in either our liberty or use of our property (Section 5.4).[14]

Lockean Justice

In contrast to Hobbesian theories of justice, which seek to derive justice from a rational bargain among essentially equal, free, and self-interested agents, Lockean-inspired theories insist that legitimate contracts specifying systems of mutual advantage and just governments are constrained by the prior moral rights of individuals. As John Locke says, we have natural rights to "Lives, Liberty and Estates."[15] These rights are what Mill called "moral rights" (point [2], Section 8.1) and so their justification does not depend—as they do in Hobbes's theory—on being a part of the established legal system. Indeed, for Lockeans, to be just, a legal or political system must respect these basic moral rights to life, liberty, and property. Even in the state of nature, Locke argued, people would recognize that each had a claim right to his or her life, liberty, and property. Locke thus disagrees with Hobbes; the state of nature was a *"State of Liberty,"* but *"not a State of License,"* because each would recognize that he was not free to attack the "Life, the Liberty, Health, Limb or Goods of another."[16] These natural rights are basic elements of ideal justice: actual political arrangements must respect them.

Equal claim rights to noninterference and protection of one's body and property are the core of Lockean-inspired classical liberal justice. Classical liberal justice also lays great stress on the role of promising and contracts in justice (Mill's point [4], Section 8.1). The conception of justice inherent in the classical liberal market society is, essentially, the justice of keeping one's agreements within the bounds of basic negative claim rights to liberty and the rights involved in private property. The classic liberal, then, tends to think that Cephalus was basically right in saying that justice is a matter of telling the truth and paying your debts (Section 1.1), as long as we remember that this takes place against equal basic rights to liberty and property. This explains the central place of commutative justice in classical liberalism (Section 2.1). Once again, we can see that the classical liberal justice is shaped by the pivotal role of negative liberty and individualism. Justice is by and large a characteristic of relations between equally free individuals; it is not about whether the social whole conducts its affairs in a just or appropriate manner.

Classical Liberalism's Ambivalence Toward Desert Claims

Classical liberals are ambivalent about the idea of desert (Mill's point [3], Section 8.1). In some ways, desert is central to their theory of justice. Overall, and in general, classical liberals have believed that one of the virtues of private property and the market system is that they tend to reward the industrious. As John Stuart Mill said, "Private property, in every defense of it, is supposed to mean the guarantee to individuals of the fruits of their own labour and abstinence."[17] One deserves the fruits of one's own labor, and it is generally seen as a real virtue of private property market systems that producers are rewarded for their productive efforts. Nevertheless, classical liberals have been wary about transforming this observation about the general tendencies of markets based on private property into a strict criterion of justice-in-holdings.[18] For the most part, classical liberals have not maintained that a person's property holdings are just if and only if she deserves those holdings. Any such criterion of justice, they have insisted, is incompatible with a strong defense of negative liberty. If a person is to be free to dispose of her property as she sees fit, she will be free to give it to undeserving others, such as her children. If no one is to have undeserved property, the freedom of people to dispose of their property as they see fit must be greatly limited. Moreover, classical liberals would almost always insist that theories endeavoring to reward people according to their overall deservingness are overly rationalist. In a well-defined context, such as a mathematics competition, we may be able to say who deserves the prize, but it is impossible to determine a person's overall deservingness, or even overall economic deservingness. Is a doctor more or less deserving than a computer programmer? Is a great artist more or less deserving than a second-rate air traffic controller? Because, says the classical liberal, there is no way to make such determinations, the attempt to apply desert to an individual's overall economic standing leads to incessant meddling with the market with no clear idea of what should result. Success in the market is determined by a combination of skill and luck, and "while, as in a game, we are right in insisting that it be fair and that nobody cheat [see Mill's point (5)], it would be nonsensical to demand that the results for the different players be just."[19]

8.3 Monistic Revisionist Liberalism: Social Justice and Contributions to the Common Good

Desert, Social Contributions, and Distributive Justice

Claims about desert have played a much larger role in the revisionist liberalism inspired by T. H. Green and L. T. Hobhouse, the so-called "new liberalism" of the first part of the twentieth century. With its much stronger rationalist underpinnings, this version of revisionist liberalism has been at the forefront of theories of distributive justice that seek to reward people according to their deserts or merits. To many revisionist liberals, a competitive market society can be just only if its competition rewards the deserving—those who produce or at least make the effort to produce.[20] Although many contemporary advocates of the welfare state associate it with an egalitarian needs-based distribution (Sections 6.4, 7.3, 9.1), its early proponents tried to show how the equal provision of needs was consistent with people getting what they deserve. Hobhouse, for example, argues,

The principle of distribution by needs would be generally recognized as broadly a principle of equality. We have now to consider the ground of differentiation. Differences arise in a system in which all have a part, and a claim to equal consideration, from the necessities from the system itself. For example, captain and sailors have an equal interest in the safety of the ship, but for the sake of that safety differences must be recognized as will ensure that the captain's orders will be carried out. In general terms, the common good is maintained by the services of its members. . . . Every one of whom a function is required may claim on his side the conditions necessary to its performance, e.g. if he has a certain political responsibility he must be furnished with adequate powers, if he has to do hard and muscular work, he must have food and rest in proportion. If he is a brain-worker he needs air and exercise to keep him fit. . . .

We may then define Distributive Justice as equal satisfaction of equal needs, subject to the adequate maintenance of useful functions.[21]

We see here Hobhouse's moral collectivism and his tendency to tie justice to the common good (Sections 1.4, 3.4). What one needs depends on one's social function, and so the equal satisfaction of needs must be adjusted to what one must have to effectively contribute to society. Thus far, the argument is cast entirely in terms of what one needs in order to contribute to society, not what one deserves. Hobhouse, however, wishes to reconcile social justice as needs provision with social justice as desert. In advocating a "civic minimum"—a minimum level of resources—Hobhouse was insistent that this was not charity but the working class's just *rewards for contributing to the common good*; consequently, he tell us that the civic minimum paid to a contributing member of the community must be his "true and full property with unlimited right of disposal." Hobhouse explicitly contrasts such contributors to "dependents"—"the helpless, the defective, the idler"; contributors have a claim based on desert for a decent existence whereas dependents "are a charge upon the humanity of the community" and are provided with an allowance "for the specific purpose of meeting their needs."[22] In the history of the development of the welfare state, this was a critical argument. The first elements of the modern welfare state, old-age pensions (such as the Social Security system) and unemployment insurance, were often advocated on the grounds that they were the just rewards of those who had previously contributed to the common good. Old-age pensions and unemployment insurance were not charity: they were the just deserts of workers who had made social contributions. That the provisions of the welfare state were deserved rewards was especially important in its expansion in the United Kingdom and the United States after the Second World War; educational and housing assistance were viewed as deserved

compensations for those who had contributed to the common good by
fighting fascism.

Underlying the new liberal's desert-based conception of social justice
is not only a rationalist supposition that the government can reliably determine the deservingness of individuals, but a monistic notion of what
is valuable and a collectivist conviction that there is a common good and
those who contribute to it are especially deserving. To reward a person
for doing something presupposes that what he does is a good or valuable
thing. For desert to be the guiding principle of social justice, then, we
must have a socially recognized notion of what is valuable. To some,
what is valuable is simply production. But of course, not all production is
valued by everyone: many insist that the production of pornography,
large cars, water jets, or modern art is not valuable at all. Hayek dismisses the very idea of social justice as rewarding desert for just this reason, emphasizing the classical liberal pluralist position that there is no
such thing as "value to society." "Services can only have value to particular people (or an organization), and any particular service will have different value to different members of the same society."[23] For a society to
adopt a notion of social justice as the systematic rewarding of people according to their deserts, there must be a socially sanctioned idea of what
is valuable. Typically, those who employ desert-based ideas of social justice appeal to what is of value to society or what promotes the social or
common good. New liberals were usually very clear that in contrast to
the individualism of classical liberalism, their policies were based on the
good of the "social organism as a whole" or the interests of "organized
society as a whole."[24]

Development, Liberty, and Welfare

Thus far, I have stressed the collectivism of the new liberal account of social justice: justice mandates that one should receive what one needs to
contribute to the common good and be rewarded according to one's contribution to the common good. This gives the impression that the individual's rights and duties are totally subservient to the good of society.
But Hobhouse's collectivism is moderated by his conception of the common good as the harmonious development of human nature. The good of
the individual (her self-development) is thus in harmony with the good
of society (the self-development of everyone); indeed, we have seen (Section 7.3) that for Hobhouse one can only develop one's own nature in a
society where other people are also developing their personalities. Thus,
the monistic harmony between individual and social good, and ideas of
self-development and positive liberty, are at the core of his new liberal
theory of social justice (see Section 4.3). Hobhouse argued that if we are

to assist each other in developing our capacities, we need to provide the conditions necessary for development for everyone. Social justice, as Hobhouse sees it, concerns the equal provision of the conditions for the growth of all citizens.

The first condition for growth is claim rights to basic liberties. But, Hobhouse emphasized, liberty is not the sole condition for development. Because, Hobhouse argued, we should understand society as a cooperative endeavor, we should cooperate to assist each other in developing our personalities. This, then, reinforces the necessity of the "civic minimum"—a minimal level of income necessary if a person is to develop. A society devoted to the development of all its citizens would also guarantee all citizens have adequate health care: those who are sick are unable to develop their potential. Education also becomes a major concern of the state (Section 4.3). Notice that in this theory of liberal justice, negative claim rights to noninterference do not have the core position that they occupy in classical liberal theory. The very aim of nourishing development and true freedom requires a complex of negative claim rights to noninterference and positive claim rights to income, education, and so on. Although the new liberals do not reject classical liberalism's devotion to negative freedom, they stress that much more is required to promote development than simply ensuring each citizen her negative liberty.

Civil Justice and Facilitatory Social Justice

Justice as giving people what they deserve is related to justice as awarding positions on the basis of merit. They are not the same idea, however. To claim you deserve something is typically to focus on some *past accomplishment* of yours: a person who has given a lot of effort in a good cause deserves some recompense. At least in the most clear-cut cases, desert says "thank you" for some past action. But to select on the basis of merit is typically *forward looking:* the selection aims to pick the person who will, in the future, do the best job. Of course, if someone has worked very hard to prepare herself, say, by diligently practicing to make the baseball team, we might say she deserves a chance; but if we are selecting on the basis of merit we will consider only her competency to play baseball—how well she will do as a member of the team.

For John Passmore, selection according to competency is the heart of "civil justice," according to which "except by way of punishment or a result of incapacity, no person ought to be excluded from participation in any form of desirable activity unless there is, of necessity, competition for entrance to it, when the more competent ought always to be preferred to the less competent." [25] This is a strongly *meritocratic* conception of justice; it conceives of society as a vast mass of competitions, each of which should be run such that the most competent win. Although such meritocratic ideals are often associated with classical liberalism, this seems a mistake. To be sure, classical liberals have supported selection according to merit in relation to competition for government or public positions, as required by the equality of opportunity (Section 6.4). But although selection according to merit has its place in public institutions with specific defined purposes and goals, classical liberals have insisted that it cannot be applied to society as a whole, for society as a whole does not share common notions of desirable activities or what constitutes excellence in performing them. And again, say the classical liberals, any attempt to apply a meritocratic notion of justice throughout society is bound to require large-scale interferences with the liberty and property of citizens. Consider, for example, the status of religious schools. Is it unjust for Catholic schools to hire a math teacher just because she is Catholic, even though a Baptist candidate might be a better math teacher? According to the idea of civil justice, it seems that the Catholic hiring authorities must show that, in some way, the Catholic math teacher is really more competent. But if the schools are the property of the Catholic Church and it funds its own schools, why should not the Catholic Church be free to spend its money as it sees fit?

Passmore's ideal of civil justice is allied to rationalism insofar as it understands all of society in terms of bureaucratic organizations that possess goals they seek to achieve, and so possess standards of competency measured by ability to meet those goals. On the face of it, civil justice appears to be hostile to egalitarian social justice (see Sections 6.4, 8.4, 9.1): civil justice stresses the distinction between the more and less competent and allows that, justly, there will be losers in fair competitions. Proponents of egalitarian social justice, in contrast, typically seek to assist the "losers" or worst-off members of society. On closer inspection, however, we can see that civil justice easily endorses a moderately egalitarian notion of social justice. Passmore observes,

> In its most moderate form—let us call it facilitatory social justice—the advocates of social justice do not reject outright the leading assumptions of civil justice. They do not deny either that some forms of activity are particularly desirable or that when a process of selection is inevitable, competence is the proper criterion. But they go beyond civil justice by demanding that a society should take positive steps to *facilitate* the wider participation of its members in desirable activities and the selection of the potentially most competent persons in any competitive situation. Such facilitation takes the form of so modifying the socio-economic circumstances which disadvantage particular individuals that those circumstances no longer act as a shackle.[26]

To see how civil justice can give rise to facilitatory social justice, think about the common metaphor of life as a race. If life is a race, or a series of races, then civil justice demands that the winners be the best entrants—those who are best at running. But if some people are unable to train for the race because they are too poor to take time off of work or cannot afford good running shoes, then we might question whether the best are really being selected. Perhaps the person best suited to the job never received adequate training. If we limit ourselves to those who have had the opportunity to train, can we say that we have selected the best? Should not a fair competition equally prepare the equally talented? This gives rise to a notion of social justice that emphasizes a thoroughgoing equality of fair opportunity (Sections 6.4, 8.4). Government provision of equal educational opportunities, child care, and head start programs all become part of the expanded ideal of rewarding people according to their merit.

Although Passmore accepts that the ideal of civil justice can be extended to include facilitatory social justice and its attendant ideal of equality of fair opportunity, he argues that civil justice is opposed to the use of quotas in awarding scarce positions. The proponent of civil justice can "protest against any attempt to rule out blacks, or women, as incompetent *en masse* to enter any particular occupation." But he will reject the idea that justice requires that social groups must be "represented in proportion to their numbers in any form of desirable activity."[27] For, Passmore insists, we simply do not know whether, say, mathematical abilities are equally distributed between men and women or between Asians and Europeans. There is, Passmore says, no reason why all talents must be equally distributed among all social groups—whether they are or are not is a matter to be investigated. Given this, we cannot infer that just because the proportions of, say, men and women in a certain occupation are not the same as their proportion in the general population, there must be an unjust competition. Only if one knew that the competencies for all occupations were equally distributed among all social groups could one infer that an instance of "under-" or "over-" representation is, ipso facto, a case of civil injustice. Passmore is not enough of a rationalist to claim that he can make such a strong claim to knowledge, hence he rejects quotas as a violation of civil justice.

8.4 Pluralistic Revisionist Liberalism: A Revised Social Contract Among Free and Equal People

Pluralistic Distinguished from Monistic Revisionist Liberalism

Throughout this book, I have contrasted classical and revisionist liberalism. The type of revisionist liberalism on which I mainly have been focusing might be called *monistic revisionist liberalism*. At the heart of this type of revisionist liberalism is a monistic doctrine that the good of each person is to fully develop her capacities, be guided by her real will, or realize her true self. This version of monism allows that each person's true good may be somewhat different, and crucially depend on her choices—my developed personality will not be the same as yours, and it will reflect my choices. Nevertheless, this type of revisionist liberalism presupposes that there is a good life for humans, which only a liberal society can achieve. It is this monistic ideal that is the foundation of positive freedom (Section 4.3), as well as the claim that, properly understood, equality (qua equal rights) is harmonious with freedom (Section 7.3). Monistic revisionist liberalism also tends to be far more collectivist in its understanding of morality and society than classical liberalism. Thus, for instance, T. H. Green, perhaps the greatest revisionist liberal of this sort, advocated a collectivist theory of justice according to which "a right is a power claimed and recognized as contributory to a common good." For Green, a right is a recognized power that we need in order to contribute to the social good, not an individual claim that can block social projects that seek to promote the common good. Thus for Green "a right against society, as such, is impossible."[28] The heart of the liberalism of Green, Hobhouse, Bosanquet, and others was this ideal of the common good. As we have just seen, this type of revisionist liberalism understands justice in terms of what one needs to contribute to the common good, and what contributors deserve and merit.

Another type of revisionist liberalism has dominated political theory in the past thirty years. This *pluralistic revisionist liberalism*—most famously advanced by John Rawls in *A Theory of Justice* (1971)—has closer ties to the classical doctrine. Rawls's revisionist liberalism is both more individualistic and more pluralistic than the version advanced by Green and Hobhouse. Like the classical liberals (Section 8.2), Rawls starts from the supposition that we are *free and equal*. We are *equal* in that we are owed "equal consideration and respect."[29] We are *free* in the sense that each person is capable of choosing her goals in life and forming plans to achieve them. Rawls accepts a version of pluralism (Section 3.2), holding that reasonable people have various, and sometimes competing, notions about what is good—what is worth pursuing in life. Different people, that is, have different goals in life, different plans they wish to pursue. Rawls typically insists that there is no single goal—such as the pursuit of pleasure, nobility, or whatever—that every reasonable person must pursue. Rawls also endorses a strong version of *moral individualism* (Section 3.4). Not only must we recognize that each us pursues his or her own vision of what makes life worth living, but we also must recognize that "each person possesses an inviolability founded on justice that even the welfare of society as a whole cannot override."[30] For Rawls, principles of justice define the rights of individuals, rights that are so important and strong that even considerations based on promoting the overall social welfare or common good are unable to override them.

Again, we confront the complexity of political theory. The "new liberal" followers of Green and Hobhouse sought to construct a welfare state on foundations that were strikingly different from the classical liberals and which borrowed much from socialism. Hobhouse in England, and John Dewey in America, explicitly sought to move liberalism closer to socialism—not simply in its support of government policies to help the poor, but in its understanding of individuals, society, and morality.[31] In contrast, Rawlsian, pluralistic revisionism stays much closer to the classical liberal's commitments to moral individualism and pluralism: its aim is to show that, properly understood, these commitments lead to a comprehensive welfare state along the lines advocated by Hobhouse and Dewey. The contrast should not be pushed too far: the writing of Rawls and his followers displays many of the self-developmental commitments that were at the heart of monistic revisionism: the idea that the state should actively assist in the development of our distinctive human capacities is a dominant theme in Rawls as well as Green.[32] Nevertheless, whereas Green and Hobhouse believed that a wholesale reconstruction of liberal theory was required to show this, Rawls begins from premises that have much more in common with classical liberals such as Berlin and Hayek.

Rawls's Social Contract

Rawls, then, supposes that (1) we have different goals, and (2) we are not part of a collective entity, "society," to whose interests we can be sacrificed. What, then, is the nature of social life? Rawls's answer is that social relations are partly cooperative and partly competitive. They are cooperative because we all benefit from social interaction. Goods are produced and services obtained that would never exist without social cooperation. To a large extent, then, Hobbes was right (Section 8.2): society is an endeavor for mutual advantage and we all can gain through living together in peace. But as Hobbes also stressed, social relations are also competitive: each of us would like the resources—the goods and services—that are produced so that we can achieve our most cherished goals. Betty wants resources so that she can write the Great American Novel, whereas Alf wants to explore Australia. Not everyone can have all he or she wants. So, we have competing claims for the resources that are produced by social cooperation.

Because of all this, Rawls says, we require what he calls a "public conception of justice"—some standard by which we can resolve our competing claims. Ultimately, we have a choice: we can resolve our competing claims through force or by a public conception of justice that we all can accept. In almost all—perhaps all—societies that have ever existed, force has been used. Those with the necessary force—the rulers—have compelled others to live according to the laws set down by the rulers. In such societies, the conflict between citizens over the distribution of resources has been resolved by force. The alternative is a society that can agree on a moral code to adjudicate competing claims. In such a society, no one is likely to receive all she wants, but she can see that the rules that determine what she gets are fair in the sense that they are impartial (see Mill's point [5], Section 8.1) and so could be accepted by everyone.

Probably the most striking feature of Rawls's contract theory is that the parties to the social contract decide on a set of moral principles in the "original position" behind a "veil of ignorance." This means that they do not know certain facts about themselves, such as their (1) place in society; (2) natural talents (for example, intelligence); (3) "conception of the good"; and (4) society's circumstances, such as its level of economic development. They do, however, know general facts, such as the laws of economics and psychology. The aim of the exclusions is to rule out specific information. If we are meeting to determine what are the best principles of justice, Rawls tells us, some things are irrelevant, that is, information that would allow a person to propose principles that favor her. Justice is *impartial;* it does not favor some sorts of people over others—the veil of ignorance is meant to express this. An agreement under the veil of ignorance would thus be fair. Because people do not know specific facts about themselves, they are not in a position to hold out for an agreement that provides them with extra benefits—how could they, since they do not know who they are? Rawls realizes, of course, that no one ever met under these conditions, and we cannot really forget who we are; he is trying to impress on us that if we are really interested in justice and fairness, then we must think about what sort of morality everyone could accept, and so we must think about what we would accept behind the veil of ignorance, where bias in one's own favor is impossible.

One feature of the veil of ignorance that merits special emphasis is Rawls's exclusion of knowledge about natural talents. Our natural talents, Rawls says, are morally arbitrary; no one deserves greater intelligence or natural skills. Justice, then, should not acknowledge that those with greater natural talents deserve greater resources. Thus, the veil of ignorance restricts our knowledge of our own talents: as Rawls sees them, they are arbitrary from a moral point of view. (Recall here from Section 6.2 the egalitarian argument that inequalities that stem from the "natural lottery" of birth, in which people receive natural and social advantages that they do not deserve, are unjust, and call for redress.) This leads Rawls away from a desert-based theory of social justice. For most of the claims a person might make to be specially deserving—her contribution was more important, she provided a unique service, she was a high producer—stem from her natural talents or her lucky social position. Since Rawls wishes to exclude claims based on such talents, capacities, and circumstances, he excludes considerations of deservingness and merit from his theory of justice. Thus, whereas our first version of revisionist liberalism (Section 8.3) is characterized by monism and collectivism and stresses desert and selection according to merit, Rawls's liberal theory of social justice is pluralist and individualist and excludes desert almost entirely.

Rawls tells us that when evaluating each proposed set of principles, a rational contractor will consider each possible position that she may occupy in a society. She will ask, "If this set of principles is chosen, how well will I fare if I am the worst-off person in the society?" So, Rawls suggests that in deliberating about principles of justice, one will be most concerned with the question, "How does the bottom of society fare under each proposal?" Rawls calls this strategy "maximin": you *max*imize the *min*imum you might receive. For any social arrangement, the minimum you might receive is what you will get if you end up at the bottom of that society; you maximize the minimum if you select the society in which the bottom or worst-off class gets more than does the bottom or worst-off class in any alternative society. Rawls argues that you will thus select the principles of justice that result in a society with the "highest bottom"—that in which the least well off do as well as possible. Thus, as a first approximation, Rawls holds that the parties to the original position would accept his "General Conception of Justice": "All social values—liberty and opportunity, income and wealth, and the basis of self-respect—are to be distributed equally unless an unequal distribution of any, or all, of these values is to everyone's advantage."[33]

Rawls's Theory and Egalitarianism

Rawls's theory of justice is a variation on the argument for equality from impartiality that we examined in Section 6.2, combined with an argument that equal treatment requires a type of resource equality (Section 6.4). If we are to treat people equally in the sense of impartially (see Mill's point [5] above)—if our treatment of them is not to depend on accidents of birth and other irrelevant considerations—justice demands an approximation to equality of resources. We observe here a common phenomenon: roughly the same political arrangement can be advocated under the concept of justice or under equality.[34] Rawls's veil of ignorance undermines all possible arguments for differential treatment based on special talents, competencies, or past accomplishments. Consequently, by abstracting away all our individual characteristics, all that remains is our basic equality; under these conditions to be impartial must lead to equal treatment. It is this strong egalitarian element in Rawls's revisionist liberalism that led Dworkin to depict Rawls's liberalism—and, apparently by extension, all true liberalism—as based on equality rather than liberty (Section 7.3).

In two respects, however, Rawls's theory departs from resource egalitarianism. (1) Rawls allows inequalities of resources if those inequalities work to the advantage to the least well off. If we are distributing a fixed amount of resources—for example, dividing a cake—then an equal distribution will always be selected by the maximin. In an equal division, the "smallest" piece is as large as the "biggest" piece, since all pieces are the same size. Economies are, however, dynamic. People in the original position are deliberating not only how to divide a fixed stock of resources, but in what way, and to what degree, the stock of resources will grow. It seems quite certain that the stock of resources will not significantly grow under a strict egalitarian distribution. To induce the more talented to work hard, to undertake long training, to perform unpleasant tasks, and so on, it will be necessary to pay them more. Thus, it would seem that allowing some inequality of wealth and income is necessary to promote the overall increase in wealth, which is beneficial to the least well off. Consequently, Rawls allows inequality of holdings if the inequality works to the long-term advantage of the least well off. When an increase in inequality no longer results in gains to those at the bottom of society, Rawls deems it to be unjust.

The above argument supposes an individualist view of human nature (Section 3.3): the better off will not work hard—or hard enough—for the sake of the community or because they are committed to justice. Only if the more talented will benefit from the use of their talents will they develop them and work. Some socialist egalitarians have criticized Rawls on just this ground; if we suppose that people really are devoted to justice these additional incentive payments to work will not be necessary.[35] Crucially, then, Rawls's liberal, individualist conception of human nature draws him back from endorsing a thoroughly egalitarian distribution of resources. Nevertheless, Rawls's theory is sufficiently egalitarian to justify wasting resources to achieve equality (see Section 6.3). Suppose parties in the original position are faced with two possible distributions of resources, as in Figure 8.4.

Rawls's "General Conception of Justice" selects Distribution (1) over Distribution (2), since the greater inequalities in (2) do not result in additional advantages to the worst off.[36] This implies, however, that although society could have the additional resources in (2), Rawls's egalitarianism would prefer the overall poorer society corresponding to Distribution (1).

	Distribution 1	Distribution 2
Best off	$90,000	$150,000
Middle class	$60,000	$ 60,000
Worst off	$35,000	$ 35,000

FIGURE 8.4   Two Possible Distributions of Income

(2) The liberal, as opposed to the resource egalitarian, aspect of Rawls's theory comes to the fore in what he calls the "Special Conception of Justice." According to the General Conception, all primary goods—including liberty and opportunity—are to be distributed equally unless an unequal distribution maximally advantages the least well off. But Rawls adds,

> If the parties assume that their basic liberties can be effectively exercised, they will not exchange a lesser liberty for an improvement in economic well-being. It is only when social conditions do not allow the effective establishment of these rights that one can concede their limitation; and these restrictions can be granted only to the extent that they are necessary to prepare the way for a free society. The denial of liberty can be defended only if it is necessary to raise the level of civilization so that in due course these freedoms can be enjoyed.[37]

Rawls insists that

> Beyond some point it becomes and then remains irrational from the standpoint of the original position to acknowledge a lesser liberty for the sake of greater material means and amenities of office. Let us note why this should be so. First of all, as the general level of well-being rises (as indicated by the index of primary goods the least favored can expect) only the less urgent wants remain to be met by further advances. . . . At the same time the obstacles to the exercise of the equal liberties decline and a growing insistence upon the right to pursue our spiritual and cultural interests asserts itself. Increasingly it becomes more important to secure the free internal life of the various communities of interests in which persons and groups seek to achieve, in modes of social union consistent with equal liberty, the ends and excellences to which they are drawn.[38]

Rawls argues that except if one finds oneself in an impoverished society (in which case some sacrifice of liberty for economic advancement may be justified), one will insist on equal liberties and opportunities. This leads to the Special Conception of Justice, which specifies his famous two principles of justice:

First Principle: "Each person is to have an equal right to the most extensive system of equal basic liberties compatible with a similar system of liberty for all.

Second Principle: "Social and economic inequalities are to be arranged so that they are both
    (a) to the greatest benefit of the least advantaged . . .
    (b) attached to offices and positions open to all under conditions of fair equality of opportunity."[39]

Rawls holds that the first, liberty, principle is "lexically prior" to the second, egalitarian, principle: the first must be met before the second comes into play. But Rawls's notion of freedom does not include economic liberty or private property; these core elements of classical liberalism are unprotected in his liberal theory of justice. Indeed, Rawls does not endorse freedom in general, advocating instead the traditional list of specific liberal freedoms (Sections 5.4, 7.3). Within the egalitarian second principle, the principle of fair equality of opportunity (Section 6.4) is similarly prior to clause (a), the egalitarian distribution of resources. Rawls's theory of justice, then, combines (in order of priority) equal liberty, equal fair opportunity, and (qualified) equal resources.

8.5 Summary

I began in Section 8.1 by sketching the terrain of justice—some of the important elements of our practice of justice that a theory of justice must organize and explain. I focused on two well-known sketches of the elements of justice: Mill's five aspects of justice (legality, moral rights, desert, free agreement, and impartiality) and Hohfeld's analysis of the relations between liberties, claims, duties, powers, liabilities, immunities, and disabilities. Section 8.2 analyzed classical liberal theories of justice, which place equal negative claim rights to liberty, claim rights to property, and contracts at the heart of justice, giving desert a somewhat ambiguous role. Underlying this theory of justice is the classical liberal's core value of negative liberty and its supposition of equal freedom, as well as its commitment to individualism, pluralism, and skepticism about our ability to know what people really deserve. Section 8.3 analyzed a monistic revisionist liberal conception of justice, which puts much greater stress on collectivism and rationalism. Crucial to this understanding of social justice is that those who contribute to the common good deserve rewards and that people should be given what they need to be effective contributors. The allied ideas of civil justice and facilitatory social justice were also examined. I stressed that although a theory of justice emphasizing merit is often associated with classical liberalism, and although selection of civil service positions by merit has been endorsed by classical liberals, the generalization of selection by merit to all social positions presupposes a view of society that is much closer to Hobhouse's revisionist liberalism than to Hayek's classical liberalism. Contrasted to Hobhouse's collectivist desert theory is Rawls's pluralist egalitarian revisionist liberal conception of justice (Section 8.4). For Rawls—and here he follows the classical liberal tradition—justice is composed of the rules that free and equal people would accept. But in Rawls's version of the social contract, the equality rather than the freedom of the parties is salient; knowing nothing about their specific natures, values, or way of life, they select principles that stress their equality, especially in the distribution of wealth, income, and opportunities. We now turn to examining some leading nonliberal theories of justice.

Notes

1. John Stuart Mill, *Utilitarianism,* in John Gray, ed., *On Liberty and Other Essays* (New York: Oxford University Press, 1991), chap. 5, para. 4. All the quotes from Mill in Section 8.1 are from *Utilitarianism,* chap. 5, paras. 5–10.

2. See James M. McPherson, *The Battle Cry of Freedom* (New York: Oxford University Press, 1988), pp. 80–82.

3. See Hannah Pitkin, *Wittgenstein and Justice* (Berkeley: University of California Press, 1972), chap. 8.

4. J. R. Lucas, *On Justice* (Oxford: Clarendon Press, 1980), p. 209.

5. See Michael Slote, "Desert, Consent and Justice," *Philosophy and Public Affairs,* vol. 2 (Summer 1973), pp. 323–347. David Miller considers a third principle, "compensation," according to which a "man's reward should depend on the costs which he incurs in his work activity." *Social Justice* (Oxford: Clarendon Press, 1976), p. 103. Compare Norman's view of "equal benefits" in Section 7.3. For a very good analysis of theories of distributive justice that pays attention to principles of desert, see Julian Lamont, "Distributive Justice," in Edward N. Zalta, ed., *Stanford Encyclopedia of Philosophy* [online at http://plato.stanford.edu].

6. Immanuel Kant quoted in James Rachels, *The Elements of Moral Philosophy,* 3rd ed. (New York: McGraw-Hill, 1999), p. 127.

7. For Hohfeld's classic analysis, see his "Some Fundamental Legal Conceptions As Applied in Judicial Reasoning," *Yale Law Review,* vol. 23 (1913), pp. 16–59. I am drawing here on L. W. Sumner, *The Moral Foundations of Rights* (Oxford: Oxford University Press, 1987), p. 27. For helpful explications of Hohfeld's analysis, see R. E. Robinson, S. C. Coval, and J. C. Smith, "The Logic of Rights," *University of Toronto Law Review,* vol. 33 (1983), pp. 267–278; Michael Freeden, *Rights* (Minneapolis: University of Minnesota Press, 1991), chap. 1.

8. I am again following Sumner, *The Moral Foundations of Rights,* p. 30.

9. Thomas Hobbes, *Leviathan,* Michael Oakeshott, ed., (Oxford: Basil Blackwell, 1948 [1651]), chap. 13. Emphasis added.

10. Ibid., chap. 13, para. 9.

11. Ibid., chap. 13, para. 13.

12. Ibid., chap. 18.

13. David Gauthier, *Morals by Agreement* (Oxford: Clarendon Press, 1986); see James Buchanan, *The Limits of Liberty* (Chicago: University of Chicago Press, 1975). I consider Neo-Hobbesian contractualism in more depth in my *Social Philosophy* (Armonk, NY: M. E. Sharpe, 1999), chap. 5.

14. On the idea of harm, see my *Social Philosophy,* chap. 8.

15. John Locke, *Second Treatise of Government,* in Peter Laslett, ed., *Two Treatises of Government* (Cambridge: Cambridge University Press, 1960 [1689]), sect. 123.

16. Ibid., sect. 6.

17. John Stuart Mill, *Principles of Political Economy,* Sir William Ashley, ed., (Fairfield, NJ: Augustus M. Kelley, 1976 [1871]), p. 209 (Book 2, chap. 1, sect. 3).

18. Compare here Gallie's comments on commutative justice in Section 2.1.

19. F. A. Hayek, *Law, Legislation and Liberty,* vol. 2: *The Mirage of Social Justice* (Chicago: University of Chicago Press, 1976), p. 71.

20. See David Miller's now-classic study of social justice, where he maintains that desert-based theories of justice are especially appropriate to market societies: *Social Justice.*

21. Hobhouse, *The Elements of Social Justice* (London: George Allen and Unwin, 1922), pp. 110–111.

22. Ibid., pp. 138–139.

23. Hayek, *Law, Legislation and Liberty,* vol. 2: *The Mirage of Social Justice,* p. 75.

24. The first quote is from J. A. Hobson, *The Science of Wealth,* 4th ed., revised ed. R. F. Harrod (London: Oxford University Press, 1950), pp. 168–169. The second is from John Maynard Keynes, "The End of Laissez-Faire," in his *Essays in Persuasion* (London: Macmillan, 1972), p. 275. For a fuller treatment, see Gerald F. Gaus, "Public and Private Interests in Liberal Political Economy, Old and New." in S. I. Benn and G. F. Gaus, eds. *Public and Private in Social Life* (New York: St. Martin's Press, 1983), pp. 195ff.

25. See J. A. Passmore, "Civil Justice and Its Rivals, " in Eugene Kamenka and Alice Erh-Soon Tay, eds., *Justice* (London: Edward Arnold, 1979), p. 26.

26. Ibid., p. 36.

27. Ibid., p. 46.

28. See T. H. Green, *Lectures on the Principles of Political Obligation and Other Writings,* Paul Harris and John Morrow, eds. (Cambridge: Cambridge University Press, 1986), pp. 79, 110.

29. See John Rawls, "A Kantian Conception of Equality," in Robert M. Stewart, ed., *Readings in Social and Political Philosophy* (Oxford: Oxford University Press, 1986), p. 188. See Section 7.2.

30. Rawls, *A Theory of Justice* (Cambridge, MA: Harvard University Press, 1971), p. 1.

31. See my "Liberalism at the End of the Century," *Journal of Political Ideologies,* vol. 5 (2000), pp. 45–65.

32. I consider the similarities of Rawls to these earlier theorists in *The Modern Liberal Theory of Man* (New York: St. Martin's Press, 1983).

33. Rawls, *A Theory of Justice*, p. 303.

34. As Hobhouse observed, "Justice is a name to which every knee will bow, Equality is a word which many fear and detest. Yet the just was rightly declared by Aristotle is be a form of the equal." *The Elements of Social Justice*, p. 94.

35. See G. A. Cohen, "The Pareto Argument for Inequality," in Ellen Frankel Paul, Fred Miller Jr., and Jeffrey Paul, eds., *Contemporary Political and Social Philosophy* (Cambridge: Cambridge University Press, 1995) pp. 160–185; and "Incentives, Inequality and Community," *Tanner Lectures on Human Values* (Salt Lake City: University of Utah Press, 1992).

36. The issue is more complex than indicated here. For complications, see Rawls, *A Theory of Justice*, pp. 65ff.

37. Ibid., pp. 542–543.

38. Ibid.

39. Ibid., pp. 302–303.

9

JUSTICE, SOCIETY, AND COMMUNITY

9.1 Marx on Societies and Their Justice

Socialism and Justice

Socialist justice is often equated with egalitarianism, especially the equal distribution of resources, welfare, or the satisfaction of needs, based on a claim that humans are fundamentally equal.[1] Our discussions of equality in Chapter 6 and Section 7.3 have covered most of the ground of "socialist justice." In its conceptual structure, equality, not justice, is the core idea. Insofar as socialists endorse theories of justice, these are typically developments or extensions of revisionist liberal theories. Particularly striking is the way in which many socialists have come to embrace Rawls's theory of social justice, although perhaps putting more emphasis on the egalitarian features and criticizing the ways that Rawls allows inequality.[2] In discussions of social justice, the line between egalitarian revisionist liberal and moderate socialist views is often murky, indeed, almost nonexistent.

One of the main aims of this chapter is to explain why socialism accords a less prominent place to justice in its conceptual structure. Now, one obvious and plausible explanation is the tremendous influence exercised by Karl Marx in socialist thinking. Although Marx was, of course, a vehement critic of capitalism, it is unclear whether he was prepared to employ the concept of justice in criticizing capitalism or whether he advanced a socialist conception of justice. "Does Marx have a theory of justice?" Let us examine three competing answers.

The Scientific Socialism Answer: The Study of Power Relations

The first answer—which is short and sweet—takes very seriously Marx's claim that his theory of socialism is "scientific" and not moralistic. According to this (fairly standard) view, Marx was a social scientist investigating how capitalism managed to transfer productive power from the working class to the capitalists. It will be recalled from Section 5.3 that, in the language of C. B. Macpherson, capitalist private property rights transfer the "labour power" of the workers to the owners. In capitalist systems of production, the owner purchases the worker's labor power for a certain period of time—the owner of private property pays the workers a wage, and in return for the wage, everything that the worker produces becomes the property of the capitalist. The owner purchases that ability for a certain time and puts it to work. "The ability, the labour-*power*, is transferred. The actual work is *performed* by the non-owner. But in a very real sense the actual work is *owned* by the owner of capital."[3] Marx called this process "exploitation." The key to understanding capitalism, Marx argued, was that the worker's labor power creates more value than the worker receives from the capitalist in wages. The wage contract gives the capitalist all the value that the worker produces in a day, but the worker only gets a part of that back in wages; the difference between what the worker produces and what he gets paid is the *surplus value*. Capitalism "exploits" the workers because the surplus value goes to the capitalist, not the worker. "The time during which the labourer works," wrote Marx, "is the time during which the capitalist consumes the labour power he has purchased of him."[4]

On this "scientific socialism" reading, Marx's theory is an analysis of the power relations inherent in capitalism and their economic, social, and political effects. The concept of power, not that of justice, is crucial. According to this interpretation, Marx is not concerned with the "morals" of capitalism: he is concerned, very simply, with a scientific analysis of it. To be sure, he believes that it will be overthrown by the workers, and Marx no doubt is happy about this, but what Marx likes or dislikes is not part of his theory.

Support for this view derives from Marx's own claim that his theory was scientific as well as his criticism of earlier socialists. In the *Communist Manifesto*, Marx and Engels criticized what they called "utopian" socialists, who "want to improve the condition of every member of society, even the most favored. Hence, they habitually appeal to society at large, without distinction of class; nay, by preference, to the ruling class. For how can people, when they once understand their system, fail to see in it the best possible plan for the best possible state of society?"[5] This idea—that all moral people will favor socialist proposals once they understand their inherent justice—is not treated kindly by Marx and Engels. Revolution and socialism, they repeatedly insist, will be created by the objective conditions of the working class, not by moralistic socialist preaching. In an essay of his own, Engels explicitly contrasts "utopian socialism" to the "scientific socialism" that he and Marx devised. Consider what Engels says of three non-Marxist socialists—Claude Henri de Rouvroy, Comte de Saint-Simon (1760–1825), Charles Fourier (1772–1837), and Robert Owen (1771–1858):

> One thing is common to all three. Not one of them appears as a representative of the interests of that proletariat which historical development had, in the meantime, produced. . . . They do not claim to emancipate a particular class to begin with, but all humanity at once. . . . They wish to bring in the kingdom of reason and eternal justice. . . . For, to our three social reformers, the bourgeois world, based upon the principles of these philosophers, is quite irrational and unjust. . . . If pure reason and justice have not hitherto ruled the world, this has been the case only because men have not rightly understood them.[6]

Engels is echoing Marx's and his argument in the *Manifesto* (but, as is typical, putting it in a somewhat cruder way), criticizing the very idea of a socialism based on claims of "injustice." As Engels sees it, with Marx's work "socialism became a science"[7](Section 3.2.). And in a science, worries about justice have no place; science is about facts, not values (see Section 1.2).

This interpretation of Marx, although by no means the last word, draws on three fundamental commitments of Marxism: (1) its rationalism (Section 3.2), (2) its "social environmentalist" view of human nature (Section 3.3), and (3) its collectivist analysis of persons-in-society (Section 3.4). If a person's nature is essentially shaped by her society, and we are to explain individual facts in terms of social facts, the scientific explanation of human behavior should focus on a person's place in the overall social system. How a person acts will not be determined by her abstract views of justice—which, as Marx said, are supposed to appeal to the oppressor as well as the oppressed. If the oppressor—the capitalist—was actually influenced by such appeals, his behavior would not be determined by his role in the social system, but by his individual conscience or will. Marx is so critical of "utopian," socialists just because they assume that appeals to what is right or just actually can make a political difference. "Utopian socialism" employs a liberal-like appeal to an individual's sense of right and wrong; as we have seen throughout this book, liberalism puts great stress on individual choice and autonomy. For the liberal, what moves a person to act largely depends on her own choices. Hence for the liberal, to convince others that something is unjust can be politically effective. For scientific socialists following Marx, this is entirely wrong: it is too individualistic, and supposes that people's actions are to be explained by their individual choices and values, not by their overall role on the social system. Thus, an enduring strand in socialist thought is suspicious of all appeals to individual conscience, and so of appeals to justice.

The Relativity of Justice

According to the first interpretation, then, Marx has no concern (or, it would seem, patience) with the idea of justice. In "The Critique of the Gotha Program," though, Marx appears to advocate a different position—that "right can never be higher than the economic structure of society and its cultural development conditioned thereby."[8] This idea has been developed by Allen Wood, who argues that Marx held a conception of justice according to which each mode of production has a notion of justice appropriate to it. In *Capital*, for instance, Marx says,

> The justice of transactions which go on between agents of production rests on the fact that these transactions arise out of the production relations as their natural consequence. The juristic forms in which these economic transactions appear as voluntary actions of the participants, as expressions of their common will or as contracts that may be enforced by the state against a single party, cannot, being mere forms, determine this content. They only express it. This content is just whenever it corresponds to the mode of production, is adequate to it. It is unjust whenever it contradicts it.[9]

Marx's point seems to be that a transaction is just when it is appropriate to the prevailing "mode of production"—the current system of power relations, property rights, and productive technology. A "just" action or policy "harmonizes with and performs a function relative to it. An unjust action, by contrast, is one which 'contradicts' the prevailing mode, which clashes with it or is dysfunctional relative to it."[10] Although Wood himself resists calling this a relativist conception of justice, it is indeed relative in the sense that what is just in a particular society is relative to the mode of production of that society. If this is Marx's understanding of justice, what would he say about the exploitation of the workers under capitalism? Could that be just? Surprisingly enough, at one place Marx suggests precisely that: "What is a 'just distribution'? Do not the bourgeois assert that the present distribution is just? And isn't it in fact the only distribution based on the present mode of production?"[11] So, it would seem that the conception of justice appropriate to capitalism—a capitalist conception of justice—would hold that exploitation is just. And within the capitalist mode of production, *it would be just.*

Despite initial appearances, this interpretation of Marx is not a radical departure from the first. Both stress the importance of the collectivist supposition that before one can understand an element of a system, one must understand the functioning of the overall social and economic system. Understanding the workings of the whole is prior to understanding the individual unit. Thus, if we are to understand appeals to justice, we must see how a certain conception of justice functions within an economic system. We will then see how the capitalist conception of justice fits into the capitalist system and plays a role in it. Note how this analysis of justice ties justice very closely to legality (see Mill's first point, Section 8.1), or what might be called "official state justice." The legal system will express the notion of justice that is appropriate to the mode of production. On the other hand, this interpretation dismisses "ideal justice" (Mill's second point, Section 8.1) in its "conceptual map," because such idealizing suggests the liberal individualist view that a person's actions can be determined by notions about what is right or wrong that do not reflect his actual social position or society's conception of justice.[12]

Marx's Theory of Justice?

In response to Wood's interpretation, it has been argued that Marx was satirizing capitalism in the above passage, and so it is not to be taken at face value.[13] A number of other contemporary political and moral philosophers have argued that Marx did indeed present an "ideal" theory of justice.

Marx's theory of exploitation, and much of the rest of his work, is filled with a moral fervor and outrage. As one Marxist philosopher, Jon Elster, points out,

> Quite generally, almost any page of *Capital*, opened at random, conveys the strong impression that Marx is arguing the case in moral terms. More specifically, he frequently refers to capitalist extraction of surplus value as theft, embezzlement, robbery, and stealing. These are terms that immediately imply that an injustice is being committed. Moreover, the sense in which it is an injustice cannot be the relativistic one. Marx insists that, with respect to capitalist conceptions of justice, exploitation, unlike cheating and fraud, is fair. The sense in which extraction of surplus value is unfair must refer to a nonrelativistic, transhistorical conception. This argument is one important piece of evidence that Marx thought capitalism to be unjust. . . . Capitalism is an unjust system because some get more and others less than they have contributed.[14]

As Elster sees it, Marx's concept of exploitation is a moral notion. Capitalism is unjust because it extracts from the worker what the worker has produced. And it is indeed difficult to read *Capital* without sensing Marx's moral outrage at such an unjust economic order. On this reading, the injustice of capitalism is its transfer of powers (Section 5.3), resulting in the transfer of the fruits of the worker's labor to the capitalist. Note that this is essentially a *desert-based* criticism of capitalism: workers do not receive the fruits of their productive activities. The laborer produces the product (which has value), but the capitalist receives the product; consequently, the worker does not receive the full product (or value) that he has produced.[15]

So, it seems that Marx has a theory of *in*justice insofar as he advances a variety of criticisms against capitalism, all of which have the point that under capitalism the worker does not get what is properly his; and so capitalism is unjust. To a large extent, Marx's "theory of justice" is a theory about the *injustice* of capitalism. Some political theorists have maintained that we miss a great deal by looking only at the positive ideal of justice. In fact, we might have a much better feel for injustice—for identifying victims and unfairness—than for developing a positive idea of justice.[16] And this seems the case with Marx, in particular, and socialism, in general: its strength is its account of perceived injustices of capitalism. As Marx's theory of exploitation makes clear, the most basic socialist criticism of the capitalist market order is that it is fundamentally unfair. Capitalism, runs the criticism, is a system in which those who actually produce and labor receive extremely meager rewards, whereas the great benefits accrue to those—the owners—who do not actually provide any useful labor. The capitalist, then, makes his living by extracting labor from the workers: the worker receives a wage, but the capitalist keeps the bulk of what has been produced. As we have observed, this indicates that capitalism is unjust because workers do not get what they deserve. Marx—and again he is joined by contemporary socialists—argues that, under capitalism, the basic human needs of workers go unfulfilled whereas capitalists have incredible wealth to satisfy their slightest whims. Thus, on both the criterion of desert and that of need, Marx and socialists in general insist that capitalism is unjust. We should also recall that the socialist insists that it fails dismally in terms of freedom. At the heart of capitalism lie unequal power relations, and so by its nature it cannot secure freedom as power (Section 5.1); and because under capitalism workers are under the power of capitalists, neither can capitalism offer the workers positive freedom as autonomy or self-rule.

If capitalism is unjust, what is just? The answer would appear obvious: justice is giving the worker the fruits of his labor. Marx, though, apparently sees this as an imperfect sort of justice, suited to the transition from capitalist society to a true communist society:

What we have to deal with here is a communist society, not as it has developed on its own foundations, but, on the contrary, just as it *emerges* from capitalist society; which is thus in every respect, economically, morally and intellectually, still stamped with the birth marks of the old society from whose womb it emerges. Accordingly the individual producer receives back from society . . . exactly what he gives. . . . The same amount of labor which he has given to society in one form he receives back in another.[17]

This principle of distribution can be summed up as "to each according to his contributions." If this principle is followed, exploitation is eliminated and workers will get what they deserve. Yet, Marx was not satisfied with this criterion:

In a higher phase of communist society, after the enslaving subordination of the individual to the division of labor, and therewith also the antithesis between mental and physical labor, has vanished; after labor has become not only a means of life but life's prime want; after the productive forces have also increased with the all-round development of the individual, and all the springs of cooperative wealth flow abundantly—only then can the narrow horizon of bourgeois right be crossed in its entirety and society inscribe on its banner: From each according to his ability, to each according to his needs.[18]

When the higher phase of communism has arrived, "to each according to his contributions" can be replaced with "from each according to his ability, to each according to his needs." And as others have argued, that looks like a theory of how a just socialist society would distribute resources.[19]

This higher phase of justice, Marx suggests, can come about only when humans are no longer "alienated." Recall from Sections 3.3 and 6.3 Marx's notion that the human essence is to "objectify" its ideas into objects. We are planners and doers: we take ideas in our heads and create real things out of them. Thus, working, in the sense of creating, expresses the human essence. Now, Marx insisted that under capitalism this human essence is repressed and its expression distorted: people do not labor in order to express their humanity, but for the most brutish of reasons—to stay alive. Because capitalism robs the worker of his product, he can find no satisfaction in work. Thus, under capitalism we only work in order to get "external" benefits such as pay. Humans still infected with this capitalist mentality, Marx suggests, would not be ready to live according to the dictum "to each according to his needs, from each according to his ability," since people corrupted by capitalism will only work if rewarded. Thus, the first stage of communist justice is to give people what they deserve; as alienation is overcome, and people learn to love rather than hate labor, the higher phase of socialist justice can be achieved.

Does Marx, then, offer us a theory of justice? The problems in answering this question stem from a tension in Marx's own writing between two views of human nature (Section 3.3). If we focus on Marx's social environmentalist and collectivist views, the concept of justice fades; the interpretations of Marx stressing either the scientific nature of his socialism or the relativity of justice seem persuasive. But Marx also advocates a strong view of human essence that is not determined by one's society and one's place in it. This view—more apparent in Marx's earlier writings—points to notions of ideal justice, in which people receive the fruits of their labor and conditions exist for the flourishing of human nature.

Steven Lukes, however, has argued that all these different facets of Marx's views on justice form a single, coherent, multilayered account. According to Lukes, there is no simple and straightforward answer to our query, "Did Marx think capitalism unjust, or didn't he?"[20] Lukes identifies four layers of Marx's account of justice.[21] (1) The first layer is the analysis of capitalist norms as they function in capitalist society, which is stressed by the scientific and relativist interpretations of Marx. "In the first place, he did offer a functional account of the norms by which capitalist exploitation is judged just. . . . These norms . . . prevail because they sanction and stabilize capitalist exploitation and thus the capitalist system." (2) Second, however, Marx offers a criticism of capitalist norms from "within." Capitalism, Marx says, cannot live up to its own image of itself. It fails to be just even on its own understanding of justice. It is not the realm of free and fair exchange that it claims to be, but a system that enslaves workers and is unfair to them. (3) "But thirdly," says Lukes, "Marx also offered an 'external' critique of capitalist exploitation and of the norms and perspective from which it appears just. That critique is in turn made from the perspective of communism's lower phase: capitalist exploitation is from this standpoint unjust because it violates the principle 'To each according to his labour and contribution.'" (4) Last, says Lukes, Marx adopts a perspective that is critical of the very idea of justice. "From that standpoint, the very attribution of justice and injustice is a mark of class society, a sign that society is still in its prehistorical phase." As Lukes understands Marx, the perspective of the higher phase of communism—"from each according to his ability, to each according to his needs"—leaves behind not only capitalist justice, but the entire concept of justice, and seeks to replace it with an emancipatory, communitarian (Section 3.4), moral vision. Insofar as the notion of justice presupposes individuals in conflict who make claims on each other, Marx's collectivist and cooperative conception of society (Section 7.4) seeks to leave behind the very concept of justice.

9.2 Socialism and the Democratic Community

Beyond the Welfare State: Equality of Freedom and Power

It is tempting, but I think ultimately mistaken, to understand Marx as offering a theory of distributive justice along the lines of revisionist liberals such as Rawls (Section 8.3). Rawls, and some moderate socialists, are interested in providing principles that identify just and unjust distributions of resources, welfare, opportunities, and so on. These criteria of distributive justice are typically associated with the modern welfare state, for which revisionist liberals have been the main advocates. But the welfare state cannot secure equal liberty as power to act (Section 5.1) because, says the more radical socialist, it cannot secure equality of power. According to effect theories of power (Section 5.2), inequality of power relations are constitutive of, and endemic to, capitalist market societies (Section 5.3). Thus, so long as capitalism endures, freedom and equality will be unachievable however much the welfare state undertakes to redistribute resources, opportunities, or whatever. The aim of *equalizing power* calls for radical democratic control of social life. At least as understood by the socialist tradition, the core of democracy is political equality (Section 6.4), where this means not simply equal votes, but real, substantive equality of political power. It is clear why socialists are drawn to such a conception of democracy. For the socialist, it is the inequality of power that is the root cause of all the inequalities and injustices of capitalist distribution; only by eliminating the inequality of power can these evils be rooted out. This, then, points socialist justice toward a radical conception of the democratic community in which all are free because all equally possess political power (itself an ingredient of freedom, Section 7.3) and all power is controlled by democratic processes in which everyone has an equal role. True democracy—which alone expresses the equality and real freedom of all citizens—would thus require the abolition of capitalism. As Macpherson observes,

> a fully democratic society requires democratic political control over the uses to which the amassed capital and the remaining resources of the society are put. It probably does not much matter whether this takes the form of social ownership of all capital, or a social control of it so thorough as to be virtually the same thing as ownership. But more welfare-state redistribution of national income is not enough: no matter how much it might reduce class inequalities of income it would not touch class inequalities of power.[22]

Rather than looking for the socialist justice in revisionist-liberal–like principles of distributive justice, it is better to focus on the ideal of a fully democratic community. Not only does this ideal include the equality of power that is the heart of socialism, but it is consistent with "socialism as a doctrine that takes human social or communal existence more seriously than the excessive individualism that they [that is, socialists] associate with liberalism."[23] Given our nature as communal beings, a just society will not simply be one in which each gets her fair share, for that entire conception of justice has an individualist slant. Rather, a just society will be a political community in which the basic equality of its citizens results in a democratic life in which all equally participate in collective decisions. Proclaimed the English socialist G.D.H. Cole (1889–1959): the individual is "most free where he co-operates with his equals in making laws."[24]

Given this picture of the just society as the fully democratic society, we should not expect radical democratic socialist political theorists to advance specific principles of justice. To endorse any set of principles as *the* correct principles of justice is to preempt the voice of the democratic community. For example, if the socialist embraces Rawls's principles of distributive justice (Section 8.3), then these principles determine what justice requires; a just democratic community must conform to these principles. That, though, is to set limits on what the democratic community can decide; the political theorist is overriding the voice of the people. Seen in this light, Marx's reluctance to advance a theory of justice is well grounded; the only worry is that even his fragmentary remarks on justice (to each according to his needs, from each according to his abilities) say too much, for they instruct the democratic community of the future how it is to decide (see Section 10.4).

The ideal of the just society as one with equality of power explains the common socialist enthusiasm for extending democratic decisionmaking throughout all social life. Democracy is not simply a political ideal, says the socialist: it should inform large organizations, including business corporations. Following Cole, a number of socialists have embraced the idea of industrial democracy.[25] There are numerous variations of the industrial democratic ideal: some involve trade unions, others propose worker management along the lines once practiced widely in Yugoslavia. On this latter model, firms were owned socially, or by the state, but run democratically. The workers set up firms by borrowing from state banks; typically all the worker-members elected a workers' council to make the main policy decisions regarding the firm. The workers' council did not undertake day-to-day management, but hired mangers (who earned significantly more than did the workers who were, officially, their employers). For our purposes, however, the details of the Yugoslav model are not crucial: the important point is the extension of the democratic ideal throughout social life.[26]

Not only large organizations such as corporations, but, on this ideal, the family itself should manifest an equality of power (between adult members, at any rate). We can see here the socialist roots of much contemporary feminist thought, for one of the main themes of feminism is the injustice of unequal power relations in the family, which reinforces unequal power between the sexes throughout the social order. Feminists have often criticized socialism for not paying sufficient attention to the inequality of "patriarchy"—male rule—but the two political theories have a common core: justice understood as equality of power. Because of this, much feminist thought is antiliberal. Although liberal feminists endorse equal civic status between men and women, and equality of opportunity (Section 6.4), they do not endorse equality of power. Moreover, liberal principles of justice provide only the basic rules for social life between equally free people (Section 8.1, 8.3). Given this framework of rules, says the liberal, people must be free to make their own consensual arrangements in their private affairs, based on their different values and ideals.

Reconciling Socialism and Democracy

We have seen that the aim of equalizing power, and so promoting equal effective freedom, provides a case for extensive democratic decision-making. Power is something to be used to achieve ends, and so to equalize power is to equalize the ability to achieve ends; it does not tell us what those ends should be. On radical democratic views, if the people, under conditions of equal power, choose a rule or policy, then it is just. The democratic tendencies of socialism thus reflect what might be called a *volunterist* conception of justice: it is the people's voluntarily choosing something—making a democratic decision—that renders it just. Now this volunterist stance seems at odds with socialism's commitment to rationalism and its commitment to social equality, equality of resources, and equality of welfare. What if the people choose to go against reason— what if they choose inequality, competition, and private property? The volunterist, democratic commitments of socialist justice would tend to side with the people's choice (although socialists hope that the people would not make such choices), whereas the rationalist commitments of socialism and its critique of capitalism as inhumane would lead it to reject the decision of the people.

This point can also be understood as a possible tension between *procedural* and *substantive* justice. According to procedural justice, whatever is the outcome of a just procedure is itself just. Thus, if a participatory democracy, based on real equality of political power, follows a just procedure, then whatever the democratic procedure chooses is necessarily just. On the other hand, substantive justice identifies certain criteria for just distributions or outcomes, such as "to each according to his needs, from each according to his abilities." Now, a thoroughgoing procedural conception of justice cannot be combined with a purely substantive conception of social justice. The pure procedural conception maintains that an outcome is just if and only if it has been arrived at by the correct procedure; the substantive conception insists that regardless of the procedure that generated the outcome, that outcome is just if and only if it accords with the principles of social justice. Although, of course, in some cases the just procedure may lead to the substantively just outcome, this cannot be guaranteed; when the two conflict, considerations of justice will yield inconsistent judgments. And as we have seen (Section 2.3), consistency is necessary for an adequate political theory.

Joshua Cohen and Joel Rogers seek to resolve this tension in democratic-socialist theory by expanding the conditions for genuine democracy so as to include socialist economic organization. "To choose democracy," they write, "is to choose a form of social association which manifestly respects ... capacities [for reasoned social choice] within an order of equal freedom."[27] But because "the taking of profits under capitalism subordinates one class of individuals to another and thus ... subverts the conditions of equal freedom,"[28] capitalism subverts democracy. Democracy requires reasoned deliberation under conditions of equal freedom and power, and it is precisely this, Cohen and Rogers argue, that capitalism makes impossible. Consequently, true democratic decisions presuppose certain conditions, including "civil liberties, distributional measures of equality, full employment, ... a humane foreign policy, ... public control of investment, workplace democracy, and ... equality of opportunity."[29] All these conditions are said to be part of a *genuine democratic procedure:* there can be no conflict between justice as democratic decisions and substantive egalitarian-socialist justice, because truly democratic decisions can only occur in an egalitarian socialist society.

Democratic socialists, then, seek to resolve the apparent tension between their faith in democratic proceduralism and substantive egalitarianism by expanding the idea of democracy to include not only political equality understood as one person, one vote, but a genuine equality of political power (at least among groups), social equality, freedom as power, and freedom as autonomy. True democracy presupposes the socialist core values, thus eliminating any conflict. We witness once again the monistic inclinations of socialist thought: just as liberty was interpreted to include equality (Section 7.4), democracy is interpreted in a way that includes the socialist concepts of freedom, equality, and justice.

The Contrast to Liberal Democracy

The especially intimate tie in socialist thought between democracy and the just community is brought out by contrasting the socialist-egalitarian to liberal understandings of democracy. Jürgen Habermas, a leading contemporary exponent of democratic egalitarianism, explains the contrast thus:

> The dispute has to do with how to reconcile equality with liberty, unity with diversity, or the right of the majority with the right of the minority. Liberals begin with the legal institutionalization of equal liberties, conceiving these as rights held by individualized subjects. In their view, human rights enjoy normative priority over democracy and the constitutional separation of powers has priority over the will of the democratic legislature. Advocates of egalitarianism, on the other hand, conceive the collective practice of free and equal persons as sovereign will-formation. They understand human rights as an expression of the sovereign will of the people, and the constitutional separation of powers *emerges* from the enlightened will of the democratic legislature."[30]

As Habermas explains it, liberals give priority to substantive justice: democratic procedures are designed so as to promote and protect substantive rights. In contrast, he indicates, egalitarians emphasize procedural justice, and conceive of substantive justice as arising out of just procedures. We must be careful here, however: as we have just seen, egalitarians such as Cohen and Rogers interpret true democracy in a rich way, such that it presupposes the essence of socialist justice.

For socialists, then, "democracy" does not describe simply a set of formal decision procedures but a type of egalitarian community. In contrast, classical liberals understand democracy simply as a set of political institutions characterized by equal voting rights, frequent elections, competition by political parties, the right to form political parties, and so on. Importantly, in contrast to socialism, democracy is not itself a sort of freedom, but a useful instrument for protecting negative liberty from oppressive governments. Recall that according to Hayek, democracy "is an ideal worth fighting for to the utmost, because it is our only protection . . . against tyranny. Though democracy itself is not freedom . . . it is one of the most important safeguards of freedom."[31] Hayek, however, reminds us, "Liberalism is concerned with the functions of government and particularly with the limitation of all its power. Democracy is concerned with the question of who is to direct government. Liberalism requires that all power, and therefore also that of the majority, be limited."[32] It thus follows on the classical liberal view that liberalism is "incompatible with unlimited democracy, just as it is incompatible with all other unlimited government."[33]

For the classical liberal, democracy is not a way to reveal the voice of the people. Given the individualism and pluralism lying at the core of classical liberalism, it denies that "the people" speak with a single voice or have a common interest—individuals speak with a dizzying variety of voices and often have clashing interests—and even if it made sense to talk of "the people" having a voice or a general will, classical liberals have spent great effort showing that democratic institutions are especially unsuited to reveal what that might be.[34] Moreover, classical liberals can be deeply critical of the ways in which democracy functions; it can lead to waste and favor short-run gains over long-term benefits, and it often puts political power in the hands of the incompetent. Perhaps the classical liberal view is best summed up in the famous remark of Winston Churchill: democracy is the worst form of government, except for all the others.

Revisionist liberalism gives a much more prominent place to democracy; for the revisionist liberals, the right to equal civic status (understood at least as one person, one vote) in political decisions is itself a fundamental requirement of justice (see Section 6.4). Democracy is not simply an effective way to protect basic substantive rights, the right to participate in democratic decisions is itself a basic requirement of justice. Democratic participation enhances self-development and induces people to think about the common good rather than their narrow self-interests. The right to political voice is a complex of liberties, claims, and *powers;* the last (powers) is worth noting, as a right to participate in political decisions is necessarily a right to participate in changing the rights and duties of other people through legislation, and so qualifies not simply as a liberty or claim, but what Hohfeld calls a "power" (Section 8.1).

Although revisionist liberals are much more enthusiastic democrats than are classical liberals, they join their classical counterparts in insisting that the basic liberty rights of individuals limit legitimate democratic choice. Revisionist liberals also hold dear the basic liberties identified by the Bill of Rights: even a democracy giving each person an equal voice cannot justly violate these basic rights. Substantive justice thus clearly sets limits on procedural justice in liberal theory, keeping democracy away from the very core of the liberal conceptual map.

9.3 Three Conservative Approaches to Justice

Tradition, Convention, and Justice: Antirationalist Conservatism

In *The Subjection of Women* (1869), John Stuart Mill argued for a "perfect equality" between the sexes. Although his focus was on legal rights (and so equal civic status, see Section 6.4), he sought to push his egalitarian case further; he argued that family relations should be a "school in equality." Mill, of course, realized that this view directly opposed tradition and custom, which attributed differential and hierarchical positions within the family. But for Mill, that inequality was upheld by custom and tradition was no real justification for it. If custom and tradition opposed reason, then custom and tradition must give way. As Mill saw it, for the most part custom and tradition simply were the reflections of past injustices; that men had subjugated women in the past provides no good reason why women should accept an inferior status today. As I have previously indicated, this is a quintessential rationalist claim (Section 3.2). Custom and tradition are understood as the embodiments of superstition, unfairness, and caprice; only the rigorous application of impartial standards of justice verified by reason can tell us whether these past practices are to be condemned or continued.

Conservative criticism of rationalism is in large part a criticism of this rejection of tradition. Reason, the conservative believes, is not up to the task of reconstructing society in the light of abstract principles of justice. Indeed, reason itself depends on tradition. Although to some extent reason's deliverances can be conveyed in the preferred rationalist manner—abstract principles and rules (Section 3.2)—there are often "overtones, elements of 'tacit knowledge,' and insight where the principles and rules are inappropriate, which are not teachable by articulated assertions but which are required by intimate association and empathy with the acts of exemplification in the persons who perform them."[35] In Michael Oakeshott's terms (Section 3.2), reason involves practical knowledge, which can only be gained through the actual practices, for example, of scientific, political, or legal inquiry, and association with those who excel at it. More radically, some conservatives have argued that the very idea of reason depends on tradition and culture. What is rational or reasonable in, say, thirteenth-century England is not the same as in twenty-first–century England, much less twenty-first–century Japan. Can we say, for example, that the belief in angels is equally rational in all three cultures? According to Alasdair MacIntyre, a contemporary conservative-communitarian (Section 3.4),

It is of the first importance to remember that the project of founding a social order in which individuals could emancipate themselves from the contingency and particularity of tradition by appealing to genuinely universal, tradition-independent norms was, and is not only, a project of philosophers. It was and is the project of liberal, individualist society, and the most cogent reasons we have for believing that the hope of a tradition-independent rational universality is an illusion derives from the history of that project. For in the course of history, liberalism, which began as an appeal to the alleged principles of shared rationality against what was felt to be the tyranny of tradition, has itself been transformed into a tradition.[36]

On this antirationalist view, then, the place to look for justice is in one's own traditions and practices. This is not to imply, however, that the conservative can say nothing in general about justice. David Hume, agreeing with Hobbes (Section 8.2), tells us that all societies require rules of justice, a settled way of distinguishing "mine" and "thine." Hume, though, rejects the claim that these rights are established through a social contract. They arise, Hume argues, by *conventions*. A convention, says Hume, expresses our common interest in settled rules and allows us to coordinate our actions. Knowing that you accept the conventional rules of property allows me to act in a predictable and consistent way, which in turn allows you to do so.

> After this convention, concerning abstinence from the possessions of others, is entered into, and everyone has acquired a stability in his possessions, there immediately arises the ideas of justice and injustice; as also those of *property, right* and *obligation*. The latter are altogether unintelligible, without first understanding the former. Our property is nothing but those goods, whose constant possession is established by the laws of society; that is, by the laws of justice.[37]

It is important to stress that Hume believes that such conventions arise slowly, on the model of a language, rather than a once-and-for-all social contract (Section 8.2). Conventions and traditions *evolve;* they are not the result of one person's rationality, but the ongoing development of a society's wisdom.

Note that the Humean conception of justice ties justice to legality rather than to ideal justice (see Mill's points [1] and [2], Section 8.1). In the last sentence of the above quotation, Hume actually *identifies* the laws of justice with the laws of one's society: it is the actual laws of one's society that provide the conventions that make possible a settled distinction between mine and thine. Although Hume believes that rules of justice serve social utility (Sections 1.4, 6.2, 7.1, 8.1) insofar as they allow for a settled social life, he opposes anyone who would employ considerations of ideal justice based on furthering social utility to overturn current conventions. Moreover, although Hume can see how abstract reason points to the ideal of distributing material goods according to deserts, he believes that experience shows such a rationalist criterion is unworkable, as people disagree on merit and deservingness.[38]

This Humean orientation of much conservative thought helps explain the conservative preference for the *common law* over *legislation*. In the Anglo-American tradition, law has two different sources. Legislation, with

which we are all familiar, is the result of deliberate efforts of the legisla-
ture to enact general laws, often with the stated aim of furthering the social good. The very idea of general legislation has a rationalist bias: legis-
lators apply their reasoning to bring about certain results, within the
constraint of general laws (see Section 5.4). The other source of law is the
common law. It has developed over centuries in response to specific
problems brought before the courts. In making a decision, the courts—at
least according the ideal of the common law—do not seek to engage in
social engineering or bring about abstract social goods. They respond to
specific problems with interpreting specific laws, or specific problems
raised by the application of the laws. Each of the decisions, arrived at
to solve a specific problem, forms the precedent for further judicial
reasoning—later courts seek to make their decisions consistent with
earlier decisions. The result is a slow evolution of the laws of justice.
Rather than change to conform to abstract ideals or theories, the laws of
justice change in response to real cases in specific contexts.

Virtue and Conservatism: Antipluralist Conservatism

Liberalism and the Death of Virtue.   Consider an interpretation of the liberal project that has been advanced by conservative-communitarians
such as MacIntyre. The liberal aim, the story runs, is to develop a social
morality that does not require that we agree on what is good, what ends
are most worth pursuing, or what sort of life is a good life. In the ancient
world, and in traditional societies, it has been said, there was indeed
agreement on these matters. The Greeks, for example, upheld an ideal of
what a good person was, and this ideal united their community. Disagreements within their community—moral conflicts—could be resolved
by calling on this shared understanding of what constitutes a *virtuous*
person. As Aristotle saw it, humans possessed a natural end—a *telos*. To
achieve this end, to be a person of a certain sort, was the good for humans. Virtues, then, were those character traits that were conducive to
this end or a part of it. Nobility, courage, temperance, and fortitude were
such virtues, whereas the vices—injustice, intemperance, deceitfulness—
were traits of humans that prevented them from achieving that perfection natural to humans.

   Now, continues the narrative, a society that understands human life in
this way constitutes a community. It is not a mere collection of self-
seeking individuals, but an association that shares a common moral life
based on a shared conception of what it is to be a human and what ways
of living suit humans. But liberalism, it has been argued, destroys such a
community. Liberals' pluralism commits them to insisting that there is no
rationally obvious or right answer to the question, "What is the best way

to live?" The pluralism that the liberal so cherishes destroys the basis for a true moral community. For since we can no longer say that some ways of living are more human or better than others, we cannot say that those traits that promote this way of living are virtues and those that prevent it are vices. Indeed, the liberal has no conception of virtue and vice, or excellence, in human life. In place of a community bonded together by a vision of what it is to be human, the liberal puts forward a theory of moral chaos, in which whatever a person wants is acceptable. Thus, MacIntyre and other conservatives have charged that the liberal conception of justice, seeking to remain neutral among ways of living, results in nihilism—no beliefs are good or bad, right or wrong.[39]

The Enforcement of Morals. This interpretation of conservatism continues the stress on tradition, but insists that tradition is inherently antipluralist: traditions are defined by shared notions of excellence, and so a society's conception of justice must reflect this. A famous example of the divergence of liberal and virtue-conservative views of justice was the debate between liberals and conservatives over the regulation of homosexuality and prostitution in the United Kingdom in the 1960s, focused on the Report of the Committee on Homosexual Offences and Prostitution. This report—known as the Wolfenden Report—proposed a reform of the law in Britain relating to certain "victimless crimes." The report adopted an essentially liberal, Millian approach based on the harm principle (Sections 3.1, 4.3): in general it advocated that since these acts did not harm others, these so-called immoral acts should be decriminalized. There ensued a famous debate between the liberal legal philosopher H.L.A. Hart and the conservative Lord Devlin.

The Millian approach, defended by the report and Hart, maintained that acts that do not harm others, but are considered disgusting or degrading by most members of society, should not be punished by the law. Although Hart does not ascribe to Mill's harm principle in every respect, he holds that "on the narrower issue relevant to the enforcement of morality Mill seems to me right."[40] That is, Hart insisted that so-called immoral sexual behavior is not the proper subject of legal regulation. In their private lives, people should be free to do as they wish, as long as doing so does not harm others. As the report said, "There must remain a realm of private morality and immorality which is, in brief and crude terms, not the law's business."[41] The business of law is to provide a framework for living together, not to make people better or more moral.

Almost as soon as Mill defended the harm principle, conservatives attacked it. Sir James Fitzjames Stephen (1829–1894), an eminent English conservative thinker, complained of Mill's principle that it would be subversive of all that people commonly regard as morality. The only moral system which would comply with the principle stated by Mr. Mill would be one capable of being summed up as follows: "Let every man please himself without hurting his neighbor;" and every moral system which aimed at more than this, either to obtain benefits for society at large other than protection against injury or do good to the persons affected, would be wrong in principle. This would condemn every existing system of morals. Positive morality is nothing but a body of principles and rules more or less vaguely expressed, and more or less left to be understood, by which certain lines of conduct are forbidden under the penalty of general disapprobation, and that quite irrespectively of self-protection.[42]

Morality, Stephen is arguing, goes beyond merely preventing harm to others, and any political doctrine that would prohibit sanctions except to prevent harm would undermine morality itself.

Put simply, liberalism is said to destroy the moral bonds of society. Devlin, in his criticism of the Wolfenden Report, presents a similar criticism of Millian liberalism. It is not possible, Devlin argued,

to set theoretical limits to the power of the State to legislate against immorality. It is not possible to settle in advance exceptions to the general rule or to define inflexibly areas of morality into which the law is in no circumstances to enter. Society is entitled by means of its laws to protect itself from dangers, whether from within or without. . . . Societies disintegrate from within more frequently than they are broken up by external pressures. There is a disintegration when no common morality is observed and history shows that the loosening of moral bonds is often the first stage of disintegration, so that society is justified in taking the same steps to preserve its moral code as it does to preserve its government and other essential institutions. The suppression of vice is as much the law's business as the suppression of subversive activities.[43]

Devlin, then, is arguing that a society is partially constituted by a code of morality, which includes public acknowledgment of conceptions of virtue and vice. This being so, it is the proper office of a government to protect this morality by legally punishing those who engage in vicious acts, such as homosexuality, prostitution, and the selling (and perhaps the reading) of pornography.

Devlin thus criticizes Mill and the authors of the Wolfenden Report for failing to see that a society is founded on notions of what constitutes good and bad people. This "shared morality" is part of the historical traditions of a society. A rationalist such as Mill, who would reject this in the name of abstract principles, simply does not understand what a society is. A society without a shared morality would disintegrate—it would find that the cement that bound it together was gone, and all that remains is a collection of rootless and confused individuals. And of course, that is precisely what the conservatives charge that Millian morality has produced. Our society, the conservative maintains, is composed of individuals who have no sense of the traditions of the community; no sense of the shared values that constitute that community; and, ultimately, individuals with very few values at all. So, for Devlin, it is not wrong to enforce a shared morality of a society, and this includes matters concerning sexual relations, taking drugs, harming oneself, and so on.

In his liberal reply, Hart distinguished what he calls the "moderate" and the "extreme" forms of Devlin's argument:

> According to the moderate thesis, a shared morality is the cement of society; without it there would be aggregates of individuals but no society. "A recognized morality" is, in Lord Devlin's words, "as necessary to society's existence as a recognized government" and although a particular act of immorality may not harm or endanger or corrupt others nor, when done in private, either shock or give offence to others, this does not conclude the matter. For we must not view the conduct in isolation from its effect on the moral code; if we remember this, we can see that one who is "no menace to others" nonetheless may by his immoral conduct "threaten one of the great moral principles upon which society is based." In this sense the breach of the moral principle is an offense "against society as a whole," and society may use the law to preserve its morality as it uses it to safeguard anything else essential to its existence.[44]

This, says Hart, is the most moderate interpretation of the conservative argument that a shared morality is necessary to the existence of a society. The argument is, in short, that to weaken the shared morality of a society does, in fact, lead to weakening the society itself. But Hart simply disputes this supposed fact. No reputable historian, he says, has ever held that departures in sexual morality, even when these deviant practices are engaged in within the privacy of one's home, threaten society's very existence. Allowing divergence in one area of morality—that concerning sexual practices—need not lead to a breakdown of consensus on other parts of morality more central to public life. As Hart says, morality is not a "single seamless web," such that a break in one area will leave the rest in tatters.

Faced by the lack of evidence in support of the moderate thesis, Hart argues that conservatives sometimes resort to what Hart calls the "extreme thesis":

> The extreme thesis does not look upon a shared morality as of merely instrumental value analogous to ordered government, and it does not justify the

punishment of immorality as a step taken like punishment of treason, to preserve a society from dissolution or collapse. Instead the enforcement of morality is regarded as a thing of value, even if immoral acts harm no one directly, or indirectly by weakening the moral cement of society.[45]

Whereas the above quotation from Devlin seems to endorse the moderate thesis, Hart indicates that Stephen supports the extreme thesis. As indicated in the above quotation from Stephen, the punishment of immorality is seen as simply the right and proper thing to do; no claim is made that such behavior has bad consequences by weakening society (as the moderate thesis holds); it is simply held that immoral behavior, including immoral sexual behavior, ought rightly to be punished. This, of course, is a strongly anti-Millian, and, indeed, an antiliberal position. It asserts that the proper office of coercion in a society is to endorse a certain way of living and discourage those who would act differently.

Conservatism and Collectivism: "My Station and Its Duties"

Our analysis of political concepts began with Plato's inquiry into the nature of justice (Section 1.1); we have yet to consider Plato's favored conception of justice. Plato thinks that justice involves the correct ordering or harmonious arrangement of the whole; a just man's soul is organized so that each element performs its proper task; correspondingly, a just state is organized so that each part properly fulfills its function, leading to the healthy working of the whole. The focus of justice is not, then, individual rights in the sense of claims that are owed to individuals, but those duties, powers, and claims that the individual must possess if she is to perform her proper social function. And because societies are complex wholes and not simply aggregations of individuals (Section 3.4), these functions will be differentiated. Not everyone has the same function. Plato thus divides his ideally just state in classes—the guardians who rule; the military class that is to enforce the decisions of the guardians; and the economic class of farmers, those in trades, merchants, and so on. Each class in a just state, then, will have the rights and duties that are necessary for it to perform its function. "We have laid down as a universal principle," says Socrates, "that everyone ought to perform the one function in the community for which his nature best suited him. Well, I believe that that principle . . . is justice."[46] Justice demands that one perform the duties of one's station or function in the community.

This, broadly speaking, Platonic theory of justice has exercised great influence in conservative political thinking. Samuel Coleridge (1772–1834) explicitly understood the state as a "moral unit, an organic whole."[47] Consequently, Coleridge maintained that an individual's rights and duties are determined by his or her place in the whole. A similar view, stressing the embedded nature of humans (Section 3.3) and our place in the social organism, was offered by F. H. Bradley (1846–1924):

> To know what a man is . . . you must not take him in isolation. He is one of a people, he was born into a family, he lives in a certain society, in a certain state. What he has to do depends on what his place is, what his function is, and all that comes from his station in the organism. . . . We must content ourselves by pointing out that there are such facts as the family, then in the middle position a man's own profession and society and, over all, the larger community of the state. . . . We must say that a man's life with its moral duties is in the main filled up by his station in that system of wholes which the state is, and that this, partly by its laws and institutions, and still more by its spirit, gives him the life which he lives and ought to live. . . . In short, man is a social being.[48]

It is a person's place in his family, profession, community, and state that determines what justice demands of him and what is owed to him. Given this view of society and justice, we can understand the conservative's antipathy to equality (Section 7.5). Since the community is a complex system in which different people perform various functions, and since justice requires that one have the rights and duties necessary to perform one's function, it will not result in a system of equal rights and duties, much less rights to equality of resources or welfare. It might be said that we equally have claims to those rights we need to perform our social functions, but these rights will be different and unequal.[49] Not only is this collectivist interpretation of justice inegalitarian, it also seems prone to limiting liberty. Plato's theory is infamous in this regard—his ideal, just state abolished the family in favor of mandatory communal rearing of children. We need not, however, go all the way back to Plato; Thomas Carlyle (1795–1881) voiced deep worries about classical liberal conceptions of a free society. Carlyle harshly criticized the individualism behind classical liberal liberty and the market order, "which has to purchase itself by social isolation, and each man standing separate from the other, having 'no business with him' but a cash account," all of which amounts to little more than the "liberty to die from starvation."[50]

> Liberty? The true liberty of a man, you would say, consisted in his finding out, or being forced to find out the right path, and to walk thereon. To learn, or to be taught, what work he was actually able for; and then by permission, persuasion, and even compulsion, to set about doing the same! That is his true blessedness, honour, "liberty" and the maximum of wellbeing: if liberty be not that, I for one have small care about liberty.[51]

Conservatives such as Carlyle have been attracted to medieval society rather than liberal capitalism. In an organic, hierarchical order, each fulfills a function, and society seeks to ensure that a person has what he needs to do his job well, unlike liberal market society, which leaves a person to sink or swim according to his talents and luck.

The moral and methodological collectivist tendencies of much conservative thought seem in tension with conservatives' valuing of liberty. We saw that one reason that conservatives reject equality is their perception that it is hostile to liberty (Section 7.5), but liberty itself is not firmly anchored in this sort of collectivist conservatism. To be sure, given English society and its traditions, some civil and political liberties are central to that tradition (Section 5.4); but a conservative analysis of nonliberal traditions (say, eighteenth-century France or twentieth-century Russia) would not provide a general case for individual freedom. And even in the Anglo-American tradition, it is not clear that the conservative case is for liberty for everyone; as Carlyle suggests, it implies liberty for the wise with deference from their inferiors.

A morally collectivist picture of the just society is not uniquely conservative. Especially in the nineteenth and the first half of the twentieth centuries, there was a widespread reaction to the individualism of classical liberalism: conservatives, monistic revisionist liberals (Section 8.3), and socialists all proposed conceptions of a just society that understood societies themselves as (to use Rousseau's words) a "public person." This collectivism led to conceptions of justice that departed from classical liberalism in three main ways. First, citizens not only have duties to other citizens and to the government, but they have *duties to society as a whole*. The collectivity becomes itself a rights holder against citizens, and citizens have duties of justice to their society, such as to perform their station or to contribute to this common good. Second, this collectivist orientation to justice leads to a morally crucial difference between those who are members and those who are not members of society. Foreigners and aliens are not part of the community; they do not owe the same duties to it, nor do they have the same claims against it. If justice depends on one's role in the community, those outside the community are, from the perspective of justice, at the periphery of the practice of justice, perhaps even entirely excluded. Moreover, subgroups that do not fit into the larger community or refuse primary allegiance to the common good—for example, communists, Jews, Catholics, Jehovah's Witnesses, atheists—may also be relegated to a second-class status. Third, as the community becomes a moral or public person, it may come to hold rights and duties against other communities. Thus, collectivist liberals seeking to defend cultural diversity—and so who wish to ensure that some ethnic or cultural groups are not accorded second-class status because they do not fit into the wider community—hold that these various communities have rights against each other. For example, it has been argued that the French-speaking *community* in Canada has rights to maintain its cultural identity, rights that the English-speaking *community* must respect.[52]

9.4 Summary

This chapter has explored a variety of socialist and conservative accounts of justice. The common theme running through these theories is a conceptual connection between justice and the organization of society, and the nature of the community. We began in Section 9.1 by examining Karl Marx's views on justice. Marx seemed suspicious of claims relying on ideal justice; they appear to presuppose a liberal moral individualism insofar as people's motivations are not determined by their place in the economic system but by their individual sense of justice. I also argued that because Marx ties justice closely to legality and the nature of society, he tends to see justice as relative to economic systems—capitalist justice is thus fundamentally different from socialist justice. Marx does, though, give us some clues about ideal socialist justice: he seems to hold that it would first give workers what they deserve (thus overcoming capitalist exploitation), and once the corruption of capitalism had been left behind, and so alienation was overcome, resources would be distributed according to need.

I noted in the discussion of Marx his reluctance to provide detailed principles of justice to guide socialist society. Except for its insistence on the abolition of capitalism, socialism has in general been less ready than liberalism to advance principles of justice. One reason for this, explored in Section 9.3, is socialism's deep devotion to equality of power and its resulting commitment to radical democracy. If power is to be equalized, so must political power; this leads to a democratic ideal of the just society. This, however, implies that the principles of a just society must be a matter of the popular will of the egalitarian cooperative community.

Section 9.3 considered three conservative approaches to justice. *Justice as tradition or convention* conceives of justice as essentially the legal justice of an existing society and is generally critical of appeals to ideal justice. This conception of justice is strongly antirationalist: it places its faith in the gradual evolution of norms of justice employed in a society rather than any philosopher's arguments about justice. *Justice as virtue* is more rationalist, insisting that the traditions of a society are based on conceptions of virtues and vice, and it is crucial to a just society that these notions be enforced by society. We considered at some length Lord Devlin's argument for the legal suppression of homosexuality and prostitution as an example of this approach to justice. Last, the most collectivist conservative approach to justice is exemplified in the idea that a just society is one in which people are able to, and do, perform the *duties of their stations*. Given the complex nature of society, these stations are differentiated, involving various and unequal rights. These three conservative approaches are variations of the themes of collectivism, traditionalism, and anti-rationalism; they are not mutually exclusive alternatives, but can be combined in a variety of ways to produce variations of conservative justice.

Notes

1. See, for example, James P. Sterba's comments in his edited volume, *Justice: Alternative Political Perspectives*, 2nd ed. (Belmont, CA: Wadsworth, 1992), p. 7.

2. A good example is Kai Nielsen, *Equality and Liberty: A Defense of Radical Egalitarianism* (Totowa, NJ: Rowman and Allenheld, 1985).

3. C. B. Macpherson, *Democratic Theory: Essays in Retrieval* (Oxford: Clarendon Press, 1973), pp. 64–65.

4. Karl Marx, *Capital,* in Robert C. Tucker, ed., *The Marx-Engels Reader,* 2nd ed. (New York: W. W. Norton, 1978), p. 363.

5. Marx and Engels, *The Communist Manifesto,* in *The Marx-Engels Reader,* p. 498.

6. Frederick Engels, "Socialism: Utopian and Scientific," in *The Marx-Engels Reader,* p. 685.

7. Ibid., p. 700.

8. Karl Marx, "Critique of the Gotha Program," in *The Marx-Engels Reader,* p. 531.

9. Marx, quoted in Allen Wood, *Karl Marx* (London: Routledge and Kegan Paul, 1981), pp. 130–131.

10. Ibid., p. 131.

11. Karl Marx, "Critique of the Gotha Program," quoted in Wood, *Karl Marx,* p. 136. In Tucker, *The Marx-Engels Reader,* a slightly different translation is given, referring to "fair" rather than "just" (p. 528).

12. For a Marxist effort to account for both official state justice and ideal justice, see Milton Fisk, *The State and Justice: An Essay in Political Theory* (Cambridge: Cambridge University Press, 1989).

13. Ziyad I. Husami, "Marx on Distributive Justice," in Marshall Cohen, Thomas Nagel, and Thomas Scanlon, eds., *Marx, Justice and History* (Princeton: Princeton University Press, 1980), pp. 46–47. See also Wood's reply in the same volume.

14. Jon Elster, *An Introduction to Karl Marx* (Cambridge: Cambridge University Press, 1986), p. 95.

15. See G. A. Cohen, "The Concept of Exploitation," in *Marx, Justice and History,* pp. 135–157.

16. See Judith N. Shklar, *The Faces of Injustice* (New Haven: Yale University, 1990).

17. Karl Marx, "Critique of the Gotha Program," p. 530.

18. Ibid., p. 531.

19. See Edward Nell and Onora O'Neill, "Justice Under Socialism," in Sterba, ed., *Justice: Alternative Political Perspectives*, pp. 87–97. Compare, however, Steven Lukes, *Marxism and Morality* (Oxford: Oxford University Press, 1987).

20. Lukes, *Marxism and Morality*, p. 59.

21. All quotes in this paragraph are from ibid., p. 58.

22. C. B. Macpherson, *The Life and Times of Liberal Democracy* (Oxford: Oxford University Press, 1977), p. 111.

23. Christopher J. Berry, *The Idea of a Democratic Community* (New York: St. Martin's Press, 1989), p. 77.

24. Quoted in Carole Pateman, *Participation in Democratic Theory* (Cambridge: Cambridge University Press, 1970), p. 36.

25. For an analysis of Cole's views, see A. W. Wright, *G.D.H. Cole and Socialist Democracy* (Oxford: Clarendon Press, 1979).

26. For a general discussion, see Robert A. Dahl, *A Preface to Economic Democracy* (Berkeley: University of California Press, 1985).

27. Joshua Cohen and Joel Rogers, *On Democracy: Toward a Transformation of American Society* (Harmondsworth, UK: Penguin, 1983), p. 147.

28. Ibid., p. 148.

29. Ibid., p. 147.

30. Jürgen Habermas, "Popular Sovereignty as Procedure," in James Bohman and William Rehg, eds., *Deliberative Democracy: Essays on Reason and Politics* (Cambridge, MA: MIT Press, 1997), p. 44.

31. F. A. Hayek, *Law, Legislation and Liberty*, vol. 3: *The Political Order of a Free People* (London: Routledge and Kegan Paul, 1979), p. 5.

32. Hayek, "Liberalism," in his *New Studies in Philosophy, Politics, Economics and the History of Ideas* (London: Routledge and Kegan Paul, 1978), p. 143.

33. Ibid.

34. See, for example, William Riker, *Liberalism Against Populism* (San Francisco: W. W. Freemen, 1982).

35. Edward Shils, *Tradition* (Chicago: University of Chicago Press, 1981), p. 22.

36. Alasdair MacIntyre, *Whose Justice? Whose Rationality?* (Notre Dame, IN: University of Notre Dame Press, 1988), p. 335. See also John Gray, *Enlightenment's Wake* (London: Routledge, 1995), chaps. 1, 10.

37. David Hume, *A Treatise of Human Nature*, L. A. Selby-Bigge and P. H. Nidditch, eds. (Oxford: Clarendon Press, 1978), Book 3, Part 2, sect. 2. Emphasis in original.

38. See David Miller, *Social Justice* (Oxford: Clarendon Press, 1976), pp. 166ff.

39. Alasdair MacIntyre, *After Virtue* (Notre Dame, IN: University of Notre Dame Press, 1981). It is important to stress that some conservatives dissent from this view. For a conservative who embraces a version of pluralism, see John Kekes, *A Case for Conservatism* (Ithaca, NY: Cornell University Press, 1998). It is at best contentious whether this historical account is accurate. For a critical examination, see Derek L. Phillips, *Looking Backward: A Critical Appraisal of Communitarian Thought* (Princeton: Princeton University Press, 1993).

40. H.L.A. Hart, *Law, Liberty and Morality* (London: Oxford University Press, 1963), p. 6.

41. Quoted in ibid., pp. 14–15.

42. James Fitzjames Stephen, *Liberty, Equality, Fraternity,* quoted in Louis Blom-Cooper and Gavin Drewey, eds., *Law and Morality* (London: Duckworth, 1976), p. 14.

43. Patrick Devlin, *The Enforcement of Morals* (London: Oxford University Press, 1968), pp. 12–14.

44. Hart, *Law, Liberty and Morality,* pp. 48–49. The quoted passages are from Devlin, *The Enforcement of Morals,* pp. 13, 8.

45. Hart, *Law, Liberty and Morality,* pp. 51–52.

46. Plato, *The Republic,* Francis MacDonald Cornford, ed., trans. (Oxford: Oxford University Press, 1945), p. 127 [IV 432].

47. Samuel Coleridge, *On the Constitution of the Church and State,* John Barrell, ed. (London: Dent, 1972), p. 117.

48. F. H. Bradley, *Ethical Studies,* 2nd ed. (Oxford: Clarendon Press, 1927), pp. 173–174.

49. See Crane Brinton, *English Political Thought in the Nineteenth Century* (New York: Harper and Row, 1962), p. 82.

50. Thomas Carlyle, *Past and Present* (London: Dent, 1960), pp. 211, 204.

51. Ibid., p. 204.

52. For a good selection of essays on this topic, see Will Kymlicka, ed., *The Rights of Minority Cultures* (Oxford: Oxford University Press, 1995).

10
POLITICAL AUTHORITY

10.1 Conservatism and Political Authority

On Being "An Authority"

The crux of accepting another person as an authority seems to be that you "surrender your judgment" to the authority. In *Casablanca*, Ingrid Bergman tells Humphrey Bogart that he will have to "do the thinking for both of us." She surrenders her judgment to him: she will allow *her actions* to be determined by what *he decides*. If we value liberty and autonomy (Sections 4.1, 4.2), we will be suspicious of authority: when a person is guided by another in this way, she is other-ruled rather than self-ruled. It is for just this reason that many anarchists reject the very idea of political authority. If our core value is autonomy or liberty, it might seem that we should never surrender our judgment to others: we should always have the right and responsibility of acting on our own judgment.[1]

It seems, though, terribly difficult to avoid ever surrendering your judgment. Consider a trip to the doctor, when the doctor tells you that you have an ailment and prescribes a treatment. Most of us do not have the expertise to evaluate the doctor's diagnosis and prescription; even if she seeks to explain it to us in detail, few of us have the background in biology and physiology, or the clinical experience, to really make a judgment about what should be done. To a very large extent, we follow the doctor's judgment. Of course, we may get a second opinion, but then we are following another's doctor's opinion. To be sure, we do not totally surrender our judgment: if the doctor tells us that we need to stand on our head for a week to cure our headache, few will take that judgment seriously. But within a wide range, we rely on the doctor's judgment, because we believe it is superior to our own. As Richard B. Friedman, a leading theorist of authority, observes,

> The basic purpose of this sort of authority is to substitute the knowledge of one person for the ignorance or lesser knowledge of another person, al-

though what the person who defers thereby comes to possess as a surrogate for his ignorance is not knowledge, but "true belief" in the sense of belief that is indeed justified, though the believer knows not why.[2]

We should distinguish relying on such authority from merely asking for advice. One specialist may ask the advice of another in a complicated case. The specialist may want to make sure that she has not overlooked anything in her deliberations, so she may consult another. But she does not surrender her judgment to the other; she retains the final decision about what should be done, a decision that she will make on the basis of her own extensive knowledge, supplemented by the advice of others. When I go to the doctor, however, I am not merely asking for advice to supplement my own deliberations; the doctor's deliberations *supplant* what I originally thought and I take over her beliefs as if they were my own. I confidently tell my family and friends that I have "iritis," though I am not really sure just what it is or how the doctor knows I have it. Yet, as Friedman points out, because I do not really have the knowledge that would justify those beliefs—I cannot actually replicate the doctor's reasoning—I take them on largely trust. I have "true beliefs" about what course I should take, but I do not have the knowledge on which those beliefs are based.

As Friedman stresses, "One person defers to another on some matter because he lacks the knowledge or insight that he assumes the other possesses."[3] At the heart of this type of authority relation is an *inequality of knowledge*. The authority relation does not create this inequality, it recognizes a *prior* inequality. "It is because of the superior insight of some person that he should be acknowledged as 'an authority' by others: the deference relation is supposed to reflect the antecedent concrete 'personal' differences between the parties."[4]

Being "An Authority" and the Art of Politics: Platonic Collectivism

The idea of being "an authority" has, as Friedman points out, been employed in political philosophy. Tocqueville, the great French political theorist of the nineteenth century (Section 7.1), held that society could not exist without common beliefs. And Friedman tells us, Tocqueville "makes quite clear in an extended discussion of this matter that he means beliefs held on the 'principle of authority,' that is, 'on trust and without discussion.'"[5] Being "an authority" will be particularly important to an account of political authority if it is held that the art of politics is a special art and those who know it best should rule. As far back as Plato, political theorists—especially those who are conservatively inclined—have justified political authority because some are "an authority on politics." Plato insisted that politics is an art, and like any art, such as medicine or carpentry, it should be practiced by those who have the necessary knowledge and skill. Those drawing on this conception of political authority have, like Plato himself, often compared the state to a ship at sea; a ship needs a crew with diverse skills, but it also needs a captain who has the necessary skill and knowledge to safely navigate the many perils confronting the ship. The sailors submit to the authority of the captain because the captain has the skill and knowledge to preserve the ship; in the same way citizens ought to surrender their judgment to those who know the art of politics. Thus, says Thomas Carlyle, the wise deserve to be the masters of others.[6]

Notice that this is an application of Plato's collectivist theory of justice (Section 9.3). If justice demands that each person perform his or her rightful function, and have the rights and powers necessary to do so, then justice demands that those who have the skill to rule and manage the state have the rights and powers—the authority—to do so. Certainly, says the conservative, the skill needed to run a government is greater than the skill needed to build a house; and no one thinks that everyone is equally skilled in house building. Indeed, when building a house we take great care to ensure that we find the most skillful builder. If we take all this trouble with a house, we should not be any less careful with the affairs of government. Those who are skillful should run the government, and others should acknowledge their authority in these matters. Hence the politically skilled should rule, and others should accept their authority and obey.

Oakeshott on Political Authority: Antirationalist and Anticollectivist Conservatism

The version of conservatism we have thus far considered supposes that there is a goal or end of political life, and some should have authority over others because they are more competent at achieving this goal. Many reject this view of political life. Politics, we may say, is not an art like medicine, for medicine has an aim, a goal—health. And it is just because medicine has a goal that expert knowledge is useful, for the *expert knows the best way to achieve the goal*. But it is often said, politics has no goal; people in society have a wide variety of different goals and values. Because there is no political goal corresponding to "health," we cannot treat the politician as an expert who knows the best route to a goal. Just because there is no single political goal, politics cannot be the art of achieving that goal.

One of the interesting features of Oakeshott's conservatism is that he agrees that politics does not have a goal such as health, or making us all better people, or whatever. But Oakeshott says, it is those who do not understand politics—the politically naïve voters of today's democracies, for example—who fail to see this. Those who fail to grasp the real nature of politics, who think there is some common goal to be achieved, are always seeking some political utopia. He writes,

> To some people, "government" appears as a vast reservoir of power which inspires them to dream of what might be made of it. They have favorite projects, of various dimensions, which they sincerely believe are for the benefit of mankind, and to capture this source of power, if necessary to increase it, and to use it for imposing their favourite projects upon their fellows is what they understand as the adventure of governing men. They are, thus, disposed to recognize government as an instrument of passion; the art of politics is to inflame and direct desire. . . .
>
> Now, the disposition to be conservative in respect of politics reflects a quite different view of the activity of governing. The man of this disposition understands it to be the business of government not to inflame passion and give it new objects to feed upon, but to inject into the activities of already too passionate men an ingredient of moderation; to restrain, to deflate, to pacify and to reconcile; not to stoke the fires of desire, but to damp them down.[7]

The politically inexperienced, Oakeshott argues, are those who are likely to conceive of politics as aiming at some great goal, be it social justice, equality, or peace on earth. Not understanding the limited possibilities of politics, the politically inexperienced see politics as the way to solve all of our problems (and, of course, they become disappointed and cynical when they discover that this is impossible). To a conservative, in contrast, "Governing is understood to be a secondary activity."[8] Politics is not itself directly concerned with promoting goals, but is the art of arranging social life so that various goals can be pursued by different people with conflicting aims.[9] Yet, although it is in this sense a second-order activity—an activity devoted to regulating other activities without an end of its own—it still is a specific art, and so one that requires practical knowledge.

"Politics," says Oakeshott, is "the activity of attending to the general arrangements of a set of people whom chance or choice have brought together."[10] This "attending to" their affairs requires knowledge of their political traditions; it requires amending, preserving, and extending those traditions in the ongoing effort to attend to the problems of life among diverse people. Consequently, those who do not grasp the political tradition are unable to effectively exercise political authority. Although Oakeshott's antirationalist case for political expertise differs from Plato's monistic collectivism, both identify politics as an art that cannot be successfully practiced by the inexperienced. Thus, neither Plato nor Oakeshott—nor any conservative—is enamored of democracy; for it gives political power to those who are without political knowledge, with the result that they let loose their passions in the political realm (see Section 3.3). The art of political rule involves the art of restraining passions and enthusiasms, which continually threaten to engulf politics. And in most conservative writings, there is a clear indication that the mass, or the majority, are prone to such passions.

10.2 On Being "In Authority"

The Contrast with "An Authority"

Friedman tells us,

> A person can be said to "have authority" in two distinct senses. For one, he may be said to be "in authority," meaning that he occupies some office, position, or status which entitles him to make decisions about how other people should behave. But, secondly, a person may be said to be "an authority" on something, meaning that his views or utterances are to be entitled to be believed (including, to complicate matters, beliefs about the right and wrong ways of doing things).[11]

The notion of "an authority"—which we have been examining—concentrates on belief and knowledge, whereas the idea of someone who is "in authority" points to her entitlement to regulate action. If you accept someone as "an authority," your beliefs are guided by her judgment; if you accept your doctor as an authority on medicine, you believe her when she tells you that you have a certain disease and what you should do about it. But to accept someone as "in authority" is to obey her directives, not necessarily to believe that what she says is correct. As Friedman puts it, when one acknowledges another as being "in authority," instead of acting on one's "private judgment" one acts on the will of another. You follow the will of another even if it conflicts with your own private judgment: on this matter you say the person "in authority" will decide what is to be done. Her will replaces your decision. Particularly important in this regard is that your obedience to the directives of the authority is not dependent on your agreeing with her wisdom. Indeed, the whole point of recognizing another as being "in authority" is that the validity of her directives is not dependent on your agreeing to their soundness. As Friedman says,

> The idea being conveyed by such notions as the surrender of private judgment or individual judgment is that in obeying, say, a command simply be-

cause it comes from someone accorded the right to rule, the subject does not make his obedience conditional on his own personal examination of the thing he is being asked to do. Rather, he accepts as a sufficient reason for following a prescription the fact that it is prescribed by someone acknowledged by him as entitled to rule. The man who accepts authority is thus said to surrender his private or individual judgment because he does not insist that reasons be given that he can grasp and that satisfy him, as a condition of his obedience.[12]

In many ways, following the directives of someone who is "in authority" is much more puzzling than doing what you are told by "an authority." If someone is "an authority," she knows more than you do, and things will turn out better if you follow the directives of a more knowledgeable person. But why would we ever follow the directives of someone who is "in authority," given that such authority makes no claim to be any wiser or any more knowledgeable than are we? After all, if the person with authority does not have special knowledge of political matters, why are we obeying him? Why should we accept direction of our actions by someone who does not know any more than we do?

Equality and Coordination Problems

To grasp why we might follow someone who is simply "in authority," consider

a situation in which a collection of individuals wish to engage in some common activity requiring a certain degree of coordinated action but they are unable to agree on what the substance of their coordinated action should be. And because they cannot agree, it follows that if each insists on following his own views, the common activity will be made impossible. Since the cost of insisting on following one's own judgment is chaos, it may then appear reasonable for each man to sacrifice his own judgment as the basis of (some part) of his behavior and also to forego pressing his own views on all others, even though he regards his own views as fully justified and theirs as mistaken; and instead accept someone to make binding decisions for all, or to establish some procedure, such as election lottery or hereditary lineage, designed to define who is to have the right to make binding decisions upon all.[13]

In this case, we all want to engage in some cooperative activity, but we each have different ideas about how to go about it. Our situation is not simply a onetime conflict that might be subject to negotiation; we will find ourselves in constant disagreement as we go about the activity. If

ALF

		Left	Right
	Left	Alf: 2 Betty: 1	Alf: 3 Betty: 3
BETTY	Right	Alf: 4 Betty: 4	Alf: 1 Betty: 2

FIGURE 10.1   A Coordination Problem

each insists on the right to decide for herself, we will not gain the benefits of cooperation; instead of cooperation we confront endless disputes or chaos, in which each does his own thing, and so activity remains uncoordinated. We will, in short, find ourselves in Hobbes's state of nature (Section 8.2).

The case for a coordinator is clarified in Figure 10.1. Alf and Betty are confronted with four possibilities: they each drive on the right, they each drive on the left, Alf drives on the right/Betty on the left, Alf drives on the left/Betty drives on the right. The numbers in the cells indicate how each ranks that option. In this case, Alf is a right-handed person who has a slight preference for a traffic code according to which he drives on the right side of the road, since he finds it slightly easier to shift gears with his right hand. Thus, Alf's first choice is for everyone to drive on the right. Betty, on the other hand, is left-handed and, for parallel reasons, would prefer a traffic code that instructs people to drive on the left. Her first choice is for everyone to drive on the left. We can see, however, that neither wishes to go it alone and drive on the side he or she most prefers regardless of what others do: that would lead to Alf driving on the right and Betty on the left—a disaster, since they will eventually crash! What is most important is that they drive on the same side of the road, even if it is not the side that is most favored. Either coordination point (right/right; left/left) is vastly preferred by both of them to options in which they fail to coordinate. Both, then, would benefit from a coordinator who proclaims which side of the road to drive on. Even if, say, the coordinator selects the right-hand side, which is Betty's second choice, Betty has every reason to obey, since she benefits from achieving coordination. In this sort of case, then, it is not relevant whether the coordinator chooses wisely (there probably is no correct answer to this problem); what is important is that the coordinator instructs everyone on what to do.

We require this type of coordinator, then, when we disagree about what is best or what we most prefer. When we all agree on what is to be done, the problem is not severe: our individual judgments converge. But that is rare in complex activities involving many people; typically we each have different judgments about what should be done. In this common case, we can only continue our cooperative activity if some people act in ways that conflict with their personal judgments about what is best to do or what they would most prefer. That is, it is necessary that they act on the judgments of the authoritative coordinator rather than their own judgment about what is best.

This case for authority, then, directly follows from Hobbes's analysis of the state of nature in which each person follows his own private judgments, leading to war (Section 8.2). There can be no justice or order in such a condition. To create a just and peaceful society, Hobbes argues, we must create someone who has authority—someone "in authority"—to resolve our disputes and direct us in what we should do. This does not mean, however, that we must accept the authoritative coordinator's opinions about what is best. For cooperation to continue, it must be the case that people can say, (1) "Well, φ isn't the option that I think is best, but that's what the coordinator says we should do, so I'll do it." And that is very different from (2) "Well, if the authoritative coordinator says that φ is the best way, it must be. I guess I was wrong to think not-φ." Friedman's point is that "in authority" concerns (1); it does not require (2), which is a case where one thinks that the coordinator is "an authority" about φ-ing. Again, the merits or demerits of the particular decision are irrelevant to the decision to obey in case (1); you do not obey because the authority has the right answer, but because he gives an answer that allows for a coordinated solution. Friedman writes,

> From this standpoint, then, the basis of the claim to obedience made by a person "in authority" is of a very special kind. The claim does not derive from any special personal characteristics of the person invested with authority, such as superior power of judgment or special knowledge (as in the case of being "an authority"). His claim to be obeyed is simply that he has been put "in authority" according to established procedure, rather than that his decisions are, on independent grounds, meritorious, or superior decisions.[14]

Friedman takes the argument one step further. Not only does the concept of being "in authority" not presuppose that he who is in authority is also "an authority," but the two ideas of authority involve different presuppositions. The argument that we have just examined for having an authoritative coordinator of actions starts from the premise that we are equally free (Section 6.3) and are not willing to defer to the judgments of others. It is because each person has his own opinions, and does not think that others are especially wiser than is he, that the basic problem develops. Each person thinks that he knows the best way to act, and because others disagree they fail to coordinate their actions. No one thinks that any of the others is especially wiser, so each keeps to his own opinion. Still, some one thing must be done if their activity is to be coordinated. So they develop some procedure whereby they select someone to coordinate their actions even though they continue to disagree about what is best. So, following once again Hobbes's analysis of the state of nature (Section 8.2), Friedman argues that it is precisely because each of us considers ourself to be equally free—we do not recognize the natural superiority of anyone to rule over us—that we argue and disagree, and so need someone to be "in authority." In contrast, he argues that the idea of "an authority" involves a basic *in*equality; someone knows better than the others, and so they should not only accept her directions about how to act, they should accept her opinions too.

Obedience When You Think the Authority Is Wrong

Friedman's analysis of political authority is enlightening. He explains what is perhaps the most important feature of political authority: that we have reason to obey even when we think that it is wrong. If, as conservatives are apt to think, political authority is based on being "an authority," accepting the authority of the state seems servile. For you must not only accept its directions, but you must alter your judgments to conform to its dictates. You must say to yourself, "If the government says that such-and-such is the best policy, then I guess it must be the best. The government knows its business." Most of us, however, are not prepared to say that: we are not prepared to abandon our political judgments. We continue to evaluate government policies as good or bad. Yet, this might seem to mean that we only obey laws when we agree with them. "I'm not going to abandon my judgment," you might say, "so only if I think a law or a policy is good will I follow it." But that would seem to undermine political authority entirely. Laws are then little more than suggestions put forward by the government for the evaluation of each citizen.

Friedman points to a way out of this difficulty: we are not faced with the choice of either (1) abandoning our independent judgment and becoming servile subjects, or (2) adopting anarchism, that is, denying that the government could ever have authority over us. A third alternative is to follow the directions of the government so as to achieve coordination, without abandoning one's judgment: one puts someone "in authority" but denies that he or she is "an authority" on politics.

10.3 Liberal Political Authority

The Pure Coordination Theory of Justice and Authority

As I have stressed, Friedman's analysis of the notion of being "in author-ity" fits well with Hobbes's theory. Recall Hobbes's account of the state of nature and justice (Section 8.2). Hobbes demonstrates how unlimited lib-erties in the state of nature would lead to conflict and insecurity. Thus, he argued, rational individuals would consent to a sovereign who would in-stitute rules of justice. It is important for Hobbes that any rules of justice are better than no rules of justice, thus everyone can see it would be bet-ter to live under *any system of justice* than to continue life in the state of nature. But to gain the benefits of a system of justice—a system of rights that distinguishes "mine" and "thine"—we need to coordinate on the same system. Thus, Hobbes maintains that we must appoint someone, or some body of people, to be in authority and thus have the power to lay down common rules of justice.

The coordination theory of political authority also makes sense of the idea that a crucial task of political authority is to provide for *public goods* such as clean air, defense, police, and so on. It has long been recognized that a private property–based market will not supply these "public goods" in sufficient quantities.[15] Consider, for example, the case of clean air. Suppose that in the state of nature, three-quarters of the population managed to agree to cut emissions, and this resulted in much cleaner air. Of course, there will be costs that these three-quarters of the population will have to bear: they will have to buy emission control devices, or drive less, or in some other way alter their activities in ways that cost. Suppose, however, they do so. We can immediately see that the one-quarter who did not cut their emissions gain the full benefits of the restraint by the other three-quarters: the one-quarter of noncooperators get *all* the benefits of clean air, without bearing any of the cost! One feature of public goods is that nonpayers cannot be excluded from enjoying the good; *if anyone gets the good, everyone else can get it for free.* Seeing that the noncooperating one-quarter of the population get the clean air without paying any of the cost, some of our cooperators are likely to decide to stop paying their share of the costs. Why should they have to pay when others get it for free? Why not get it for free themselves? Reasoning thus, we might expect an increas-ing number of cooperators to switch to the noncooperator camp, with the result that eventually so few cooperate that air quality goes down. Yet, it may well be the case that everyone prefers clean air to dirty air, but all purely voluntary schemes fail because too many people seek a "free ride"—they seek to get the benefits without paying the cost, with the re-sult that the benefits are not achieved at all. Thus, one important liberal argument for political authority is that we would all benefit from a coordinator—someone in authority—who could direct everyone to do his or her part in a cooperative scheme that everyone wants, but which cannot be achieved as long as contributions remain purely voluntary.

If we accept the Hobbesian pure coordination theory of justice and political authority, political authority is unlimited in the sense that all citizens have good reason to follow any rule laid down by the political authority. In this case, the sovereign's rules of justice or policy always "preempt" your own views about what is just: you follow the sovereign's reasoning to the extent that you exclude your own views about justice when considering what to do.[16] The reason for this should be clear: since our overriding aim is to coordinate our actions according to common rules, it is better to follow even a bad directive of the authority than ruin cooperation and risk a return to the state of nature by following different rules than those laid down by the political authority. Moreover, since justice is tied to legality (Sections 8.1, 8.2), no one can reasonably claim that the rules laid down by political authority are unjust. It is important, however, to stress that the sovereign makes no claim to be correct or have the best views about justice, and on the Hobbesian account your obedience in no way supposes that the sovereign is "an authority" about anything. The important thing is to *do* what the sovereign says, not at all to believe what he says.

Locke, Kant, and Umpires

Although the pure coordination theory is extremely helpful in explaining the puzzle of why equally free people would surrender their judgment to others, and so is helpful in constructing a liberal theory of political authority, it seems to put too much weight on coordination. As we saw in Section 8.2, Hobbes's theory ties justice *too closely* to legality. Most liberals have insisted that there are some moral rights that constitute the basis of ideal justice, to which legal justice must conform.

If we reject the Hobbesian position that political authority *defines justice*, what is the relation between principles of justice and political authority? Suppose that we all accept certain substantive principles of justice, such as the classical liberal rights to life, liberty, and property. Locke held that even if everyone acknowledged these natural rights, disputes will still arise as to what justice demands. People would interpret these rights differently; in disputes each individual would be likely to incline toward interpretations that favor his interests over those of others. To avoid this "inconvenience," Locke argued, it is necessary to appoint an "umpire" to resolve disputes about the requirements of justice. Peaceful social life requires an authoritative interpreter of justice. Immanuel Kant agrees:

Although experience [and, we might add, Hobbes] teaches us that men live in violence and are prone to fight one another before the advent of external compulsive legislation, it is not experience that makes public lawful coercion necessary. The necessity of public lawful coercion does not rest on a fact, but on an a priori Idea of reason, for, even if we imagine men to be ever so good natured and righteous before a public lawful state of society is established, individual men, nations and states can never be certain they are secure against violence from one another because each will have the right to do what *seems just and good to him*, entirely independently of the opinion of others.[17]

Kant goes on to insist that justice is absent in the state of nature because each relies on his own judgment about what is just, and thus "when there is a controversy concerning rights *(jus controversum)*, no competent judge can be found to render a decision having the force of law."[18] Because conflict and injustice arise if each person always relies on his own interpretation of what is just, Kant insists that if one "does not wish to renounce all concepts of justice," one must "quit the state of nature, in which everyone follows his own judgments" and subject oneself to a "judge."[19] The liberal theories of Locke and Kant, then, are first and foremost justifications of an "umpire" (Locke) or "judge" (Kant) whose task is to provide public, definitive resolutions of conflicting judgments about justice. To escape the state of nature, in which each relies on his own moral judgments, we require rule by an "Umpire, by settled standing Rules, indifferent, and the same to all Parties."[20]

Umpires: "In Authority" or "An Authority"?

Must the liberal umpire be "an authority" about justice or is it enough to be simply "in authority" to make decisions about what we should do? To better grasp what sort of authority is needed, let us focus on a particular case: suppose two people, Alf and Betty, are in the state of nature, and they disagree about the nature of liberal justice. For example, Alf may insist that although liberal justice makes some provision for private property rights, property is subject to taxation in order to redistribute resources to the least well off along the lines suggested by John Rawls (Section 8.4). In contrast, Betty may maintain that the liberal contract gives no significant scope for redistribution. What are they to do? Of course, we hope that they will discuss their differences and present their arguments; but given the complexity of political debate, especially concerning interpretations of contested notions such as property and distributive justice, we should expect continued disagreement.

One possibility is that they will go to a sage: someone who is "an authority" about justice.[21] The sage, priest, elder, or moral philosopher is, on this view, taken to have superior insight into justice. Now, although sometimes we do seek the advice of those whom we consider more wise, the liberal supposition of the basic freedom and equality of all makes it terribly unlikely that everyone will defer to the same sage about justice. The entire liberal project in political theory—and in this way it radically differs from most conservative views—rests on the supposition that there are no natural moral authorities to whom everyone should or would defer. The liberal recognizes "no high priests of morals."[22]

In terms of Friedman's analysis, Alf and Betty may well conclude that they do not need "an authority" on morals; they require only that someone be "in authority" to end the practical dispute. But on reflection, it does not seem that Alf and Betty simply seek a coordinator who tells them what to do, with no claim that the coordinator's views are correct or right. In our case, because Alf and Betty's practical controversy about what *to do* is based on a moral dispute about *what is just*, it seems doubtful they would be satisfied with an umpire who makes no attempt whatsoever to track the underlying issue about justice. After all, they conceive of themselves as disagreeing about what to do because they disagree about what is right; to resolve the former without reference to the latter treats their moral dispute as if it were no more than a conflict of preferences, like our driving example in Figure 10.1.

It would seem, then, that Alf and Betty must reject the pure coordinator notion of authority—Friedman's notion being simply "in authority"—because it makes no attempt to relate the resolution of the practical controversy to the proper solution of the disagreement about justice. But also, they reject the sage account of political authority—trying to find someone who is "an authority" about justice—because as free and equal people they will surely disagree about who the proper authorities are. Locke's notion of an "umpire" provides a third alternative. Consider more carefully the idea of an umpire in a game. Players require an umpire because they have practical disputes based on their different views on how the rules of the game apply to particular situations. Often, the dispute is simply about fairly straightforward matters of fact such as whether or not Betty hit the ball in foul territory. But this is not always the case. Consider the concept of a "strike zone" and what constitutes a "called strike." The boundaries of the strike zone are contested—we might even say essentially contested: some players and umpires insist that the zone is wide, others advocate a narrower conception. Neither in law nor in sporting matches do rules apply themselves: they need to be interpreted, and the application requires practical judgment. The umpire, then, makes her practical determinations on the basis of her judgments concerning the rules of the game. This makes the umpire appear to be something of a sage. But players typically do not, and nothing about accepting an umpire requires that they must, see the umpire as a sage. Players certainly may, but usually do not, take the umpire's decisions as reasons to believe: they usually do not see her as "an authority" in the sense that they defer to her judgments about what to believe. Players usually believe just what they did before the umpire decided—that is why they so often argue with umpires—but they accept her judgment as a resolution of the practical dispute insofar as they do what she says. They may argue, but in the end they do what the umpire says. Yet, they expect the umpire to deliberate about what to do on the basis of the rules and the facts. Although the problem is essentially a practical one, the umpire's resolution is to be based on her determinations concerning the facts and the rules of the games.

Umpireship, then, constitutes a mix of expertise (being "an authority") and practical directives (being "in authority"). The umpire's aim is to produce practical decisions that best track what the rules require. Yet, players need only conceive of her as a practical authority (they see her as being "in authority," not "an authority"). Indeed, the players must accept the umpire's practical authority even when they are confident her decision is wrong. Unless they were prepared to do so, they could not proceed with the game. Situations always arise when players reasonably disagree about what is the appropriate thing to do, and that is precisely when an umpire is needed. Unless they are prepared to follow the umpire's decisions in these cases, the umpire could not do her job. To be sure, there are limits. At some point, we say things like, "These just are not even reasonable calls. This ump is either blind or has been paid off." Even when we disagree with an umpire, we can usually grasp how someone seeking to apply the rules of the game would make that decision. But if an umpire consistently acts in ways that, as far as we can tell, have nothing to do with the rules of the game, we will sooner or later conclude that she is either incompetent or corrupt. We can say, then, that the players only accept the practical authority of the umpire for decisions within some range of reasonable decisions.

The difference between Locke's umpire account and Friedman's coordination theory is fundamental: Locke's umpire view ultimately leaves each citizen the right to judge when an authority loses its claim to be an interpreter of justice and hence no longer need be obeyed. One of the most controversial features of Locke's *Second Treatise* is his claim that each citizen retains a right to revolt against a political authority that has lost its claim to be a judge of justice. Although we need an umpire to resolve disputes about the nature of justice, each of us must still examine the merits of the umpire's decisions to see if they are beyond the bounds of reason. To accept the authority of an umpire is not to accept a tyrant; if the case for governmental authority is based on our need to resolve conflicting interpretations of justice, a government that no longer is concerned with justice loses its authority. In the history of political philosophy, this has been a controversial position. To some, such as Hobbes, it undoes everything that the argument for authority was meant to accomplish. If authority was meant to end the arguments about what is to be done, many political theorists have concluded that citizens should not decide, on the merits of each decision, whether to obey. But I have argued that the Lockean position does indeed follow from the umpireship model; our understanding of umpireship implies that the umpire must remain within the bounds of reasonable decisions. (A baseball umpire who declares, "Strike two, you're out!" loses his authority to call the game.) And if that is true, then the "inconvenience" of each person relying on his own opinion is not completely removed; for one must still rely on one's own opinion as to whether the political authority is acting within the bounds of reasonable interpretations of the principles of justice.

10.4 Democratic Authority and the Management of Collective Affairs

Socialism and Anarchism

Authority conflicts with equality. If someone has authority over others, that person is in the position to direct or command others—that person's judgment "preempts" the judgment of those over whom she exercises authority. This is manifestly inegalitarian. Conservatives, of course, are not troubled by this, since they are critical of equality (Section 7.5). It is much more of a problem for liberals; in many ways the chief project of liberal political theory has been to show that equally free people would consent to rules of justice that constrain their freedom, as well as submit to a political authority to interpret and enforce justice. Now, as I have previously remarked, much socialist thought is very close to revisionist liberalism (Section 8.1) and embraces a view of the state as the authoritative interpreter of justice; insofar as it does so, such socialist thought adopts an essentially liberal theory of political authority. We also have seen, however, that radical socialist thought—for example, that inspired by Marx—has refused to build its case on principles of justice (Section 9.1). Indeed, socialism's valuing of equality of power (and so of freedom as power) leads generally to a privileged place for democracy in socialist thinking about justice (Section 9.2). But if equality of power is a core value, it seems almost impossible to justify political authority.

The core commitment to equality has led some socialists to anarchism. As we saw above (Section 10.2), some liberal-inclined thinkers so value liberty and autonomy that they insist on the illegitimacy of any political

authority. In a similar way, some socialists so value equality of power
that they too renounce all authority. Mikhail Bakunin (1814–1876)—who
fought Marx for leadership of the international socialist movement—was
adamant that the inequality inherent in all political authority corrupted
the nature of humans and destroyed social cooperation.[23] Thus, it was
not simply the destruction of capitalism, but political authority and the
state, at which Bakunin aimed. In his controversy with Bakunin, Marx
himself seemed to accept that, ultimately, communist society would abolish political authority in the sense of authority of one person over another; although there still would be a central administrative authority in
a fully communist state, the "administration of things" would replace the
"domination of people."[24] Just as in many ways conservatism is a critique of the ideal of equality rather than an interpretation of it, socialism
often takes the form of a rejection, rather than an interpretation, of political authority.

Democracy and Socialist Authority

Anarchists such as Bakunin reject political authority as corrupting; because Marx places so much weight on economic forces as the true deter-
minants of a society, he tends to downplay the role of political authority.
What became known as "democratic socialism" was a rejection of Marx's
beliefs that socialism was the inevitable result of economic forces. Instead, argued socialists such as Eduard Bernstein (1850–1932) in Ger-
many and G.D.H. Cole in Britain, socialism was an egalitarian ethical
ideal and required political action to implement it. Thus, to democratic
socialists, parliamentary democracy and its attendant political authority
are necessary to bring socialism about.

As soon as socialism accepts political authority as legitimate and necessary, however, its tension with equality immediately arises. How can
anything that is intrinsically inegalitarian, such as political authority, be a
necessary part of a thoroughly egalitarian ideal such as socialism, which
seeks equality of power and social equality? The key, once again, is democracy, understood in such a way as to reconcile authority with both
freedom and equality. Recall that in their analysis of socialist democracy
(Section 9.2), Cohen and Rogers insisted that a genuine democratic community presupposes equal freedom and some sort of equalization of
power and resources among classes. Under such conditions, they argue,
the members of the community can deliberate and debate about "the direction of social life" and "conditions of their own association":

> That members of the order together determine the institutions, rules and
> conditions of their own association means that they themselves are sover-

eign. This sovereignty is *freely* exercised in the sense participants in the order have, and are recognized as having, the capacity to form reasoned judgments about the ends of social life. . . . Sovereignty is *equally* exercised in the sense that the views of each member of the democratic order are accorded equal weight in public deliberation.[25]

Following Rousseau, Cohen and Rogers understand the democratic community as exercising political authority over itself, and so political authority actually expresses both freedom and equality. Each member of the community, argued Rousseau, is not only a citizen subject to the laws but also a member of the "Sovereign," the supreme political authority. Supreme political authority, then, resides in the community as a whole, of which everyone is a member. Laws—acts of the Sovereign—are thus acts of the entire community (considered in their active role as citizens) legislating for the entire community (in their passive role as subjects). Thus, all genuine acts of authority *come from all and apply to all*. An act of sovereignty is not, then, the act of a superior talking to an inferior, it "is the will of the body of the people," the group deciding what is best for the group.[26] As such, it does not involve an inequality between those with political authority and those subject to it: everyone exercises political authority, and everyone is subject to it. Critical to Rousseau's analysis is that the verdict of the majority is not simply the will of the majority imposed on the minority—for that would be yet another form of slavery and dependence—but the expression of the general will and the common interest. Recall Rousseau's analysis of the relation of freedom and the general will (Section 5.4). If (1) a free person acts on his true will, (2) each desires the general will or common good of the community; (3) because the democratic process reveals this common good (4) each person wills the democratic verdict and so (5) each person is free when she submits to the verdict. Further, since (6) the democratic verdict is based on equality of civil and social status because each has the same political rights and (7) the law is general and applies equally to all citizens, (8) equality is reconciled with authority. Rousseau is so fascinating just because he seeks to show that the political concepts we have examined—liberty, equality, justice, democracy, and authority—can be achieved, without conflicts or trade-offs, given the proper political arrangements. Rousseau's theory is perhaps the clearest example of a thoroughly monistic view of political concepts.

Rousseau depicts the authority of the democratic sovereign as "an authority" about the general will. To be sure, the democratic sovereign is *not always* correct about the general will: "The people is never corrupted, but it is often misled, and only then does it seem to will what is bad." As Rousseau puts it, the democratic majority sometimes expresses only "the will of all" rather than the general will. "The general will studies only the common interest while the will of all studies private interest, and is indeed no more than the sum of individual desires. But if we take away from these same wills the pluses and minuses which cancel each other out, the balance which remains is the general will." Thus, argues Rousseau, "From the deliberations of a people properly informed, and provided its members do not have any communications among themselves, the great number of small differences will always produce a general will and the decision will always be good."[27] Rousseau, then, holds that insofar as the democratic majority has genuine authority, it speaks for the general will, and democracy is justified because under the proper conditions it is a reliable, though by no means perfect, way to arrive at the general will. Thus, if democracy is properly functioning, confronted by the verdict of the majority the minority should change what it believes to be right. According to Rousseau, each person in the minority should conclude, "If my particular opinion had prevailed against the general will, I should have done something other than what I had willed, and then I should not have been free."[28] The people, in the form of a properly constituted democracy, is thus "an authority" on the general will, although, like most authorities (such as doctors) it can sometimes be mistaken.

The tension between procedural and substantive justice in democratic socialist thought (Section 9.2) leads to a similar tension in its analysis of political authority. In the passages I have been examining, Rousseau depicts democracy as a reliable way to discover the common good: the democratic majority is "an authority" about the general will, and thus we should "surrender our judgment" to it. This, then, assumes that we possess a substantive understanding of a just outcome, and democratic decisionmaking is an "expert" method to achieve this outcome. Cohen agrees: following Rousseau, he insists that people should reason together about the common good of the community.[29] But we have seen that democratic socialism tends to depict democratic outcomes as procedurally just: a law or policy is just simply because it has been arrived at by democratic methods. On this view, the democratic majority is not "an authority" about justice, its will *defines* justice. Insofar as Rousseau and democratic socialists define justice in terms of the democratic will of the people, the authority of the people goes far beyond mere expert authority: it is more like the authority of God, whose will determines justice. As it has sometimes been put: *Vox populi, vox dei,* "The voice of the people is the voice of God." In the face of the pronouncements of such authority, the individual citizen has no grounds for objection or complaint. If it is the true voice of the people, its will is necessarily just and must always be obeyed. In itself, the people as a whole cannot conceivably be wrong about justice. Hence the conservative jibe that in Rousseau's society "each morning the citizen would look into the mirror while shaving and see the face of one ten-millionth a tyrant and one whole slave."[30]

Rationalism and Expert Authority

I have been stressing the egalitarian commitments of socialism, and how this leads to a thoroughly democratic account of legitimate authority. But socialism displays a strong rationalist strain that leads in precisely the opposite direction, toward rule by an elite who have the necessary understanding of society and skills to run it. Recall that according to Engels, one of Marx's great achievements was to base socialism on a scientific understanding of society rather than ethical claims (Sections 3.2, 9.1). Now, science is the realm of expert knowledge. The scientist has special techniques and has studied a specialized area of knowledge, with which the average person is not acquainted. The scientist is thus "an authority" on her area of expertise (Section 10.1). Scientists, of course, may be wrong, and they disagree with each other, but the lay person is seldom in the position to participate in these debates among authorities.

If socialism is a science that reveals the laws of capitalist production, the laws of economic, social, and political change, we should not expect lay people to really grasp these laws or their implications. To be sure, Marx himself apparently believed that explicit understanding of the laws of economics was not necessary: those very laws would cause the increasing impoverishment of workers, which would lead them to develop a revolutionary consciousness, working for a socialist revolution without themselves understanding Marxist theory. But as the nineteenth century progressed and turned into the twentieth, it became increasingly clear that this revolutionary consciousness was not developing. Instead, workers were joining trade unions and democratic socialist parties, seeking simply to reform capitalism and institute something like a welfare state.

Lenin, the leader of the Russian revolution of 1917, saw this reforming socialism as denying "the antithesis in principle between liberalism and socialism."[31] Lenin did not believe that the workers would spontaneously develop a revolutionary consciousness; according to Lenin, insofar as the workers develop any "spontaneous" consciousness, it would be the capitalistic ideology that their problems can be solved through trade unionism and some sort of reformist liberalism. Lenin thus makes the proclamation that turns socialism away from democratic egalitarianism to rationalism and hierarchy: "Without revolutionary theory there can be no revolutionary movement."[32] If knowledge of socialist revolutionary theory is necessary for effective political action, then political leadership rests in the hands of those who know the theory. Lenin thus advocates leadership by a "vanguard" party, controlled by the elite who understand socialist theory and thus are in the position to advance the workers' cause. Note that few workers will themselves be part of this elite, for they are unlikely to be conversant with the socialist theory. Lenin's extreme rationalism thus leads to a socialism that rests political authority in those who are an authority on socialist theory and practice; it is their task to lead the workers toward an egalitarian social state.

Lenin thus proposes to combine a high degree of political inequality in a hierarchical political structure with a commitment to social and economic equality (Section 6.4). This became the official version of socialism in the former communist states of eastern Europe and Asia, and still remains influential in the political cultures of China, North Korea, and Cuba. From its very inception—and this view easily can be traced to Marx himself—its critics have doubted whether this starkly inegalitarian conception of political authority could be joined to socialist equality. The result, they predicted, would be a socially and economically inegalitarian society favoring the political elite over the masses, in whose interests they were supposed to rule. And these predictions were largely borne out. Although the communist societies were probably more economically egalitarian than most (but they were by no means remarkably egalitarian), they demonstrated marked social inequality resting on great political inequality. Lenin's dream that rule by the vanguard party would fade away as the workers developed socialist consciousness was never achieved: the inequality of authority remained a defining feature of these societies.

Political Inequality and Socialist Planning

The tendency of socialism to embrace hierarchical political authority, despite its deep commitment to equality, has deeper roots than Lenin's conviction that left to themselves, the workers would embrace reformist rather than revolutionary politics. Most versions of socialism have been critical of not simply private property but the very idea of market society. A long-standing criticism of capitalism is that the market is chaotic and wasteful. According to a standard Marxist view,

> Under capitalism the production and distribution of goods is quite unorganized. What does this mean? It means that all the capitalist entrepreneurs (or capitalist companies) produce commodities independently of one another. Instead of society undertaking to reckon up what it needs and how much of each article, the factory owners simply produce upon the calculations of what will bring them most profit and will best enable them to defeat their rivals in the market. . . .
>
> The first reason, therefore, for the disharmony of capitalist society is the anarchy of production, which leads to crises . . . competition and wars.[33]

The Marxist solution, and this was often put explicitly, was to organize all of society along the lines of an "immense cooperative workshop." To quote again from a book called *The ABC of Communism*,

> We must know in advance how much labour to assign to the various branches of industry; what products are required and how much of each it is necessary to produce; how and where machines must be provided. These and similar details must be thought out beforehand, with approximate accuracy at least; and the work must be guided in accordance with calculations. . . . Without a general plan, without a general directive system, and without careful calculation and book-keeping, there can be no organization. But in the communist social organization, there is such a plan.[34]

Doing away with market coordination, and replacing it with a consciously planned economy, expresses socialist rationalism and its faith in the power of human reason to understand and control society. In comparison to conscious planning, market coordination seems haphazard; it subjects us all to the whim of uncontrolled forces. To Marx, this violates not only reason, but freedom, which can "only consist in socialized man, the associated producers, rationally regulating their interchange with Nature, bringing it under the common control."[35] Clearly, however, this rationalist demand to control and plan requires giving experts the authority to organize and plan the economy. Although some socialists have hoped to combine radical democracy with economic planning, this hardly seems plausible: economic planning presupposes specialized economic and organizational knowledge. Thus, it seems inevitable that efforts to eliminate or even reduce the role of the market inevitably lead to increased political-economic authority of experts. Many contemporary socialists accept this, and so have endeavored to develop forms of socialism that rely on market coordination (compare here the classical liberal view in Section 5.3).

10.5 Summary

This chapter has examined the concept of political authority and its ties to the concepts of liberty, equality, democracy, and justice. Richard Friedman's analysis of the distinction between "an authority" and "in authority" provided our focus. Section 10.1 argued that political authority understood as the right of those to rule who are "an authority" on politics is fundamental to most conservative theories. Understood thus, political authority is inegalitarian; it is based on the inequality of knowledge between those who rule and those who are ruled. Friedman (Section 10.2) contrasts this to political authority understood as someone "in authority": such a person is empowered to give directives that preempt our own decisions about what we should do. This is the authority of the coordinator. Rather than being based on an inequality, this conception of authority arises out of our freedom and equality, and so our disagreements over how to conduct cooperative arrangements. Precisely because we conceive of ourselves as equally free, we require a coordinator to direct our actions to mutually beneficial outcomes.

Section 10.3 examined two accounts of authority associated with the liberal tradition: Friedman's coordinator, who directs our actions but provides no reasons to accept her pronouncements as correct, and the Lockean umpire, who seeks to umpire disputes about justice and moral rights. Although both models have played important roles in liberal political theory, I argued that the umpire model better accounts for the relation of liberal justice and liberal authority. Given the liberal position that equal liberty (and, typically, property) rights are fundamental to a legitimate state, these provide limits on what a justified authority may command. Moreover, because these ideal moral rights are abstract and vague, they need to be interpreted and expressed in legal justice (see Mill's points [1] and [2], Section 8.1). That, according to the Lockean umpire model, is the main task of political authority. As I argued, such a conception of authority combines aspects of being "in authority" with being "an authority" on justice.

Section 10.4 turned to the problematic place of political authority in socialist thought. On the one hand, socialism's strong egalitarian commitments lead it to be skeptical of the very idea of political authority. It seems that only when such authority is democratic, and so arises out of the equality of all citizens, can socialism embrace it. Moreover, given the close relation of democracy to socialist theories of liberty, equality, and justice, we observed that the ideal democratic state appears to hold out the possibility for a harmonious realization of all key socialist values. Yet, the rationalism of socialism also draws it to conceptions of authority that share much with the conservative views with which we began. Those who are experts on the social good, economic planning, or socialist theory seem to have claims to direct the activities of their less well-informed fellow citizens. Thus, we have the paradox of socialism: the political theory that in some ways seems most averse to authority was employed to justify some of the most authoritarian states in history.

Notes

1. See Robert Paul Wolff, *In Defense of Anarchism* (New York: Harper and Row, 1970).

2. Richard B. Friedman, "On the Concept of Authority in Political Philosophy," in Richard E. Flathman, ed., *Concepts in Social and Political Philosophy* (New York: Macmillan, 1973), pp. 142–143.

3. Ibid., p. 143.

4. Ibid., pp. 143–144.

5. Ibid., p. 123.

6. Thomas Carlyle, *Past and Present* (London: Dent, 1960), p. 212.

7. Michael Oakeshott, "On Being a Conservative," in his *Rationalism in Politics,* expanded ed. (Indianapolis, IN: Liberty Press, 1991), pp. 431–432.

8. Ibid., p. 433.

9. This is very close to the liberal ideal, especially as articulated by the value pluralist. See Sections 3.2, 4.3, 8.2.

10. Michael Oakeshott, "Political Education," in his *Rationalism in Politics,* p. 44.

11. Friedman, "On the Concept of Authority in Political Philosophy," pp. 122–123.

12. Ibid., p. 129.

13. Ibid., p. 140.

14. Ibid., p. 141.

15. I consider the reasons for this more fully in my *Social Philosophy* (Armonk, NY: M. E. Sharpe, 1999), pp. 187ff.

16. On the idea of exclusionary reasons, see Leslie Green, *The Authority of the State* (Oxford: Clarendon Press, 1988), chap. 2.

17. Immanuel Kant, *Metaphysical Elements of Justice,* John Ladd, trans. (Indianapolis, IN: Bobbs-Merrill, 1965), p. 76. Emphasis in original.

18. Ibid.

19. Ibid.

20. John Locke, *Second Treatise of Government,* in Peter Laslett, ed., *Two Treatises of Government* (Cambridge: Cambridge University Press, 1960), sect. 87.

21. See E. D. Watt, *Authority* (London: Croom-Helm, 1982), chap. 6.

22. Jan Narveson, *The Libertarian Idea* (Philadelphia: Temple University Press, 1988), p. 125.

23. For a selection of his writings, see Sam Dolgaff, ed., trans., *Bakunin on Anarchy* (London: Allen and Unwin, 1971). For Bakunin's disputes with Marx, see Paul Thomas, *Karl Marx and the Anarchists* (London: Routledge and Kegan Paul, 1980), chap. 5.

24. Karl Marx, "After the Revolution: Marx Debates Bakunin," in Robert C. Tucker, ed., *The Marx-Engels Reader,* 2nd ed. (New York: W. W. Norton, 1978), p. 545.

25. Joshua Cohen and Joel Rogers, *On Democracy: Toward a Transformation of American Society* (Harmondsworth, UK: Penguin, 1983), pp. 149–150. Emphasis in original.

26. Jean-Jacques Rousseau, *The Social Contract,* Maurice Cranston, trans. (London: Penguin Books, 1968), Book 2, chap. 2.

27. Ibid., Book 2, chap. 3.

28. Ibid., Book 4, chap. 2.

29. Joshua Cohen, "Deliberation and Democratic Legitimacy," in James Bohman and William Rehg, eds., *Deliberative Democracy* (Cambridge, MA: MIT Press, 1998), p. 69.

30. See Robert Nisbet, *Conservatism* (Milton Keynes, UK: Open University Press, 1986), p. 48.

31. Vladimir Ilyich Lenin, *What Is to Be Done?* in James E. Connor, ed., *Lenin on Politics and Revolution* (Indianapolis, IN: Bobbs-Merrill, 1968), p. 32.

32. Ibid., p. 35.

33. N. I. Bukharin and Preobrazhensky, *The ABC of Communism*, quoted in Michael Ellman, *Socialist Planning* (Cambridge: Cambridge University Press, 1979), pp. 8–9.

34. Ibid. p. 9.

35. Marx, *Capital*, in *The Marx-Engels Reader*, p. 441.

CONCLUDING REMARKS:
FROM POLITICAL CONCEPTS
TO POLITICAL THEORIES

Throughout Part II of this book, I have tried to show how liberal, conservative, and socialist interpretations of political concepts are shaped by, first, the analysis of other political concepts, as well as by, second, commitments to rationalism or pluralism, collectivism or individualism, and views of human nature. We have seen, for example, how a classical liberal analysis of negative liberty supports classical liberal suspicions about most forms of equality, how the notion of equally free people is the basis of its theory of justice, and how this leads to a certain view of political authority. We have also seen the way in which much socialist thought endorses interlocking conceptions of liberty, equality, justice, authority, and democracy, which stress how all these political ideals, if properly understood, can be harmoniously achieved, without the conflicts and trade-offs that are so central to classical liberal thought. I have also stressed how a great deal of conservative thought focuses on the themes of inegalitarianism, antirationalism, and the historical and customary dimensions of human life. We have, then, developed some rough conceptual maps of our enduring political theories, which have related the analysis of one concept to that of others, as well as to their differing views on some of the fundamental issues in political theory.

Think back to our starting point: Plato's query, "What is justice?" This looked at first as if it was a request for a definition or an essence. By now, we can appreciate that Plato was proposing a rationalistic and collectivist political theory. For Plato, justice involved the proper ordering of the collectivity, with one's rights and duties related to one's place in that collectivity; naturally enough, political authority ought to be invested in those who have the expert political knowledge. Equality, of course, has little importance in such a political theory, except insofar as we are equally members of the community; and democracy is entirely wrongheaded. Insofar as freedom involves doing what is rational to do, the members of such a state are free. On all these issues, Plato may be right or wrong. But our inquiry into whether he is right or wrong will not take the form of an isolated analysis of the term "justice." It will involve wide-ranging examinations of his views about reason, human nature, and the nature of society, as well as the value of liberty and equality; questions about how liberty and equality relate to each other, and how they relate to justice and political authority; and whether all of Plato's positions on these matters cohere or whether they conflict. Having started out with the analysis of a political concept, we will have ended with an analysis of a political theory.

Although I have sought to show how the liberal, socialist, and conservative traditions form enduring, coherent views of politics and society, I have also tried to point to the internal diversity within each enduring theory. As I have stressed throughout, political theorizing is not done according to a formula; interpretations of political concepts can be combined in different ways, as can positions on rationalism, collectivism, and human nature. For example, although in many ways Plato's account of justice is clearly conservative, stressing a version of "my station and its duties," it also is highly rationalist: Plato's "philosopher kings" have knowledge of the workings of society and what is best for it. Thus, we have a sort of rationalist conservatism, a view that is very different from Burke's and Oakeshott's conservatisms. The liberal and socialist traditions, we have seen, are no less complex: classical liberals stress individualism, whereas Hobhouse described himself as a collectivist; some socialists are radical egalitarians and anarchists, whereas the followers of Lenin developed an elitist and authoritarian theory of political authority. And the enduring traditions overlap: at times it can be difficult to distinguish between a revisionist liberal and a moderate socialist, or a resolutely antirationalist classical liberal such as Hayek and a conservative such as Oakeshott. Like political concepts, our enduring theories are not characterized by a common essence, but by crisscrossing family resemblances (Section 1.4). Nevertheless, it should be clear by now that, by and large, classical liberals endorse constellations of political conceptions that fundamentally differ from the sort of conceptual clusters that have dominated socialist and conservative political theories. Hence it should not be surprising that conceptual disputes seem so intractable. What is at stake is not the meaning of a word, but a view of the world.

INDEX